CULBERTSON

CULBERTSON

THE MAN WHO MADE CONTRACT BRIDGE

John Clay

WEIDENFELD AND NICOLSON
LONDON

Contents

PREFACE

I first played bridge when I was twelve. Culbertson was still in vogue in bridge circles in those days. Years later wanting to write a biography, I thought back to Culbertson. I read his autobiography, *The Strange Lives of One Man*, published in 1940, which covers the first forty-seven years of his life, and hunted around for other material on him. I was surprised to discover how little had been written about his unusually dramatic life. No previous biography existed. Then I heard that his closest associate and colleague, Albert Morehead, had been due to write his biography but had died quite suddenly of cancer in 1966. Morehead proved to be an important link for me since his obituary of Ely Culbertson in *Bridge World* in January 1956 cleared up what might otherwise have remained lingering doubts about the authenticity of Culbertson's own account of his life. Morehead wrote, 'In 1940 Culbertson published *The Strange Lives of One Man* in which he told many adventures. He told them with the greatest frankness, and as accurately as his memory permitted. Even among those who worked in his organization and knew him well, there were many who still would not believe the autobiography was fact and not fiction. I, who was closest to him and knew him best, could not overcome large areas of doubt; yet time after time I later encountered absolute proof that it had all happened exactly as he said.'

While researching this book I took the opportunity to check as many of these facts as I could with Culbertson's family and friends. My conclusions became the same as Morehead's, and I have followed the same sequence for Culbertson's early years as he gives in *The Strange Lives of One Man*, quoting occasionally from that book to give a flavour of his fulsome style and amplifying his account where necessary to give a more complete picture.

I was greatly assisted in my task by the lengthy and always entertaining discussions I had with the remaining 'greats' of Contract bridge in the 1930s, all of whom were at one time or other Culbertson business associates or bridge partners – Richard Frey, Sam Fry, Oswald Jacoby, Alfred Sheinwold and Waldemar von Zedtwitz. The sharpness of their memory is ample tribute to the mind-enhancing qualities of top level tournament bridge! Through them I hope to have fulfilled one of my aims in this book, to show how Contract bridge evolved, took America by storm in the 1930s and created a whole new social milieu. Culbertson, the man who made Contract bridge, was behind this. He made sure that when beginners wanted to learn the game they immediately thought of Culbertson. Sadly Oswald Jacoby and Waldemar von Zedtwitz have died since this book was completed.

I owe as many thanks to Culbertson's family, notably to his son Bruce and grandson Stephen for much appreciated help and for their permission to use previously unpublished papers and photographs. My talks with them enabled me to focus on another objective of this book, to underline the importance of Culbertson's partnership with Jo, both at and away from the bridge table, as a crucial factor in his success. I wanted to show too how unusual it was for a young woman such as Jo to establish herself on equal terms with the best male bridge players of her era.

Other thanks go to the American Contract Bridge League and their then librarian Edith Simon, to Richard Goldberg, Nat Cohen, Sue Emery and Diane Hayward and other members of staff for their gracious help on an all too brief visit to Memphis, Tennessee.

Elsewhere in the USA I am particularly indebted to Dorothy Culbertson's mother, Hildegarde Baehne, for her help on a visit to Brattleboro, Vermont and then to George Coffin, Gertrude Croker (then aged 102), David Daniels, Hildegarde Durfee, Bert Gillikin, the late General Gruenther, Lee Hazen, Prince Djoli Kansil, Edgar and Betty Kaplan, Jack Korshin, Alexander Marvin, Jack Sanders of Ridgefield Press, Alan Truscott, Niccolo Tucci and Stephen White for their help in various ways.

In Europe I am most grateful to Jaime Ortiz Patino, President of the World Bridge Federation, for early encouragement with the book and to Rixi Markus for her frequent and valuable help, and to Terence Reese and Boris Shapiro for giving me their impressions of the international bridge scene in the 1930s and 1940s.

A special word of thanks to Wolf Klewe for allowing me to consult his extensive private collection of bridge books, and to Leslie Parris for supplying otherwise difficult to obtain bridge literature.

Finally this book owes much to the encouragement and support of my wife and ever-patient three children, still mercifully too young to make up a bridge four!

John Clay
London 1985

Acknowledgements

Grateful acknowledgement is made to the following for permission to reprint previously published material:

George Allen and Unwin: an extract from the *Autobiography of Bertrand Russell*, Vol 11, 1914–44 [1968].

Holt, Rinehart and Winston: extracts from *The Strange Lives of One Man* by Ely Culbertson [John C. Winston, 1940].

Hutchinson: excerpts from *Stranger on the Square* by Cynthia and Arthur Koestler [1984] and an excerpt from *The Saturday Book* [1950].

The Macmillan Company: an excerpt from *The Only Way to Cross* by John Maxtone Graham [1972].

McMaster University (The Bertrand Russell Archives), Ontario: a letter from Ely Culbertson to Bertrand Russell.

Routledge and Kegan Paul: excerpts from *I Meet America* by W.J. Brown [1941].

ILLUSTRATIONS

FOR C
'My Wife and Favourite Partner'

'I play men, not cards.'

Culbertson in 1932

INTRODUCTION

Four men are seated around a makeshift card-table. They are playing vint, a Russian card game derived from whist. One of them, the dealer, is to be executed next morning. Each player concentrates with rapt attention – not because of the high stakes but out of a sense of dedication to the task in hand. The year is 1907. They are all revolutionaries, members of the Social Revolutionary Party, in prison at Sochi, a resort on the Black Sea. Among them is Ely Culbertson, then aged sixteen. He is eager to learn the game as time is running out for him too. He is awaiting a possible death sentence for alleged revolutionary activities and will know his fate within two days.

He watches the players closely, and with growing admiration. He listens to them discussing the future of Russia, not with any sense of recrimination about their own misfortune but still trying to plan ahead in a relentless spirit of enquiry. Instead of feeling appalled by this, he is strangely elated, dimly aware that he is witnessing something vitally important to him, the first coming together of the powerful combination of cards and politics that is to shape much of his life.

Dawn approaches and the game is still in progress. The thud of hobnailed boots is heard in the corridor and their cell door is thrown open by one of the guards and a name called out. The oldest of the group, Ureniev, aged forty, gets up to leave and as he reaches the door, beckons to Ely and says, 'Goodbye, Illiusha. There is no sense in these revolutions. Concentrate on vint.'

Thirty years later, Culbertson was sitting at a bridge table in Budapest, feeling nervous and irritable. His team USA I was competing against the Austrians in the final of the World Championship, and was losing. He watched anxiously as the next hand was dealt. It was the ninety-fifth and next-to-last hand.

Neither side vulnerable
Dealer South

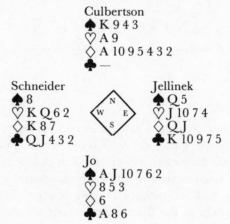

Culbertson
♠ K 9 4 3
♡ A 9
◇ A 10 9 5 4 3 2
♣ —

Schneider
♠ 8
♡ K Q 6 2
◇ K 8 7
♣ Q J 4 3 2

Jellinek
♠ Q 5
♡ J 10 7 4
◇ Q J
♣ K 10 9 7 5

Jo
♠ A J 10 7 6 2
♡ 8 5 3
◇ 6
♣ A 8 6

The bidding:

South	West	North	East
1♠	Pass	2◇	Pass
2♠	Pass	4♡	Pass
4♠	Pass	5◇	Pass
Pass			

He studied his wife and partner, Jo, as she prepared to bid. Jo looked cool and unconcerned. She opened one spade and the bidding quickly moved up to five diamonds, Culbertson's last bid, which became their contract. But something had gone wrong, Jo failed to notice that Culbertson's bid of five diamonds was an asking bid enquiring about slam possibilities. It was too late, they missed a crucial slam. The Austrian team of Frischaeur and Herbert in the second room bid and made the grand slam in spades without difficulty.

Suddenly, for the Culbertsons, their system, on which they relied and depended for years, had failed, and the match was irredeemably lost. The Culbertson supremacy, which had more or less dominated the 1930s, was now at an end. Culbertson had particularly wanted to win this match. It was the first World Championship to include all main bridge-playing countries and he was the one who had done more than anyone else to internationalize Contract bridge. A win here and he could have gone out on top and then looked back on a decade which had begun with his triumph over Lenz, and had gone on to include triumphs over other great rivals such as Sims, as well as his outstanding international successes in the Schwab Cup. It was an impressive record and he had seen his name grow into a household word, virtually synonymous with Contract bridge. A win here would have been a fitting conclusion. But Culbertson knew that things never ran quite as smoothly as this. He knew too that beneath the surface all was not well. Two or three years ago he had lost his real hunger for success, that essential factor in tournament victory. He was having to rely on skills and techniques acquired long ago, and now even his partnership understanding with Jo was collapsing. Unknown to the general public, his marriage with Jo, which in itself had symbolized so much that was modern and promising about Contract bridge, was under severe strain. Not long afterwards, at the beginning of 1938, they would be divorced.

He decided to make this his last tournament match. Instead he would go back to his first love – the study of politics that he first embarked on all those years ago in Russia.

CHAPTER I

RUSSIAN ORIGINS

Ely Culbertson is usually thought of as so very American that it may surprise people to discover that his mother was Russian, the daughter of a Cossack chieftain, and that he spent a turbulent youth in Russia engaging in revolutionary activities in the era preceding the collapse of the Tsar's regime, ending with imprisonment in Sochi. But his story starts earlier, in 1880, with the arrival of his father in the Caucasus to look for that elusive twentieth-century commodity – oil.

Ely's father, Almon Elias Culbertson, was born in 1856, and brought up in Titusville, Pennsylvania. His childhood coincided with the discovery of oil deposits that led to the mushroom growth of Oil City. The Culbertsons as a family were, as Ely liked to remind interviewers in subsequent years, 'as American as the cigar-store Indian'. His branch had lived in Pennsylvania for many years and were originally descended from Scots Covenanters who had set foot in America before the American Revolution. In later years, Ely refuted doubters about his ancestry by joining the Sons of the American Revolution. But, back in the 1860s with oil being discovered almost on their doorstep, the Pennsylvania Culbertsons were more concerned with the pursuit of money and exploited the petroleum resources under their land.

Almon's father, Elias Culbertson, and his uncle, Hamilton Culbertson, were both successful prospectors. Elias, with the money he made, bought a hotel in Titusville, but he was too generous for the harsh environment of an oil-rich town and too easy on credit. The oil gains began to disappear, the hotel got into debt. To compensate, he had to sell some of his land and it was at this point that his son, Almon, then aged twenty-four and a walking and bicycle champion of the state, decided to go and seek his fortune elsewhere. What he knew about was oil; he had watched it being drilled almost in his backyard, and he knew that in this growing industry such knowledge was invaluable. But he wanted to get away, make a life elsewhere. Word had got around in Pennsylvania of the oil strikes now being made in the Caucasus in Russia and rumours abounded of the fortunes to be made there. It was early days as yet, but there was a demand for skilled workmen and above all engineers to work there. Almon made enquiries and found that a Dr Tweddle, an Englishman in the Caucasus, was looking for a chief engineer and skilled labour to develop the 1,500,000 acres of land he had leased in 1879 from Colonel Novosiltzoff. This was not in the more prosperous southern region of the Caucasus, but in the north, in the Kuban province.

Almon arrived in the small village of Illskaya, about sixty miles from Ekaterinodar, in 1880. These villages were more like the personal fiefdoms of the local Cossack chieftain or land-owner, in this case General Rogozny, whose father had been granted land by the Tsar as a reward for his part in the reconquest of the Caucasus in the earlier part of the century. As Almon walked up the village street with his team of five American drillers and mechanics and approached the terrace of the large rambling house they could see standing beside the General his wife, his four children and his mother. In accordance with local custom the old mother was holding out a wooden plate containing bread and salt, blessed by the local Greek Orthodox priest. Almon, shy but hungry after his long journey, took the bread and ate it, noticing that the eldest daughter quickly suppressed her laughter at this. He learnt later that this bread was meant as a symbolic offering of hospitality. Embarrassed, he waited for the next move. The mother continued with her ritual welcome, bowing to the ground three times and saying, 'May God bless your entrance into our house.' They were now permitted to cross the threshold and ushered into the main hall where a feast awaited them.

Almon found himself sitting next to the General's wife with a Mr Gayton, an Englishman long resident in Russia, sitting on his right. As the meal proceded Gayton told him about the Rogozny family. There were four children altogether – Xenia, Alexandra, Glafira and one son, Yegor. The eldest daughter, the one he had seen outside, was called Xenia. She had been married, but her husband had been killed in the Russo-Turkish Wars three years previously. Then her only child had died a year later of malignant fever. Just as Gayton was telling him this, General Rogozny came up and introduced Xenia, telling Almon in French, their only language in common, that she would be his partner for the dancing which was about to start. In the background he could hear musicians playing a waltz. He stood up, asked her to dance and they took the floor. Almon was six foot three, tall and muscular. He waltzed in the vigorous, twirling American fashion but, out of the corner of his eye, he noticed that the other couples were hardly moving but gliding in a slow and decorous manner across the floor, barely touching each other. It was his second *faux pas* in quick succession, but Xenia only smiled at him. It was the beginning of their friendship.

The story of Almon's and Xenia's courtship was often recounted to the Culbertson children. It had all the ingredients of high drama and sensation belonging to something out of the Arabian Nights. Almon set up house outside Illskaya near the oilfields with his manservant Nikita. It was wild and dangerous country. Brigands often descended from the hills and his guard dog, as was the custom, had his ears and tail cut off so it would appear more ferocious. Xenia would come out to see him and they would go riding together in the foothills visiting outlying farms on her father's estate. She longed to hear of this strange and distant land of America. As Almon got to know her better, he could see she had a restless and volatile temperament. At times he was at a loss to understand her moods. At twenty-six she knew the chances of finding a second husband of her own choosing were slender – she would probably be married off to an old man or a widower, Almon presented both an enigma and challenge to her. He was unlike any of her Russian suitors, so American in his ways, but also proud, rather reserved and fearless, like a Cossack. Within her family Xenia had always been the unconventional one.

In time, after several meetings whose details the children were decorously spared, they agreed to get married. Tradition demanded that Almon had to seek her father's permission. First he made a formal demand in writing to General Rogozny to grant him an interview on a matter of 'extreme importance and urgency'. At the appointed hour in the afternoon, he stood waiting for the General, dressed in a tail coat borrowed off Mr Gayton, with white gloves and smoothly brushed hair. A faint smell of camphor emanating from the rarely used tail-coat added to his discomfort. As the servant led him to see General Rogozny, he could tell from the frigid look on his face that he both knew of his mission and disapproved of it. The General, dressed in equally formal attire, greeted him cordially and ordered vodka and liqueurs to be brought in. Pretending not to know the purpose of his visit, the General busied himself with his pipe while waiting for Almon to speak. He had already made his own private assessment of him and come to the conclusion he would make a good husband for Xenia. He had a good mind, a strong heart, he worked hard and no doubt would make a good father, but there were two conditions. First he had to become Greek Orthodox like the rest of the Rogoznys. Almon could agree to that. But the second condition was too much for him. He had to become a Russian subject (and a honorary 'Cossack') and agree to remain in Russia. This was quite against Almon's principles, as he was determined to bring his children up as Americans.

There it was left. Soon the entire household abounded with rumours. 'The Amerikanetz refuses to be baptized,' they whispered to each other.

Convention now dictated that Almon, as a rejected suitor, could no longer visit their house nor see Xenia. She too was heartbroken. Two weeks went by and then Almon heard that General Rogozny was pressing Xenia to accept the proposal of one of her suitors, a middle-aged colonel, wealthy, distinguished and apparently still of adequate vigour. By now Almon knew enough of Cossack customs to appreciate the power of a father. He decided it called for desperate measures. He arranged to abduct her, and use marriage by stealth. This was an age-old but rarely used Cossack custom. It too had clearly defined rules. The kidnapper had to be certain the girl was willing, otherwise a blood feud followed with certain death for the captor. The bride's family, once the kidnapping was known, had to do everything in their power to prevent the marriage. Almon arranged for his manservant to give Xenia's maid a letter inviting her to a final rendezvous before her impending marriage. She rode out to the meeting place expecting to see Almon alone but as she approached a band of Circassians, Almon among them, came forward to intercept her.

As they rode along Almon told Xenia that her father had told him about various ancient Cossack customs, and marriage by stealth was one of them. He had feared he would lose Xenia to her new suitor and had looked for a local priest to marry them, but all had refused, being frightened of the General. Then he had gone off into the mountains to find one there. This was where they were now headed. Xenia made a show of dissent, as custom demanded, but as they rode on through the night her protests diminished.

Back at the General's house there was a tremendous commotion when Xenia's absence was noticed. The maid tremblingly confessed and the General set off immediately in hot pursuit after the elopers. His wife went down on her knees and prayed for his safe – but late – arrival!

By the time the General and his posse reached the mountains, the young couple had already been married by the local priest. As they rushed into the house they found the couple standing in the middle of the room surrounded by the other celebrants. The General wished from the bottom of his heart he could join them, but he was forced to turn on his heel and without so much as a glance at his cherished daughter, bow to the host and sweep out again for the lonely ride back to Illskaya.

After their marriage the Culbertsons set up home in another large house about fifteen miles away from Illskaya. While Almon was increasingly preoccupied with his role as chief engineer at the oil-wells, Xenia made a conscious effort to learn American cooking and American ways.

For the Culbertsons the next few years were the happiest of their young lives. Almon succeeded in bringing up enough oil from the recalcitrant earth to make his employer's continued drilling commercially viable. The Kuban province had always been patchy and difficult terrain to work successfully and its yield was nothing like as prolific as the oilfields further south around Baku.

Their first son, Eugene, was born in 1887. They celebrated in their by now familiar mixed style, part Cossack and part American. The songs were as much of Pennsylvania and West Virginia as of the Caucasus. They even danced the Virginia reel which Almon had introduced to the Cossacks, along with 'corn likker' and the habit of chewing tobacco!

Two daughters, Natasha and Marianna, followed in quick succession but they both contracted diphtheria in their infancy and died in the same month, September 1890. Eugene managed to survive. Xenia was distraught with the death of her two daughters. She turned to religion for comfort, feeling that somehow she had brought on this calamity through neglect of her spiritual duties.

She went on a pilgrimage to the ancient monastery of Derbent on the Caspian Sea to pray before the miraculous ikon of the Holy Mary, the Protectress of all mothers. She promised to do penance and fasting. Before the year was out she was pregnant again. She prayed, read the *Lives of the Saints* and led an exemplary life. Then in the fourth month of her pregnancy, Almon received an offer to go to Romania, at a greatly increased salary, as chief engineer for a foreign company developing the oilfields outside Ploesti in the Carpathian Mountains. It was an offer he could hardly refuse, despite the inclement weather and inconvenient time of year. He went on ahead and the others followed in due course, taking the steamer across the Black Sea from Novorossisk to Constanza in Romania.

Xenia tried to re-create a Russian home in the heart of Romania. However great the superficial similarity to Russia, she felt herself to be among strangers. The time of her confinement was fast approaching and she focussed all her energy on preparing for the birth of her child, this child whom she saw as a gift from God.

Under such auspicious circumstances Illya (Ely) Culbertson made his way into the world on 22 July 1891 in the small village of Poiana di Verbilao, near Ploesti in Romania. He was born 'in a shirt', as the

Russians say, or covered in a caul – another supposed good omen. His father had him registered with the American consul as a native American citizen.

What Ely later called the shuffle of his chromosomic deck meant that he came out as a 'powerful but unbalanced' 7–4–1–1 hand. The ratio of seven coming from his Scots father, the four from his Cossack mother, and the one–one from the bizarre assemblage of ancestors he inherited. Such mixed parentage was to be a crucial element in his life – his attempts to reconcile its two halves (or the seven–four ratio) inspired many of his activities and to the end he was, in many people's eyes, as much Russian as American.

As an infant he was well looked after. As a 'special child', his mother took extra care of him. She breast-fed him to make him resistant to disease, and followed the Romanian custom of employing a male nurse, a strong, healthy, young peasant, to look after him. The Romanians believed that a male nurse gave virility to a boy.

Two years later his brother Alexander (Sasha) was born, dark and handsome, later to make his name as an international violinist. His mother could now justifiably feel she had levelled her score with death – three live children, three dead ones.

Their stay in Romania was cut short by the news that Xenia's mother had died. Her father, the General, had died the year before while out bear-hunting. They had to make the long and arduous journey back to Russia to settle the estate. It was the depths of winter. First they had to make the icy sea crossing of the Black Sea to Novorossisk, then travel in a troika across the snow tracks and through the forests, with the horses nervous and fractious at the threat of wolves.

In Illskaya they moved into the big house where her younger sister, Alexandra, now married to a Pole, Henry Kozlovsky, was living. Xenia's other sister, Glafira, was there as well – she had recently married Constantin Dolinin, a Russian aristocrat and high official in charge of the government's monopoly of vodka for the region.

For the next four years, Ely led an idyllic life. In the long Caucasian summer he ran about barefoot, played with the boys of the village, frequented a swimming hole under a giant oak tree. Sometimes he would go up into the hills with the Cossack herdsmen on horseback to tend their sheep and goats, and they would describe the Cossack way of life in their *stanitzas*, or villages, and show him their *kindjals*, knives keenly edged on both sides with a groove down the middle to drain an enemy's blood away.

At the age of six, he was photographed with his brothers. Dressed like a Cossack in his white woolly coat, with his broad trousers tucked into leather boots, a small dagger inserted into its silver sheath on his belt and a wild-looking fuzzy *papakha* on his head, Ely stands gazing out at the world with the self-assurance of someone twice his years. The photograph of the three brothers was taken as a reminder of life in the Caucasus. Almon had decided to return to America where they were to start up a new life.

The family disembarked at Philadelphia and spent their first few days there. Xenia found it a nightmare, nothing but noise and incessant bustle and unfamiliar sights. The raucous atmosphere of an American city at the turn of the century was not what she had bargained for and she longed for her native Caucasus.

They moved on to Franklin, Pennsylvania, to stay with Almon's father and stepmother. It was a regular Cossack invasion of the town, with the three little Cossack boys, their mother the daughter of a Cossack general, and all their Russian belongings including the samovar and huge pillows. During all his years in Russia, Almon had dreamt of returning to his native land with his wife and children to show them the small wooden cottages and pine-scented hills above the Allegheny river where he was brought up.

But the dream failed to match the reality, and a month later they were packing to go back to Russia. However much he had prized his homecoming he realized that now he no longer fitted into the tight framework of a small community such as this. It was as if he had needed to come the whole way back to Pennsylvania to realize how much he valued the Caucasus, with its space and breadth of opportunity. Here he was a mining engineer along with many others, but in Russia he was someone – and the pioneering spirit in him came to the fore.

Almon made enquiries and was soon offered the post of chief engineer for the newly-formed Spies Petroleum Company who were to set up business in Grozny, in the heart of the Caucasus.

Its driving force was G.R. Spies, a German with extensive oil experience. It was registered in London with a paid-up capital of £1,500,000. English interest in the Caucasus was now at its height. As investors literally fell over each other to get a stake in the Caucasus, it became like a gold rush. But Spies managed to avoid association with the more maverick companies and in time acquired a fine reputation both for the thoroughness of its methods and its enlightened management.

Much of the credit for the company's success must go to Almon as its chief engineer. His role was by no means an easy one. Not only did he have to be a technical expert in the drilling and boring for oil, but he also had to deal with the immensely complicated labour problem that the Caucasus presented. This was due to the different tribes and races employed at the wells. They were a mixture of Armenians, Tartars, Lesghines, Grozines and Osetines. They each spoke a different language, each had their own national or tribal holidays and frequently would not work or speak to each other. No wonder that Pliny wrote of the Caucasus that, 'We Romans conducted our affairs there with the aid of 150 interpreters.' The oil-wells simply reflected conditions all over the Caucasus, where adjacent valleys between mountains would frequently have two different tribes speaking totally different languages. In addition to this, the chief engineer was likely to be roused in the middle of the night if some accident had happened or there had been a blow-out. At the best of times it was hard, dirty work, but rewards were there for the taking.

One day he was talking to a Cossack who had just come down from the hills. It was the rainy season and a ray of sunlight glinted on the Cossack's muddy boots. It caught Almon's eye and, as he looked down, he saw a tell-tale black speck on them. He pulled out his pocket-knife and scraped a little mud off and then began to question the Cossack carefully, asking him to take him back to the hills, with the promise of a reward if successful. When he returned a few days later he maintained an air of great secrecy, but offered to take Ely, then aged ten, back with him. They rode for some time before stopping among some ordinary-looking grass and weeds. Almon cleared away the undergrowth to reveal a shallow pit with a few crystals reflecting the sunlight. He had found oil, his personal discovery, later named the Neklepayefsky oilfield, and the source of the royalties on which the Culbertsons were to live in comfort for the next twenty years. It was a tribute to Almon's skill as a geologist that he was able to locate it singlehandedly.

Now they were back in the Caucasus, the Culbertsons had the children's education to think of. Eugene was sent to the gymnasium in Vladikavkaz about sixty miles away, while Ely and Sasha were to be tutored at home. A French governess, a male tutor, a violin teacher and a priest for their religious upbringing were appointed. Mlle Pinchon, their governess, was prim and severe, a stickler for propriety. Ely took an instant dislike to her. She was responsible for French and good manners. Mr Nicholayev, the tutor, schooled them in Russian grammar, history, geography and science. His manner too was distant and reserved, but he claimed to justify this by a deep love of the truth. Almon was convinced he was giving his two sons the best education available, despite their protests at the unfriendliness of their teachers. They were forced to persevere, just as a generation later Ely was to impose an equally harsh regime on his own children, even though he must have remembered how dispiriting it had been for him.

The big event of the week was the Sunday outing, the family all dressed up and sitting in their landau, to the cathedral in Grozny. There was an atmosphere of suppressed excitement as they got ready. Ely loved these visits, awestruck by the mystery and ritual of the religious ceremonies. It gave him a feeling of elated power to be part of it. Even at the tender age of twelve he was drawn to situations of high drama and splendour.

In the autumn of 1904, at the age of thirteen, he was sent to the gymnasium of Vladikavkaz to join the eighteen-year-old Eugene, now in his last year. Vladikavkaz (Ruler of the Caucasus) was the nearest large town, about sixty miles away. It lay under the snow-capped mountains with the peak of Mount Kasbek clearly visible. The gymnasium was modelled on the German system, with eight-year courses, ranging from the age of ten to eighteen. Ely, with the advantages of his private tutoring, was put into a fifth-year class with pupils two or three years older than himself. He was given lodgings with the Misses Goriev, two old spinsters of noble birth, who also taught foreign languages at the school. Theirs was a world of flannel underwear, mufflers, vapour inhalers, barley soup with lemon, mustard footbaths, and a grand piano in the salon with a book of Chopin waltzes neatly opened on the middle page.

Entering the gymnasium was a perplexing experience for him. Here he was suddenly one among hundreds of pupils. It was a blow to his self-esteem. Eugene solved the problem by merging with the crowd, but Ely found himself unable to do this. He was more of a loner. Being American gave them a certain inflated status. America represented the country of the free and of modernity to the other students and they looked upon the brothers as rarities. Ely knew that his temperament had been shaped partly by his upbringing. The sense of uniqueness or difference had been early instilled into him by his mother, while his father was ambitious for him and expected high standards.

Not all his fellow pupils viewed this aloofness with favour. Rather than seek to join them and share their preoccupations, Ely opted instead to try and become a leader. He did this by sustained effort – that sense of application that was to be a hallmark of many of his bridge triumphs. It is always tempting to see the man in the child, or in this case the adolescent, but in Ely's case it seems to be true. He wasn't a natural at sports, but he taught himself to be good at them; he was always intellectually among the front rank. The other pupils began to look up to him. Then, just as typically, as soon as he had

got to the top, he became bored and began to lose interest. He cultivated another pose – that of the cynical, rather world-weary, omnis-
cient adolescent. He moved, as it were, from the front of the class to
the back row where he joined the old guard of hardened, rebellious
students. He read Edgar Allan Poe for the macabre and mysterious
in his writings, he read Goethe for his tinge of *Weltschmerz* and he
picked up whenever he could the newly fashionable author Chekhov.
Above all he wanted to identify with the university students of the
town. He affected the same foppish attitude as they displayed and
engaged in the same pursuits – drinking vodka, going to horse races
and chasing girls.

The question of girls presented quite a problem. He wanted desperately to be rid of the embarrassment of his chastity. It hardly
seemed in keeping with his wished-for image of man of the world.
Once or twice he ventured to the parts of town where loose women
were reputed to hang out, but to no avail. In polite circles he was
going through a tortured phase, finding it hard to look an attractive
woman full in the face. He was saved, in time-honoured fashion, by
his university student friends. They invited him to join them on a
Saturday night jaunt. Having fortified themselves liberally with Kache-
tian wine and vodka, they ended up in a brothel. Ely had to borrow
a student's uniform on the way as gymnasiasts weren't allowed into
brothels. Once inside, gazing at the cherub-laden stucco surroundings,
he rapidly began to lose heart. Trepidation and awe at the task ahead
soon erased the effects of the drink. The madame greeted them, and
summoned her girls. Glancing at Ely's youthful appearance, she pat-
ted him on the head and told him, 'We'll have Anita for you. She
adores young boys!' Everyone laughed and Ely felt compelled to join
in if only to conceal his embarrassment. Had he been alone he would
have rushed out there and then.

The others picked their partners and went off. Anita was brought
over. She was just as he had feared, motherly and looking like a faded
rose. He really wished the earth would open up and he could disappear, but there was no retreating now. She took him by the hand
and led him off to her room where, carefully extracting five roubles
from him, she initiated him into the uncertain pleasures of paid sex.

Afterwards in the salon his fellow students slapped him on the back
and congratulated him vociferously on reaching his manhood, but all
he wanted to do was go home and vomit – the mixture of Anita's
overbearing presence, the wine and vodka and the sense of revulsion
at what had happened were too much for him. At home he took a
long bath, feeling he had defiled the image of his mother in some
way.

But next evening he was out on the town with the same group of students. Since it was Sunday and part of the weekend they saw no reason not to go on with their celebrations. Predictably they ended up at the brothel. Ely had been drinking much more than he was accustomed to all evening and it was beginning to show. Once they got there, he sat morosely with the madame and the expectant Anita, paying no attention to her unmistakable overtures and engaging in what he thought was adult conversation. He only got progressively drunker. As the other students came back to the salon, they chaffed him for not going off with a girl. He became truculent and made remarks to one of them that caused a fight. Ely, in the manner of such incidents, contrived to do more damage to the broken mirrors of the establishment than to his opponent. The police had to be called and he was escorted to the local jail. He was only released after his mother had been notified and the local governor, whom she knew, had intervened.

But the repercussions of this incident were far-reaching. The principal of the gymnasium heard about it and his father was informed. Ely was almost certain to be expelled from his school and under the existing regulations in Russia, expulsion from one gymnasium meant that he couldn't enrol at another. His father, determined to use what influence he could on the principal, came from Grozny to see him. As Ely and his father strode along the corridors of his school, he could feel the envious glances of his fellow pupils on him, now apprised of his supposedly manly endeavours. The principal listened to Almon's arguments and agreed to let Ely be transferred – the only solution that was a way round the regulations.

Then Almon, with a sense of punctiliousness and financial rectitude that Ely failed to inherit, insisted on returning to the brothel to pay for the damage. He also wanted to rub Ely's nose in the mess he had made.

But it was goodbye to Vladikavkaz for ever, and to the Mlles Goriev who made a tearful farewell. Back in Grozny, he was brought before his parents. His father felt badly let down by this incident and his mother was seriously alarmed at the signs of excess in her devoted son. Rather than risk his consorting with more 'diseased women', she resolved to remedy this in her own particular way.

Since Ely's 'expulsion' had taken place in the middle of the academic year, his parents had to engage a private tutor for him. This was Herr Raessler, a single man in his early forties from the Baltics. Everything about him reeked of the bookish and pedantic. His pale-blue eyes and protruding teeth and air of perpetual bewilderment gave him an other-worldly look. He was writing a treatise on Spinoza, and was under the spell of Nietzsche. But Ely grew to like him, and was introduced to a wide range of literature that he might otherwise never have come across.

For the summer the family went to Kislovodsk, an inland summer resort just below the mountains, with a casino, lakes and villas belonging to rich merchants and members of the nobility. Almon remained in Grozny, but Herr Raessler, the old nurse *diadka* and their new maid Dounya came along.

Dounya had mysteriously appeared a few days before their summer holiday began. Her duties were to look after Ely and Sasha. She was extremely pretty, a Ukrainian type. Though only twenty she was already a widow, having lost her husband in 1905 in the Russo-Japanese War. Before long Ely and she were fast friends, and then one night he went to her room and they became lovers. Ely was blissfully happy – gone were the profane memories of Anita and now for the first time he could experience the delights of uncomplicated passion. Dounya was tender, playful, sometimes serious. Ely now began to work and study hard. He stopped going out, content with the way his life was going. Then, one afternoon while he was reading in the garden beneath the open window of his mother's bedroom, he heard raised voices. His father had returned a few days before from Grozny and was accusing his mother of bringing Dounya into the household like a procuress. Xenia saw no harm in her actions. Rather this, she declared, than the sort of things Ely got up to in Vladikavkaz. But the puritan streak in Almon was shocked, and Dounya was told to leave. Ely promised passionately to keep in touch with her, but she left his life for ever.

As the summer of 1906 drew to a close, Almon called his family together for a conference. He said he had some momentous news for them. He was retiring and not going back to Grozny. He had made enough money to provide for them comfortably now and in the future. Instead he wanted to devote himself to the children's welfare and education, and in particular Sasha's development as a violinist.

Almon had had this plan in the back of his mind for some time. He justified his years of toil in the gruelling conditions of the oilfields as a means of ensuring that his children had a better start in life. He had witnessed the decline of the Culbertson fortunes in the example of his father, who had gone from comparative wealth to near penury. He was determined not to repeat the same mistake. On the contrary, he wanted to see his branch of the family back where it belonged, on the crest of the wave – with Sasha as a successful artist and Ely a scientist. It was the familiar wish of the successful entrepreneur to see his children shine in more cultural and socially acceptable pursuits. Almon was a little over fifty and he looked forward to this second career.

The plan was for the family to move up to Rostov-on-Don. Eugene would go to Munich Polytechnicum, Ely to the local gymnasium and Sasha to the Conservatory. Rostov was then a city of over half a million people, sprawling along the shores of the River Don. They took an entire floor of a large apartment building with a wide marble staircase leading up from the ground floor, near the central park.

At the gymnasium, Ely was determined to cut a dash, flaunting his difference from normal students. He soon found himself among a moneyed, fast-living, card-playing set who spent their time thinking up elaborate pranks. One of these was directed at the principal and misfired. Ely was again expelled. They had been only nine months in Rostov. For Almon the blow was softened by the reassuring news of Sasha's outstanding progress, and he decided to devote most of his energies to his well-being. His marriage with Xenia was beginning to drift apart. Almon had never been entirely at home in the very Russian environment Xenia created. They now undertook an unofficial separation. Almon took Sasha to Prague to study under Profesor Sěvčík, the teacher of Kubelik, Kocian and others. Xenia went back to Ekaterinodar where her sister Alexandra was living, taking Ely with her.

CHAPTER 2

Nadya

Ely was rapidly growing up. At sixteen, he was physically and intellectually mature enough to be mistaken for a twenty-one-year-old. His mother had given him an extra allowance, as if to encourage him to hurry up and attain his manhood. Ely responded to the invitation to become a man about town. He joined the fast set, made up of the younger Cossack officers, the offspring of the wealthier families and a few university students. His days and nights were soon spent in bars and cafés, and it was in one of these that he pulled off what seemed to him a great coup. He met a young French actress and, sacrificing every penny of his allowance, had installed her as his mistress in a suite in the main hotel. Soon they were to be seen driving around town in a rubber-wheeled open phaeton, attracting admiring and envious glances from bystanders and colleagues alike.

For the *jeunesse dorée* of the town, style was everything. Caucasians, and particularly Georgians, have always been flamboyant dressers and the current fashion was to imitate the dandified posture of a Parisian student of the time. Ely, always a snappy dresser, took to this and cultivated the other pursuits that were considered indispensable – a slightly fastidious manner of speaking, proficiency in cards, billiards and fencing, as well as a cavalier attitude to eating and drinking.

But, behind all this frivolity, another side to Ely began to assert itself. To the outside world it was concealed behind a mask of aristocratic disdain, but there was both dissatisfaction and frustration at the shallowness of his adolescent life. Where, he asked himself, was it all leading to and where had his lofty ideals gone? The answer came from the external events that were already taking shape around him.

For two or three years now, the rumblings of social discontent had been distinctly felt in the outposts of the Russian Empire. The defeat of the Russian forces during the Russo-Japanese War and the humiliating destruction of the Russian fleet at Tsushima in May 1905 had visibly shaken many people's faith in the old order and brought civil unrest to a head. Trouble had simmered all that summer, with frequent strikes, agrarian outrages and assassinations. In June the famous mutiny on the battleship *Potemkin* had broken out. Eventually the

Tsar yielded and in October agreed to grant Russia a constitution. The first parliament, or Duma, was convened. But this 'October Mani-ifesto' split those who opposed it. The majority of them were prepared to accept its terms, but others, such as the first workers' Soviet, would not agree to it and there was continued resistance and street fighting in the working-class districts of Moscow well into December of that year. Order was only restored there by harsh repressive measures.

Against this background, Ely was developing his own political con-sciousness. He noticed that many of his peers were beginning to feel the same way, and were divesting themselves of the trappings of wealth in an attempt to identify with 'the people'. It was as if the young were trying to expiate the sins of their fathers, rather as at the time of the Crusades the children of the rich stripped themselves of their silken robes and made arduous pilgrimages to the Holy Land. In Russia in 1905 the generation gap was as wide as it had ever been.

For an impressionable adolescent with a touch of idealism these were stirring times. Within his own immediate group of friends in Ekaterinodar, definite changes had taken place. One of his closest friends had already joined the revolutionaries and was berated for being a traitor to his class. This espousal of radical causes was fairly widespread among younger members of the privileged classes. Many radicals, populists, terrorists even, came from families where the father could easily have been a governor general, estate-owner, merchant, senior bureaucrat or respected member of the professions.

A few days later he went to a mass meeting in the local park organized by the Social Revolutionary Party, the most popular of the left-wing parties among his student group. The Social Revolutionary Party had been founded, illegally, in 1901, at about the same time as the Social Democrats, later to subdivide into the Bolsheviks and the Mensheviks. The Social Revolutionary Party followed the populist, pro-peasant tradition of the 1870s, and advocated the use of terror in the early stages of the struggle. Their eventual aim was for peasants to confiscate the land not already held by the communes, but first they wanted to clear the way for socialism by demanding limited measures of reform – political liberty, the eight-hour day in factory and village and a constituent assembly. Their headquarters in the southern half of Russia were in Kharkov, but the party had a strong following in the Caucasus and the meeting Ely was about to attend had been called to draw attention to some of those demands.

Walking through the vast crowd assembled in the park made a deep impression on him. He stopped to listen to one of the speakers haranguing some of the gathering from a platform and watched as the upturned faces of the moustachioed peasants and working men listened in rapture to him. This speaker wore the now familiar belted shirt outside his trousers with a peaked workman's cap, but his face betrayed the nervous, ascetic quality of an intellectual and he spoke in pedantic, cumbersome phrases that can have meant little to his audience. Ely marvelled at the way they listened with unquestioning attention. It was an early lesson in crowd psychology, something he was to remember in later years when he was called upon to deal with large assemblies of people. It was an enthralling experience and Ely was overwhelmed by the feeling of solidarity and oneness with the crowd around him.

When the speaker had finished and the crowd was milling around expectantly waiting for the next thing to happen, Ely suddenly felt an urge to speak. He wanted to address the crowd and confess his secret longing to be part of them. As he tells the story in his autobiography, he waited for a moment and then went up to the platform and said to the speaker.

'Let me say a few words to them, please.'

'Are you a Social Revolutionist?'

'No, but I'm their friend.'

The nearby spectators had heard this, and encouraged him to speak, proclaiming that it was now a free country.

Ely climbed on to the platform. The voices hushed and the crowd watched him with curiosity. A few moments before he had been yearning to speak but now he was tongue-tied and embarrassed. The silence of the crowd throbbed in his ears.

'Ladies and gentlemen,' he began falteringly.

'Comrades, please,' a ferocious-looking, bearded young peasant standing at the front called out.

'Oh, yes, excuse me, comrades.' Ely tried again, smiling in his best, governess-taught way.

'We'll excuse you if you go on,' snapped the same voice.

He could tell he was making an unfavourable impression. The crowd was beginning to eye him with suspicion, with his well-tailored clothes, cane and diamond signet-ring (none of which he had thought to leave behind before coming to the meeting – an indication of his essentially romantic view of revolutionary engagement) and mumbling at his upper-class accent.

'Perhaps he's an *agent provocateur*, or in the pay of the police,' a voice called out.

'No, he's just a mama's boy.'

This last shot stung Ely hard.

'Comrades,' he began again. 'I have come here to tell you that I am the son of a capitalist –'

'You certainly look it.' The same voice again.

'Yes, I look it, but –'

He did not have time to finish. Another speaker jumped up on to the platform and pushed him aside. As Ely tried to continue, the other man placed one hand on his shoulder and called out to the crowd,

'Comrades, this man is not a spy. He has come to tell you he is ashamed of his own capitalist father. He claims to be the victim of the capitalist regime. I really feel sorry for him. Look at his pale face, the rings under his eyes and his trembling hands ...' The sarcasm was building up. 'In one night of debauchery he spends more money than any of you can make in a month of slavery. Is it for this that you are working?'

'No,' roared the crowd in unison.

The speaker took his hand off Ely's shoulder and stood back to point at him.

'These are the criminals who seduce your daughters and steal your wives. Is that what you are working for?'

'No,' they shouted back. Soon there were cries of, 'Down with the rich! Down with the Tsar!'

The speaker now turned back to Ely and asked him, 'Do you really want to be one of us?'

'Yes, I do.'

Then, with a melodramatic gesture towards the crowd, he said, 'Ask them to forgive you.'

Ely did not know what to say. Deeply embarrassed, flustered, his habitual blush surging to his cheeks, he stammered out, 'Forgive me.'

So blatant was his discomfort that some members of the crowd took pity on him, and he heard one or two cries of commiseration. As he looked at them, he noticed a well-dressed young girl standing among them looking at him with a mixture of sympathy and pity. He was momentarily distracted by her, but the earlier speaker was marshalling the crowd and telling them to get into formation for the march to the Governor's Palace.

Flushed now with heroism, Ely determined to be in the front rank, among those who would feel the first effects of any opposition. The march set off with the red flag flying, banners unfurled, the words of the Varishanka and the Internationale ringing in his ears.

> Arise, you prisoners of starvation
> Arise, you wretched of the earth
> For justice thunders condemnation
> A better world's in birth.

They soon reached the Governor's Palace and surged into the square, shouting for the Governor to appear. They had brought with them a lengthy petition, with a list of demands and complaints and a selected deputation to present it. Instead the chief of police appeared on the balcony and called out,

'I give you ten minutes to disperse.'

This was met by jeers and cat-calls, and upraised clenched fists. Mounted Cossacks, whose presence testified to the seriousness of the occasion, stood at every exit to the square except one. The police strategy had been deliberately to let the marchers into the square and then seal off the other exits. Seeing the Cossacks brought back memories of the occasion in Tiflis in August 1905 when members of one of their regiments had fired volley after volley through the open windows of the town hall when a Socialist meeting was in progress, with no apparent warning. But that massacre had only served to inflame the spirit of rebellion, none more so than in the heart of a local shoemaker's son, one Joseb Vissarionovich Djugashvili, then an active member of the Bolshevik faction of the Georgian Social Democrats, and later to be known as Stalin.

The Cossack officer in charge ostentatiously held a watch in his hand and, as the last minute approached, called out:

'Your last minute! Disperse! Move on!'

The leaders stood firm. They knew the risks, and knew that the propaganda effect of a confrontation like this, even though there might be deaths, was far greater than that achieved through individuals terrorized and beaten by the Okhrana, the Tsar's secret police, in the privacy of the jails. They both wanted and needed the publicity as the peasantry was remarkably slow in switching their allegiance from the Tsar, who remained for many of them a God-like figure unable to do any wrong.

When the time was up, the Cossacks charged. The crowd soon broke up as the horses galloped towards them, but the most steadfast among them refused to move. Ely's instinct was to flee along with the rest of them towards the only exit, but his pride and new-found heroism held him back.

A Cossack horse knocked him violently aside, but he was prevented from falling to the ground by the solid mass of men behind him. Next he heard the swishing sound of a knout's leather thongs flailing through the air and raised his hands to protect his eyes, but immediately felt a sharp pain on his back, as blow after blow followed. He was almost delirious with excitement as if those blows were beyond pain.

By now the remains of the crowd had begun to scatter quickly, and the air was rent with the gasps and screams of wounded and dying people. Beside him on the ground lay a placard proclaiming 'Workers of the World, Unite' that a young dead peasant had been carrying a moment before.

Seconds later, panic spread. He ran with everyone else out of the square, pursued by the Cossacks. He fled down a side street, and turned off into a small alleyway which proved to be a cul-de-sac. He stood huddled in a corner, trying to look inconspicuous.

As he caught his breath he heard a noise behind him. It was the girl he had seen at the meeting in the park. She told him how she had watched him take his place in the front row of the march, and had gone on it herself but when the Cossacks charged she had fled immediately from the square and hidden down the street. So began his encounter with Nadya, the young Russian revolutionary who was to transform his adolescence and leave a lasting imprint on him for the rest of his life.

They waited a while, then decided to move out. They walked cautiously along the street. Ely groaned. As they came out into daylight, the girl gasped with horror. There was a deep cut on his neck. She took out a handkerchief and deftly swabbed his wound saying, 'This will do till we get to my home.'

They headed towards the main square looking for a cab, past houses which now had their doors and windows firmly thrown open (it was a serious offence to harbour revolutionaries). Small groups stood tensely discussing what had happened just before.

They hailed an *isvoschik*, a small horse-drawn cab, and told the coachman to go to her house. As they turned the corner, they were both horror-struck to see the bodies of the dead already being carted away out of the square. As one cart passed by with a badly mutilated corpse, Ely instinctively leant forward to shield the girl's view from it. But she pulled him back impatiently saying:

'You're not a realist. You seem afraid of the truth when it's horrible.'

'Who, I, not a realist?' Ely protested, but inwardly he was sickened.

'They'll pay for it ... with blood,' he said, full of adolescent bravura.

The girl dismissed this.

'We are working for tomorrow, for the generations to come, not for today. It's not individuals that count.'

Ely studied this girl who seemed so determined and forthright, despite her tender years. She could not be more than twenty.

'But *you* count,' Ely insisted.

'I don't count either.'

'Who does then?'

'The children ... people may be evil, but children are good ... they are innocent victims.'

'And how do you propose to save the children?'

'Through science and machines.'

'But machines have no soul.'

'You're wrong. Machines do have a soul of their own, even primitive machines. We must change the system so that science can move forward and save all the children – there is no other hope.'

'You may have to do it against the will of the people,' Ely ventured.

'The people are cowardly, stupid and cruel. We too must be cruel, but wise, even lying and hypocritical if necessary. We can win only if we are strong and unashamed.'

The coachman drew up in front of a large yellow house, partly hidden behind acacia bushes and oak trees.

'My father is a doctor,' the girl said, as they walked into the house, led by an old woman who had clearly been the girl's nurse and who shook her head disapprovingly at Ely's bandaged neck.

'Another of those student revolutionaries! They'll be the ruin of you one day!'

'Is father home?'

'No, he's out on an important case. He should be back soon.' The nurse threw another reproachful glance at Ely and ushered them into the drawing-room.

Ely suddenly became very formal, clicked his heels and bowed. 'May I introduce myself? I am ...'

But the girl laughed.

'You needn't. You are Illya Culbertson. You are the *Amerikanetz* who has been making such a noise around here!'

'How do you know me?'

'Your cousin Tasya told me about you.'

Ely's heart sank. Tasya must have told her a lot else.

'You had a French mistress, and you spent your time fooling around town.'

'I know. It was pretty stupid of me.'

'Why?'

'Surely you can't think that sort of life is right?'

'It depends,' she said enigmatically.

'How do you mean?'

She looked at him seriously. 'I mean, the more you do for others, the more you have a right to do things for yourself.'

'But that's just it ... I've done nothing for others.'

She looked at him kindly.

'That was then. Now you have at last tried. I like you for that.

When you stood up to speak in the park I could see how agonized you were, but at least you tried.'

He discovered her name was Nadya Igorovna. He had never met anyone like her. She seemed such an extraordinary mixture of idealist, coquette and pragmatist. Physically she was tall and broad-shouldered, with a fashionably narrow waist. She had striking blue-green eyes and dark hair. Even in her habitual plain student's uniform, she had an indefinably aristocratic air about her. In her presence he felt decidedly inferior. Three years younger than her and intellectually her inferior, he had little to offer and suspected her kindness sprang from pity as much as anything else.

The door opened and Nadya's father came in. He was a big man, of commanding presence.

'Another bandit, Nadyushka?'

'Yes, Papa, an American one this time – Illya Culbertson.'

The doctor dressed his wound for him, a risky action since doctors who dressed the wounds of revolutionaries or criminals were required by law to report the fact to the police. Nadya's father made it quite clear that he did not share his daughter's political views and was simply acting out of compassion. He warned Ely that Nadya had the most romantic views of America and all things American, and since he was the first American she had met, she was bound to treat him like some precious object.

Ely felt it was time to leave but before doing so he asked Nadya if he could see her the next day. Her reply came instantly.

'Of course. From now on I must take care of you.'

He returned home in a state of supreme excitement. In one day he had launched himself into politics and had encountered this girl with whom he convinced himself he was head over heels in love. Hurrying upstairs, he refused dinner and went straight to his room to be alone. His mother was left to guess about what had happened.

The next morning Ely rushed over to see his cousin Tasya.

'Do you know Nadya Igorovna?'

'Of course I know her. She's very beautiful, but a bit crazy. She's not your type.'

'Why not?'

'She's much too serious – a highbrow. In fact there are rumours she's become a revolutionary.'

Tasya was a different type altogether, but she told Ely one or two interesting details about Nadya's past. Her father came from a well-off, noble family. He surprised his relations by becoming a doctor and specializing as a bacteriologist. Equally surprisingly he suddenly disappeared to Tiflis one day and came back with a Georgian princess as wife. Their marriage produced only one child, Nadya, and the mother died when the girl was only nine. Nadya had then been brought up by the nurse whom Ely had met. At the age of seventeen, three years before, she met a middle-aged, poor, ugly, pot-bellied fellow who had arrived in Ekaterinodar from nowhere, and became his mistress. He said his name was Ivanov but no one knew whether this was his real name. Nor was his claim to be a journalist true. In fact, as it later emerged, he was one of the leading revolutionaries. It was even whispered that he was a member of the Central Committee, which had its headquarters in Switzerland. Eventually he was arrested by the Tsar's police and thrown into jail. Then he escaped under mysterious circumstances and was never seen again. Nadya was deeply upset by his disappearance and was gravely ill for some time, but then she threw herself wholeheartedly into the revolutionary movement.

Through Nadya, Ely was soon admitted to the Social Revolutionary Party. But he had to be vetted first as they were still worried about *agents provocateurs*. It was some time before he could become a fully-fledged member. He hovered on the edge of the party, proud to be part of it and to be in the service of the underground political movement. How much this was out of genuine conviction and how much out of a desire to win Nadya's heart is hard to say.

Nadya put him to work and persuaded him to set up a clandestine printing-press – in his mother's garden! Xenia was very pleased to hear of his sudden enthusiasm for chemistry and wish to have a laboratory in the summer-house at the bottom of the garden. The advantage for the revolutionaries lay in the fact that the back-gate led on to an alley by the river along which they could transmit their secret packages. Indeed, it was Ely's mother who financed the whole operation. He went to her and, in a painful scene, confessed to recent gambling losses. He said he had lost 1,000 roubles and reminded her that, in true Russian fashion, this was a debt of honour that had to be settled within twenty-four hours.

Ely had to learn revolutionary discipline. Nadya made him understand that the cause was all important, that they had to win, at all costs. She belonged to that generation of students that a contemporary writer, Prince Eugène Troubetskoy, then Professor at the University of Kiev, described as 'having a passionate readiness to put themselves at the service of the social ideal and a need for self-sacrifice, a yearning for martyrdom'. He compared them, with their receptiveness to radical ideas, to their counterparts in France before 1789. Nadya's own personal heroine and model was Maria Spiridonova, a fellow Social Revolutionary Party member, who had shot and killed General

Luzhenovsky in 1906 for his role in burning down villages of rebellious peasants. For Spiridonova being a Social Revolutionary meant dedicating 'one's life, one's thoughts, one's feelings to the realization of the party's ideas; it means owning nothing but the interests and ideals of the party; utilizing every moment of one's life in such a way that the cause may be richer for it' – an indication of the passionate commitment inspired in the party's adherents at this time.

Nadya also made Ely discard some of the recklessness that he had assumed was both the way to her heart and an essential part of the revolutionary endeavour. Together they made round after round of meetings. Ely even learnt how to address meetings, standing up, a callow youth, in front of an audience of bearded working men and peasants. As his confidence grew, so Ely studied his fellow party members and found he had joined a group comprising a wide cross-section of society. The usual meeting-place was at the house of one of them for interminable discussions round a samovar in an increasingly smoke-filled room. Some he already knew, but others he recognized as being the sons or daughters of local tradesmen, professional people and occasionally the upper classes. Ely stood out as the *Amerikanetz* and was looked to as an authority on America, which they all held up as the model of freedom and democracy.

They planned revolutionary tactics and ways of combating the widening powers of the police. News had just come in of legislation introduced by Stolypin, the Prime Minister, that empowered governors general to hand over anyone accused of subversive or revolutionary activity to a special court composed of a chairman and four military or naval officers. The case was then heard in secret within twenty-four hours and concluded within forty-eight. The sentence had to be executed at once. It was a particularly repressive measure and was used widely in the Caucasus where, because of religious and nationalist (i.e. secessionist) differences, disaffection from central government was widespread. The revolutionaries counselled extra caution but for someone as young and impressionable as Ely it was heady stuff.

Nadya and he became inseparable. He idolized her, putting her on a pedestal, so that thoughts of physical possession were banished for the time being. He still could not quite believe his luck, and thought she might drop him at any moment. He avoided telling his mother about her, knowing that she would disapprove because of the involvement with any aspect of revolutionary politics. However, his mother must have got an inkling of his affair with Nadya, because now she insisted that Ely accompany her on a trip to Europe. She wanted him out of harm's way. Ostensibly she was going for treatment of her diabetes, to the spa at Karlsbad and then on to Switzerland, Austria and Germany. He told Nadya of his proposed trip and, to his surprise, she was delighted. Now he could carry important messages to colleagues in Switzerland and bring back clandestine literature. Really all Ely wanted to know was whether she would miss him while he was away. Reassured by her he took the letters from a certain Stepanov, leader of the local revolutionary committee. She made him also learn by heart two or three highly confidential messages which he was only to commit to paper once he had crossed the border and arrived in Karlsbad. He could then send them on to Switzerland.

Europe to him was like a breath of fresh air. No longer did he have to look behind him to see if he was being followed or lower his voice in the company of friends or colleagues. His father and Sasha joined them from Prague and fortunately his mother seemed to respond to the beneficial effects of the waters. He was glad to see Sasha. He had been making good progress in Prague and was now considered among Professor Sĕvčík's star pupils. He was still only thirteen but had already given concerts at Berlin and Vienna and been warmly acclaimed at each of them. Soon after arriving Ely faithfully posted his letters to Switzerland and a month later received a visit from a mysterious Russian who gave him some more sealed letters to take back plus a package of illegal propaganda.

He was worried how he was going to smuggle them through the notoriously strict Russian customs. Ely decided the safest place to hide them was the most obvious, under his overcoat carried on his arm. The plan worked. As the train made its journey across the interminable steppes, his mind was full of Nadya and of how high her esteem would be when he returned with his packages.

She was there waiting for him at the station. He greeted her awkwardly, conscious of his mother's presence as she made a little ceremony of handing him over, making some comment about him now being 'a man of the world' as he stood there in his new tailored suit from 'Old England', the top men's outfitters in Vienna. Ely was undergoing what Huysmans, later a favourite author, termed the 'painful and exquisite' emotions of adolescence.

They went back together to his house where he could retrieve the letters and hide the contraband literature in the garden pavilion. Nadya told him how things had changed quite dramatically during his two-month absence. The revolutionaries were now much more subdued. Many were on the run and others had been captured by the Okhrana. Nadya had noticed some suspicious-looking individuals hanging around her house. She feared they were from the dreaded

Black Hundreds. This was a loosely-knit organization of extreme right–wing individuals, many of them no better than thugs, who usually went around in bands of twenty or thirty. They had come into existence in 1905 as an offshoot of the Union of the Russian People, a coalition of various reactionary and extremist groups who opposed the advocates of constitutionalism and all left-wing parties, on the basis that they were anti-Russian and anti-Tsar. The Black Hundreds' preferred method of combating revolutionary movements was to use the same weapons as they did, in other words riots and acts of individual terrorism.

In the Caucasus, their following was not as great as elsewhere and their targets fewer. They were strongly anti-semitic, but there were not many Jews locally. The Black Hundreds were just as violently opposed to the intelligentsia, but the Caucasus had few universities. Instead these self-styled forces of 'lawfulness and civic order', carrying icons and portraits of the Tsar and chanting their slogan 'Beat the Jews and the intelligentsia and save Russia', would burst into high schools and insist that the students join them in singing 'God Save the Tsar'. Anyone who refused was immediately beaten up. It was noticeable that the police seemed to turn a blind eye to such goings-on. Certainly, many Tsarist officials connived in their activities and they could rely on the tacit support of the ruling class. Tsar Nicholas was, after all, the son of Tsar Alexander who once admitted that 'in the depths of his soul' he could understand those who attacked the Jews. Nicholas himself had recently replied to a declaration of loyalty by the selfsame Union of the Russian People: 'May the Union of the Russian People be my trusty support, serving for all and in everything as an example of lawfulness and civic order.'

Both Nadya and Ely had justifiable cause for alarm. If there was a shortage of targets for these marauding groups, then they, as members of the Social Revolutionary Party, would be high on their list. As Nadya and Ely talked in the summer-house that evening, he detected a note of weary resignation in her voice.

'Illiusha,' she said. 'We must face the facts. We're being beaten all over Russia.'

They went to her house and talked about the changed political situation, of how, in the wake of revolutionary disillusion, social conventions were becoming freer and there was now a move away from public concerns to more private pursuits. Gone were the revolutionary songs and in place of Marx and Engels radicals were now reading Nietzsche and Baudelaire and the French Symbolist poets. They seemed to talk of everything except what was uppermost in their minds. There was an air of imminence and expectancy, but Ely still felt unsure and self-conscious. He was still in awe of Nadya. She was like a goddess to him, however much he wanted her and loved her. Nadya was looking at him intently. Suddenly she leant forward to kiss him and said, 'I told you I would wait for you.'

But getting no response she upbraided him, 'Ech, Illiusha, what a Don Juan you are!' It had the desired effect.

'But I love you,' Ely blurted out. 'You are the dearest thing in the world to me. I want to marry you.' He rushed the last sentence for fear she might laugh at the idea.

But she replied tensely, 'We are married ... You strange, silly Amerikanetz ... let's not talk ... let's forget,' and they fell into each other's arms.

For the next few days Ely was walking on air. Now that his love for Nadya had been declared and consummated, his life was trans-figured. Even his ever-haunting fear that everything might suddenly disappear seemed to have been overcome. The more he saw of her, the more he was captivated by her. Yet his puritanical side was still shocked at her frankness about sex. He wasn't used to this. In his relationship with his French mistress, it was he who had called the tune. With Nadya it was different.

Their intellectual and political discussions still went on. Nadya told him she secretly dreamed of going with him to America, when things had quietened down in Ekaterinodar. Perhaps they would then have a baby together, and go to a university to study and prepare for higher things.

Nadya's father was away and Ely and Nadya were apprehensive about the irregular activities of the Black Hundreds. Ely made her promise not to leave the house alone, and whenever he went to visit her he always carried a revolver.

A few nights later, he was on his way to her house when he en-countered the Black Hundreds in action. He heard shouting and saw clusters of people milling around in front of a group of houses where stones had been thrown at the windows and barricaded doors battered down by fire axes. Some of the mob were shouting, 'Down with Jews', 'Down with revolutionists', 'Long live the Tsar'. There was no sign of police. The roadway was full of glass from the broken window of a Jewish jeweller's shop. Smashed pieces of furniture and pillows ripped apart in a desperate search for hidden treasure lay scattered in the street.

He rushed on towards Nadya's house a quarter of a mile away. The noise gradually died down behind him but as he turned the corner of her street he saw a crowd standing by her house. He raced forward, his heart pounding. There was a peculiar quietness and stillness to this crowd; people were talking in whispers. He recognized some of Nadya's neighbours and sensed that something serious had just happened. With immense relief he saw a policeman guarding the gate, and he pushed his way forward. But the policeman would not let him pass, despite his protests that he was a friend of the family. He demanded to see Nadya.

'She's been taken away.'

'Where? To jail?'

'No – to the morgue. She's dead.'

His heart heaved violently. His head was spinning and he did not know where to turn. In desperation he pleaded with the policeman, hoping he was mistaken. But the policeman confirmed that it was the doctor's daughter. The coachman from next door came across and told him how he had earlier seen five or six men hanging around the front of the house. His guess was that they must have got in through the back because a few minutes later a loud scream was heard, followed by silence. The police were called but they took ages coming. They broke down the door and found Nadya strangled, too late to revive her or take her to hospital. The coachman had heard rumours that Nadya was a likely target for the Black Hundreds, her activities as a revolutionary being well known.

Ely listened, though he knew enough about the Black Hundreds. He forced himself to go on talking and asking questions, still trying to keep the full horror at bay. The coachman tried to commiserate with him, but Ely moved away. He was holding back his grief and did not want to share it with anyone.

Nadya's death had a shattering effect on Ely. Suddenly everything she represented, his youthful romanticism, his hopes for the future had been taken away. Characteristically he did not want to show the deep distress he felt. He chose action instead. He had to avenge Nadya's death. His target was not the murders themselves, but the system that could allow someone like Nadya to be killed so wantonly. He needed to choose someone dramatic and he thought of the Governor of the province. The Social Revolutionary Party sanctioned individual acts of terrorism against high officials of the Tsar. It was a way of destabilizing the system. The local Governor had been one of the most ruthless exponents of the Tsar's edicts. Ely's advantage lay with the fact that his mother knew the Governor and Ely himself had met him on one or two occasions, so he might be able to gain access without too much difficulty. Now that he had settled on his method of revenge, it became easier for him to think of Nadya's death.

The day after her funeral, he decided to pay two visits. First he went to see Nadya's father. He was shocked to see how much her death had aged him. Ely didn't want to tell him his plans but wanted to reassure him that he was carrying on Nadya's work. 'They'll pay for what they did. Nadya's murder will be avenged.' But her father wasn't interested in the adolescent bravura of a young man he may have considered partially responsible for his daughter's death.

Next he went to see Stepanov, the leader of the revolutionary committee, for whom he had brought the sealed letters from Germany. Stepanov was now on the run, never sleeping in the same house two nights running. Ely had to contact a workman who led him across the railway tracks to where Stepanov was hiding in the working-class district of the town. Stepanov sat behind a table with a samovar on it. He was short, dark, with close-cropped hair and spoke with a strong Ukrainian accent.

'Sit down, *Tovarich*. I have heard a lot about you from Nadya. She was one of our best workers.'

'That's what I want to talk to you about.'

'There's not much more to say.' He smiled grimly. 'We'll add her name to the bill we're sending the Tsar.'

'That's just it. I'd like to present the bill myself.'

'How do you mean?'

'I would like to volunteer to assassinate the Governor.'

Stepanov took off his thick-lensed glasses, cleaned them, put them on again, and then told him his committee could not possibly approve of his actions. The party would be severely criticized for using someone who was both under twenty-one and an American citizen. When Ely threatened to go ahead alone, Stepanov's features changed. Gone was the friendly smile and his tone became sharper. 'That's up to you. But I hope your revolutionary conscience realizes the difference between political terrorism and the desire for revenge.'

'They murdered Nadya.'

'They were thugs. We are revolutionaries.'

Ely's pride was hurt. Here he was hoping to legitimize his youthful idealism, and it was being turned round on him.

Stepanov went on, 'Revolutions are serious businesses. They can't thrive on impulsive acts. Years of little things, accumulated every day, are what count. You have done valuable service for the party with your printing press and your smuggling and propaganda. We want you to live – not die in a sudden heroic act.'

Just like Nadya's father, he was telling him to desist. It wasn't what he wanted or expected. He tried to explain in his own way.

'Haven't you ever lost someone you loved dearly?'

Stepanov continued with his fatherly approach. 'You've got it all mixed up in you – Nadya and the Revolution. If you're in search of action, then I've got something for you. The party's still active around Sochi. Go there. They can use you. I'll give you a letter.'

He rose to say goodbye. His manner was impatient, as though he had more important tasks to attend to. Ely returned home full of agitation and uncertainty. But he had little time to ponder, for when he got there other events had preceded him. The household was in turmoil. His mother greeted him with a look that told him something serious had happened. The police had called about an hour ago enquiring after him. It transpired they had found some letters from him in Nadya's room, two of them from Karlsbad, the contents of which they considered incriminating. They had gone away only after his mother had assured them that he had left for Rostov the day before. However much she disapproved of her son's revolutionary activities, Xenia put her loyalty and devotion to him first. She was calm and businesslike as she set about helping him to escape.

She suggested he should leave immediately for Novorossisk, the port on the Black Sea about seventy miles away. There he could stay with friends and lie low for a week. This would give his mother enough time to use her influence to get him out of Russia and join his father in Prague. She had already arranged for a boat to be waiting at the back of the house to pick him up and take him down the Kuban river where there would be no police looking out for him. His bag was packed and his American passport and money ready. There was no time to waste. They embraced in a fond farewell. His mother, fighting back her tears, said:

'To think that I reared my son to be a revolutionary, who fights against my own people and my own church. *Ech*, Illiusha.'

But Ely did not intend to follow his mother's plan. He told the boatman to stop a short way down the river from his house and then wait for him. He went quickly to Stepanov's house and, after prolonged negotiation with the guards, was admitted to get his letter. Within an hour he was back in the boat. From the station he caught his train to Novorossisk and arrived there next morning. He found there was a steamer leaving for Sochi in the evening and bought a ticket.

The trip took thirty-six hours along the Black Sea coast. After arriving he booked a room in a hotel and then went for a walk in the town. He was aware of the tense atmosphere wherever he went. The town was under martial law and there were soldiers at every corner. An insurrection had just been put down and hundreds of revolutionaries had been thrown into jail to await trial by the military courts and then possibly the firing-squad. He heard that fighting was still going on in the mountains. Ely knew that he was likely to be spotted and picked up, so he went to a *café chantant* to lose himself among the singing and dancing throng. His plan was to pick up a prostitute who would take him back to her room. He knew prostitutes were good at hiding people and shielding their identity from the police.

He was too late. He had already been followed to the café by a member of the secret police. Sochi was a small town and a stranger was easily noticeable. He was stopped and taken to the police station. The police captain seemed to know immediately that he was a revolutionary. Ely tried to show him his American passport and bluff his way out of it, but he was given away by his Russian, a difficult language for any foreigner to speak without an accent. He was given a thorough grilling and then searched. In the lining of his boot, they found Stepanov's letter. It did not have Stepanov's name on it, but a signature in code. At first Ely denied all knowledge of it, saying that he was just a young American citizen and a mysterious stranger had asked him to take the letter with him, but the police captain was not fooled by this. The letter had Ely's name on it, and was addressed to Tovarich Ureniev. When Ely protested that he had never even met him, the captain assured him that he would do so shortly. He signalled to the guards to come forward and Ely was led off unceremoniously in the direction of Sochi jail, where Ureniev had recently been incarcerated.

Sochi jail was an enormous fortress of dark brick, with a huge wooden entrance-door. Inside, it was overcrowded with the recent influx of political prisoners, but, in typical Russian fashion, it was surprisingly cheerful. At times even the jailers joined in political discussions (at another Russian jail, Lev Bronstein took his better-known name of Leon Trotsky from a friendly jailer). Many of the political prisoners were facing certain execution but they seemed undaunted by this, revelling in their notoriety. They were kept apart from the common criminals who were held in a different part of the jail. Occasionally fights between the two groups would break out in the toilets.

Ely was taken to a cell in the political prisoners' wing. It was large and very neat. There were eight bunks in all, two in each corner. All but one were occupied. When he came in the other inmates were lying on them reading. There was a spotlessly clean table in the middle of the room, with books scattered around it. As soon as Ely arrived, the other prisoners gathered in a circle around him, full of curiosity. Who was he? Where did he come from? What was an American citizen doing mixed up in the Revolution? The questions came thick and fast. Their eagerness in asking him questions was almost childlike. Finally, Ely managed to ask them, 'Which one is Ureniev?'

The answer came from a tall, gaunt-looking man of about forty, with fair hair, a thin, wispy moustache and a long, narrow face. His face was deeply-lined, with an ascetic air about it.

'I am Ureniev. How did you know my name?' A faint ironic smile played on his mouth as he spoke.

'I had a letter for you,' and then Ely proceeded to tell his story leading up to his arrest in Sochi.

'You probably don't realize, Tovarich Culbertson,' he said, addressing his remarks half to Ely and half to the rest of the group, 'just how serious your position is. You could easily have been shot for carrying a letter like that. We must plan your defence.'

The others started talking among themselves and Ely felt a warmth and solidarity among them as if at long last he was being admitted to an inner circle of revolutionaries.

'Your best chance is to insist on your American citizenship. The authorities won't want to get involved in a diplomatic incident,' said one of them. It was decided that at his forthcoming interrogation he should insist that his mother and father be informed of his whereabouts.

By now it was evening and they prepared for their dinner. A guard brought in some black bread, *bortsch* and *kvass*, a local alcoholic beverage. While the table was being prepared, Culbertson walked over to the window and looked out at the Caucasus Mountains beyond. Legend had it that Prometheus had been chained on the peak of Mount Kasbek, to be pecked at by Caucasian eagles. As he held the bars on the window he noticed they were loose and shaky; he thought he could easily pull them out. He was still yearning for some heroic gesture to commemorate Nadya's death. Suddenly he heard a low whining whistle and a chipped piece of brick flashed past his face.

'What's that?' he cried.

'A bullet! Get away from the window, quick,' Ureniev shouted. His cellmates had forgotten to tell him not to go near the window, where a sentry's bullet was likely to hit him.

'Don't they warn you?' Ely asked indignantly.

'Yes, but they shoot first!' Everybody laughed.

They began their dinner. A bottle of vodka appeared from somewhere. Ureniev explained why they received special treatment. They were 'distinguished guests of the government'. More laughter, and as Ely was clearly looking bewildered, Ureniev explained, 'We're not going to have these meals much longer. We are waiting for Stolypin's necktie,' – another in-joke and a reference to the gallows.

Ureniev chuckled at the look of shocked surprise that came over

Ely's face. He did not want to believe it at first; surely there was some hope.

'No, none.' Ureniev shook his head. 'We've already been judged. We've lost. When you gamble and lose you must pay.'

Ely was taken back to see the police chief two days later and given a three-hour grilling. He managed, this time thanks to his fluent Russian, to insist that his American citizenship would bring dire consequences if anything should happen to him. He invoked a whole string of names of Russian generals and other prominent people who would come to his aid. In Tsarist days such string-pulling still had some effect. As he left, Ely had no idea what the outcome might be. The firing-squad still loomed as a possibility, or he would not have been placed in the cell with Ureniev and his comrades. However, the police chief had agreed to wait before taking any further action.

Ely managed to get a letter to his mother but, with Russian delays in communications, it was three weeks before he got a reply. It must have seemed strange and disconcerting to Ely to find himself cut off from his family. His mother let him know she was doing everything in her power to get him transferred to Ekaterinodar as the Governor there had told her he could only exert his influence if Ely was under his jurisdiction. To do this she had to go to St Petersburg to see the Minister of the Interior and get a special order from him transferring Ely to Ekaterinodar. She warned him, in her letter, that this might take two to three months.

Back in his cell, and all set for a long wait, Ely used the opportunity to get to know his cellmates. He was fortunate in that all seven of them had been leaders of their section of the Social Revolutionary Party. But the one who impressed him most and was to have a lasting influence on his life was Ureniev.

Ureniev had been a schoolmaster, one of the few professions available to someone of his background. But his real interest had always been politics. He had devoted his efforts to transforming Russian society from the old order – full of injustice and inertia – represented by the Tsar, to a new order based on science and the belief in progress. Ureniev belonged to that post-Darwinian generation for whom the belief in social change as an evolutionary process was as strongly held as the tenets of Marxist theory. Science would pave the way to a better life.

He became for Ely his mentor and father-substitute. He was warm, audacious, imaginative and concerned, in contrast to the more solid and homely virtues of Ely's real father. He taught him how to play chess and vint – and taught him also the underlying principles of both games, their inner structure and the essential strategy required to win, and by extension the application of these same principles to other spheres of thought. He valued intelligence and a trained intelligence above all else. For Ely, this is just what he wanted to know about. With his father it had always been more a question of seeking his approval, of finding ways to please him and do things in the way he wanted (when a child, Ely had built him a full imitation model oil-derrick). Now here was someone who was trying to help him with what he was interested in, and to help him take those interests a stage further. And in an adolescent, hero-worshipping sort of way, Ely also admired Ureniev's soul, the nobility of his aims and his wish to help the oppressed and down-trodden. Ureniev fired Ely's imagination. Unlike Almon who was always stern and rather forbidding, Ureniev was a mixture of the serious and the playful. He was keen on games, on laughter as well as on weightier problems. Vint was his great love and he could hardly wait for the evening meal to finish before settling down to a game.

Meeting Ureniev reconciled Ely to Nadya's death. Ureniev made him view the past like a bridge on which to build the future, telling him that there was little value in bemoaning what had already hap-pened and could not be undone. By all means, Ureniev told him, retain the memory of the past (and Nadya was enshrined in Ely's memory for ever) but use it as a stepping-stone to the future. He himself had led his life on that basis. It explained why he was now able to view the future with confidence and optimism.

One morning, not long afterwards, the knock on the door was for Ureniev and Ely never saw him again. But the memory of him lasted. With all his contradictions he was the most rounded and inspiring person Ely had met. He made a silent pact with himself that he would live by Ureniev's standards in whatever way he could. In later years, Ely was to look back on those days with Nadya and Ureniev as the most formative and influential of his life. Certainly he learnt more there than at any of the universities he subsequently attended.

His mother's industry now paid off. Ely was informed that he was going to be transferred 'for identification purposes' to Ekaterinodar. His mother had even paid for a detective and two soldiers to accom-pany him, rather than leave him to wait for the next government-organized convoy of prisoners, which might take months. Back in Ekaterinodar, the Governor arranged for Ely to be released on his mother's surety, and on condition he left the country at the earliest opportunity. Then the matter would be dropped. His mother sug-gested he joined Eugene at Munich Polytechnicum. This meant that the services of Herr Raessler would no longer be required.

As soon as news of his release from prison came through, Almon hurried back from Prague with Sasha. He lectured Ely on his dangerous way of life, and how his own hopes for him had once again been disappointed. What was he planning to do next? Ely explained the idea of going to Munich. What was he going to do in Munich? Become a writer and study revolutionary politics (the influence of Nadya and Ureniev was strongly upon him). His father demurred, and Ely thought for a moment he was going to signal his displeasure by cutting off his allowance. But no, his father had made his financial arrangements for his children when he retired from Grozny and he was not going to unsettle them now. Relieved to hear this, Ely now ventured to suggest what had been in the back of his mind all along. He would like to go to America (here it was Nadya he was thinking of) and study at university there. His father was delighted at this suggestion. He had always wanted his children to be as American as possible, particularly when it came to their education. He was worried, too, that Ely was becoming far too 'Russianized'. America, Almon told himself, should soon straighten him out. His mother agreed to this plan, even though it meant a lengthy separation from her favourite son. She was sure he would steer clear of trouble there.

When he heard of Ely's plan, Eugene wanted to go to America as well, rather than return to Munich where he had got in with the beer-hall, duelling crowd, with whom he felt ill at ease. They would both try to get into Yale. The plan was settled upon and the two young men set off for America, secure in the knowledge that they had their parents' approval and secure too in an allowance of $125 each per month, plus travelling and tuition expenses.

CHAPTER 3

TRAVELS

Ely and Eugene sailed for New York on the newly-built *Kaiser Wilhelm der Grosse* of the North German Lloyd line. At seventeen, Ely's English was still very patchy and he was held up by the immigration officials who had to call upon the services of an interpreter to verify that he really was an American citizen returning to the land of his ancestors.

One foot ashore and he was in the land of the free and of the thieving free. A stranger offered to carry his baggage and that was the last he saw of it. However, the thief had taken only the largest piece, a steamer trunk full of weighty tomes on Russian literature and political systems.

From New York they went up to New Haven and took rooms in a boarding-house. The landlady took one look at the two foreign-looking gentlemen and said, 'No ladies allowed.' Eugene's English, after his stint at Munich University, was much better than Ely's and he registered at Yale without much difficulty. But Ely had to enrol for a special English course at a preparatory school. He became part of a group of students who used to foregather in the back room of the Davenport Hotel. One of these, named Phoebe, took a shine to Ely and helped his English on and off the campus. At weekends they would go down to New York and head for Jack's Bar, a fashionable rendezvous for the young set, and then on to the German Village, a slightly sleazy night-club where the hostesses endeavoured to create an illusion of sophistication for their high-paying clientele. This was a place Ely could understand. But at New Haven, he never felt at home in the Ivy League atmosphere of fraternities, sports and bars. In Russia the burning question was always 'What is happening in Russia?' while here it was more likely to be 'What would happen to Yale if the crew lost to Harvard?' His only consolation was a twice-weekly class he attended with six American students on Russian literature, given by Mr Mendell, a Russian who eked out a living as a chiropodist.

Ely's restlessness soon got the better of him. He was still under the powerful influence of his experiences in Russia, and he had little enthusiasm for the privileged way of life Yale seemed to offer. He gave Eugene most of his allowance, took himself off to New York, and lived on the Bowery. With him (as with George Orwell later) there was a compulsion to see how the lower classes lived and experience their way of life at first hand. Whether this stemmed from guilt, the same feeling of guilt as had driven many of his compatriots in Russia into revolutionary action, or from a sense of not belonging, is hard to say.

He was clearly unsettled. He did not feel he belonged in America, just as, in a sense, he did not really belong in Russia. He was a misfit and his explorations among lower-class life, or 'real' people as he preferred to call them, was just as much a search for somewhere to belong as the scientific undertaking he claimed it to be. Ely kept himself apart in these years, as he did later on. He thought of himself as different, a potential leader perhaps. For the moment it was good to pretend he had no money, it absolved him from thinking about a career or how he really was going to lead his life.

In the earlier part of this century, the Bowery had already acquired a reputation as the meeting place for drunks, bums and labourers out of work. Ely took a room near Mott Street, and passed most of his days in and around Cooper Junction, well-known then as a civic centre and a library where he could read the works of Henry George and other social reformers. He joined the bread-lines and learnt how to panhandle for a bowl of soup at lunchtime. All the time he told himself he was discovering the inner mechanism of this broken-down segment of American society – part of his life-long attempt to understand the structure of the masses. Later he moved to the Newsboys' Lodging-house on Park Row and earned enough money each day selling newspapers to pay his keep.

In April 1908 he found a job as a helper in a bar on Seventh Avenue and took a room at the Mills Hotel, paying fifty cents a night. Between the saloon, the Hammerstein Vaudeville house and the nearby public library, Ely felt he was absorbing America in a way that would never have been possible at Yale.

Then, in June, Eugene received a cable from his mother saying she would be coming to New York, arriving on 15 June. Ely hurried back to New Haven. When the two sons saw her come down the gangplank, they knew she was a sick woman. She had aged visibly – even her usually fast-flowing speech had slowed up. It looked as if she had made the effort to come to America for a final farewell.

They stayed at a hotel in New York for a week and tried to re-create a Russian atmosphere, but without the steaming samovar. She told them news of other members of the family. Her sister Alexandra had died and her husband Henry had left and bought a villa at Menton in the South of France; his two daughters, Tasya and Shoura, were now at a finishing-school in Lausanne. Nadya's father had gone to Rostov to tend to another cholera outbreak there – and the Revolution, she was quick to tell Ely, had now virtually faded out. But the best news was of Sasha, whose concert successes were going from strength to strength. She had just come from London where he had given a performance at the Queen's Hall that had been described in the *Morning Post* as 'extraordinarily brilliant'. She showed them the clipping which, from its well-thumbed appearance, had clearly made the round of the other passengers on the ship.

Almon had stayed in London with Sasha. It was during this stay that he acquired the famous Guarneri del Gesù violin, known as 'Count Ferni' from Hills Brothers, at a cost of some £7,000. This violin was to figure prominently in Sasha's life. Xenia mentioned how Almon, after buying this extremely expensive violin, refused to take a taxi back to their hotel, as Sasha suggested, and insisted they walked instead.

They both noticed how in the middle of talking that Xenia would suddenly doze off for a while. She was only fifty-six years old. Her diabetes had worsened, and she had been to see many specialists, each proposing a different remedy.

Ely thought the fresh air of Atlantic City might make a pleasant change from the stuffy atmosphere of New York City and they went there for two weeks. Ely became a model son again, devoting his time to Xenia, watching her diet and being generally solicitous about her welfare. It seemed to make a difference for under his ministrations she picked up, but then, as often happens after a brief recovery, she had a relapse, in the first week of July. They hurried up to New Haven to rejoin Eugene. As she lay dying she pressed Ely to look after Eugene and Sasha. 'You are a Culbertson like your father ... But Eugene and Sasha are Rogoznys ... They'll need your help.' Within days she was dead aged only fifty-six. Ely fought back his emotions, characteristically keeping his grief to himself. He arranged for her to be buried in Woodlawn Cemetery, New York.

After the trauma of their mother's death, Eugene and Ely both felt the need to return to Europe to spend the summer with their father and Sasha in Pisek, Bohemia. It was a sad reunion for all of them and their mother's absence was often commented on.

Early in September Eugene and Ely returned to America. Now even more unsettled, Eugene decided he wanted to study law and transferred to Cornell University. Ely went to a preparatory school at Ithaca to try to complete his English course to get the necessary credits for Yale. He overdid it and worked himself into a state of exhaustion which prevented him from completing the course. He consulted a doctor, who ordered him to rest and take it easy.

'Read some detective stories, play cards a little, or get a nice girl ...'

'A nice girl, doctor?'

'Well, not too nice.'

But sex had, for the moment, taken a back seat. Nor did Ely want to tie himself down to a prolonged university course. He needed to venture out into the world and live among 'real' people and, in line with his earlier Russian experiences, discover what it was like to be on the receiving end of other people's ideologies. He decided he should go back to Europe to see his father first and put his plan to him, especially as he was not going to proceed with his university course.

It was the spring of 1909 and Almon and Sasha were on a concert tour. Ely eventually caught up with them in Florence. He waited a few days before breaking the news to his father. His father was not at all pleased. He had hoped Ely would at least stay put in America, complete his university course and settle down there. He was ambitious for Ely, despite the fact that he had not given him much help or support. Ely, slightly adrift, clearly felt the need for his father's approval – otherwise he would hardly have ventured all the way across the Atlantic. He half-hoped his father would be as attentive to him as he had been to Sasha. But Sasha represented something special to Almon, he embodied the future of cultural and artistic achievement that was so dear to Almon's heart. Almon could see now that he would have to shelve his ideas of Ely becoming a scientist, or even taking up a conventional career. Ely wanted to strike out on his own and be as successful in his own field as Sasha was in his. Almon was never one to stop Ely from doing something on which he had set his heart. He even increased his allowance to $150 a month, partly to provide a safety-net against possible disaster, and no doubt to try to prevent him from embarking on anything too rash.

Eugene too came to Europe for the summer, rather less enchanted with the aggressive style of American university life and finding his law studies a little too intricate for his liking. He did not want to go back and his father suggested that he became assistant to Mr Dunkel, Sasha's manager, and join them on their European rounds. That was the last Eugene ever saw of America.

As the summer went on, Ely was impatient to leave. He was tired of moving from one comfortable hotel to the next, in Hungary at one moment, Italy two days later, always with the same entourage of his father, two brothers and Mr Dunkel.

In September he caught a boat from Hamburg, bound for New York. On board he met a Canadian family from Winnipeg. The father, a grain broker, was travelling with his wife, son and daughter. Every evening they played a strange four-handed game of cards. Ely watched them with interest, noting how similar the game was to vint, which he had learnt at Sochi, except that here the dummy was exposed and the bidding seemed more limited. Every so often one of them would exclaim 'Partner, may I play?' 'Pray, do.' 'No spades, partner?' and so on. It was Ely's first introduction to Auction bridge and he was not impressed by it.

The family invited him to stay with them in Winnipeg and he made this his first stop on his way across Canada but he was impatient to sample 'real' life. He made his way to Edmonton and joined a construction team on the Grand Trunk Pacific Railway line in the northern Rockies, building the line out to Prince Rupert on the Pacific Ocean. Clearly he did not look the part of a seasoned navvy, so he was given the job of timekeeping.

Some of the camp leaders thought they would lay on a little initiation ceremony for the greenhorn Ely! They told him that the timekeeper had to have a horse to visit the work site. The worthy steed was brought out and Ely, having rashly mentioned his Cossack past, was invited to mount. Hardly had he gone ten yards than the horse started bucking wildly, carrying him all over the camp. Ely hung on for dear life. The horse eventually tripped on a tent rope and sent him thudding to the ground, fortunately without lasting injury.

To his immense surprise, he discovered that ninety per cent of the work force there were Ukrainian, specially brought over for this task, most of the engineering and executive jobs being done by American and Canadians. He was soon appalled at the conditions under which these Ukrainians, or 'Bohunks' as they were called, had to work. Labour laws, such as they were, offered little protection and because of their immigrant status, they were shamelessly exploited. They had no means of protesting, and even if they did, they might well be replaced by other workers.

Through his job of timekeeping which also gave him responsibility for the accounts at the camp stores, he saw how they were being badly treated. They got the agreed basic rate of $3 per day and the free food they had been promised. But the latter was barely edible and they were obliged to supplement it by buying food at the commissary, where they were charged extortionate rates for such basics as bacon, flour and canned goods. The contractors were clearly making a tidy profit on the side from this and the Ukrainians were spending all their wages just to keep alive. The whole point of their coming here was to save up money to take back to the Ukraine with them. Ely resolved to do something about it. He spoke their language and got them to agree to allow him to act as intermediary between them and the bosses.

He told his boss Jim MacDiarmid, a Scot, that he could not, in all conscience, stay in his post if conditions remained the same. In the meantime he used his position to organize leaders among the Ukrainians in the different camps. They were each to have a strike committee of ten members. The plan was to call a sudden strike and submit demands for better food and a reduction in the charges for company stores. With November coming, the ground would start to freeze over soon, making the job of track-laying and blasting even more difficult and the management wouldn't want to lose precious time on a strike.

A preset signal was arranged for all the camps to strike at the same moment. On the designated morning, the Ukrainian labourers got up, went to breakfast as usual, but then returned to their bunks, refusing to work. This action happened simultaneously through all the camps at the site. The company bosses at first tried to threaten and intimidate them, but the labourers refused to give in. Seeing their resolution, the bosses resorted to subtler tactics of half promises and even bribery. This didn't work either. A stalemate ensued. In the end the management were forced to make concessions. But there had been ugly moments. Fights frequently broke out, with the Canadian Mounted Police being called in to restore order.

Ely had been in the thick of it and one of the company's conditions, on settling the dispute, was that Ely and four other leaders had to leave the area. Ely felt hostility from many sides. Many accused him of betraying his fellow Americans and couldn't understand how he could sympathize with the other side, especially as they were immigrants. The whole experience was quite an eye-opener for him. He viewed it as a personal triumph; he could think of himself now as a potential leader.

Ely found his way back to Edmonton, then still a frontier town, where he hung around the bars and saloons for a few days before moving down to Calgary. Flushed with his success at the construction camp and firmly committed to seeking out adventure wherever he could, he travelled on a freight train, riding in an empty box-car, and so began his odyssey as a hobo.

In Calgary, however, he could not resist the temptation of a final luxurious bed and breakfast. Then, as if to punish himself, he sent all his spare money on to San Francisco to await his arrival. Freed from encumbrances, he could hit the high road in classic Whitmanesque tradition. He continued riding on freight cars across the American border into Idaho, heading towards Spokane. The going got tougher and tougher, as he was now joining the main highway for the drifters all converging on the golden state of California. There were literally hundreds of them, travelling in loosely-formed gangs. At times they were a frightening assembly of men, but, as always, knowledge and skill counted. Ely had to learn quickly the techniques of hobo living: to stay on a train usually meant bribing the brakeman; when the train stopped in the freight yards, he had to watch out for the 'bulls', or private railway police, whose job it was to hunt down hobos and beat them up to keep them away. Ely learnt how to get away from brakemen by running along the top of moving freight cars, even how to jump off a fast-moving freight train at one point and rejoin it further down, and, most dangerous of all, how to lodge himself, and travel, on the box-rods under the train. The latter was a very difficult technique. It meant tucking oneself underneath and lying flat by the fast-rolling wheels of the train. The incessant noise and clatter of the wheels and the debris flying up into the face, as well as the danger of being knocked off the perch or falling down between the wheels made this the most hazardous of all forms of travel. There were many deaths.

Ely soon developed his own particular style. Hobos were just as fussy about certain things as ordinary folk. Ely was very fastidious about his clothes, keeping his only suit in good repair and always wearing a clean shirt. Other than that, his baggage consisted of two pairs of socks, a spare shirt, a cake of soap, a toothbrush, a couple of books and a small quantity of salt which served as toothpowder and for flavouring any of the meals he partook of in the hobo 'jungles', as the gathering-places at stations and such-like were called.

Ely developed a technique of knocking on back-doors and asking the lady of the house if she had any work, however menial, for him to do. After a moment's hesitation, he would add that he had not eaten for three days. But his manner of delivering this spiel was done with such courtesy and charm that the housewife would invariably ask him why he was begging, since he clearly did not look the type. If she looked a suitable candidate, he would pour out a long and sorrowful tale about being the illegitimate son of a grand Russian lady and the American military attaché in St Petersburg. He was now on his way to San Francisco to locate his alleged father. It often worked, though occasionally there were terser replies to his requests.

From Spokane he moved on to Portland and down to Oregon. By September 1911 Ely had reached San Francisco. He hung up his travelling-boots, shed his hobo rags and, reunited with his money, moved into a first-class hotel.

Now, with so much first-hand experience under his belt, he wanted to study again and he entered the Boone Preparatory School in Berkeley to get his English credits. He was at last able to enrol at Stanford University. He also took the opportunity to read widely into whatever he could find on anarchism – Proudhon, Bakunin and especially Kropotkin, whose writings and belief in the spontaneous good of human nature he particularly valued. He enjoyed being in San Francisco, still recovering from the great earthquake of 1906, and entered into the carefree spirit of student life with fewer inhibitions than previously. He felt strengthened and emboldened by his time on the road. His fellow students nicknamed him 'the Duke', an improvement on the 'Slim', 'Dutch', or 'Skinny Swede' he had been called by the hobos.

In January 1912 news came through of an uprising in the Sinaloa province of Mexico. It looked just the sort of spontaneous uprising he had been waiting for; the peons had risen against their landlords, and he was impatient to be part of it. Ely set off for Mazatlan. At that time it was a town of about 30,000 inhabitants, with a small expatriate colony of Americans, English and Germans. Ely met some of these, and in particular Dick Stuart, a middle-aged American soldier of fortune, who made his money smuggling arms into South America and had now settled down in Mazatlan. He had married a local girl, and spent much of his time imbibing *pulque*, a narcotic drink made from the cactus plant. He invited Ely to stay at his villa, and introduced him to Challo, a half-Indian, half-Spanish girl who was a friend of his wife, and Ely fell for her.

Eventually he made contact with the revolutionaries through some journalists and lawyers he came across. They were planning an insurrection in the town once the Zapatistas had gained control of the surrounding hills. But the police must have got wind of Ely's involvement, for they came to his house, arrested him and put him in jail for 'plotting a counter-revolution'. He was kept incommunicado for a whole week before the American vice-consul was permitted to see him. He told him how lucky he was to be an American, otherwise he would almost certainly have been shot. For the second time his American nationality had saved him from the ultimate penalty for revolutionary activities. Prison life, however, was not too disagreeable. He was allowed visitors, including Challo, and he had plenty of time to read, mostly in Spanish. He read *Don Quixote*, a fellow knight of lost causes, from cover to cover.

Eventually, he was released on condition he leave the immediate vicinity. He made his way across to Vera Cruz on the east coast, and there, at long last and almost by accident, he became involved in real revolutionary activity. He met some radical students in one of the town's cafés, and they assured him that an uprising was going to take place the very next morning, led by Felix Diaz, the nephew of the deposed President. Why didn't he join them? Ely, new to the town, agreed. His instructions were to go to a modern warehouse close to the docks. When he got there, he found a group of about thirty men all in civilian clothes. Each carried a gun and had two belts of cartridges slung over the chest. There was one machine-gun for all of them. They went up to the roof of the warehouse, which commanded a view over most of the nearby streets and part of the docks. It was a strategic position. Just after dawn the shooting started and they could hear machine-gun fire elsewhere in the town. This was to be expected, as the uprising had been scheduled simultaneously throughout the town. As they looked over the parapet of the warehouse, they could see government soldiers advancing cautiously two blocks away. They fired a salvo at them from their machine-gun post, and the soldiers quickly retreated around the corner of the street. Then followed a period when nothing seemed to happen. Shooting could still be heard elsewhere.

Ely knew they ought to leave the warehouse and advance, but no orders came. Soon, the soldiers they had seen earlier summoned up reinforcements and, climbing on to a nearby rooftop, started firing at them. Ely had never been under fire before. But this situation, far from being frightening, was frustrating and a sore disappointment to him. They had no choice but to retreat from their rooftop, and scatter once they reached the ground floor of the building.

Ely ran back to his hotel, knowing it would only be a matter of time before he was picked up by the police. He packed his belongings and decided his only chance was to take the next boat out of the harbour. He was lucky enough to find one going to Cuba almost immediately.

There can be little doubt that, without his father's generous allowance, Ely could never have managed these action-packed experiences. He himself was never quite sure how much he was playing at life, and how much he was making a serious attempt to understand the world around him. It was a dilemma that was to remain with him for many years.

From Cuba he caught a boat to Spain, travelling steerage. On board was a small group of Spanish anarchists whom he fell in with. So keen were they to instill their beliefs on their fellow passengers that they persuaded the captain to improve conditions below decks during the relatively short duration of the voyage.

Ely was attracted by anarchism and in Madrid he kept up his

anarchist connections. Staying at a pension near the Plaza del Sol, he attended their meetings and heard rumours of an intended assassination plot on the Spanish King, Alfonso XIII. He was asked to join but something, his card-player's sixth sense perhaps, held him back. Just as well, for an assassination attempt did take place three days later. He subsequently discovered his anarchist 'friend' had been an *agent provocateur*. He was arrested, but his alibi was sound as he could prove he had been to the Prado on the day of the attempt since a 'tail' had been put on him by the police. He was told to leave the country.

The Spanish adventures had a sequel. In January 1938, he was staying at the Grand Hotel in Rome, where the then exiled Alfonso XIII was also staying. They played bridge together as partners. Ely's mind went back to twenty-five years earlier when their meeting might have been of an altogether different kind.

Ely's father and two brothers were spending the summer in Ostend and he went to join them there. He was reporting back to base, but with no particular sense of belonging to his family. Now that his mother was dead, he felt even less part of it. When in September they all left for Germany, Ely decided to go his own way. He went to Paris with the aim of finally becoming the university student he had for so long promised to be.

He enrolled at L'Ecole des Sciences Economiques et Politiques, that prestigious training-ground for future politicians, economists and diplomats. For Ely it opened up a new world. He had always been by temperament more European than American and his travels in America had confirmed that. Here in Paris with its large Russian emigré colony he felt he was among his own kind.

He lived in a comfortable pension in the rue Tournefort in the Latin Quarter. It was central, not far from the Ecole, and he saw little need to go elsewhere in Paris. He spent quite a bit of time in his favourite library, the Bibliothèque Sainte Geneviève. In front of it was the Pantheon, final resting-place of the immortals of France, with Rodin's recently completed statue of 'The Thinker' by its entrance. Many of his idler moments were spent in the nearby Luxembourg Gardens, a colourful impressionistic scene of prams and uniformed governesses, children in sailor-suits, with groups of bohemian-looking students locked in discussion or simply passing the time of day. He ate at a Greek restaurant on the corner of the place Soufflot, a small family-run affair.

At the Ecole, Ely followed a course in political history and the theory of government. He also studied statistics, which introduced him to the laws of probabilities as formulated by de Moivre and by that early advocate of the pre-emptive bid (on eternal life), Blaise

Pascal. Pascal, he was delighted to discover, also invented the roulette-wheel.

So passed his first year in Paris. He found himself a girl-friend, one of the floating population who migrate to Paris from the provinces with hopes of becoming an art student or actress. She was called Aline and came from Alsace. Neither particularly beautiful nor intelligent, she lived contentedly with Ely for a year. At the end of the academic year, news came through of the murder of the Archduke Ferdinand at Sarajevo on 28 June 1914. This was followed by an ominous quiet all over Europe and Ely thought it prudent to join the rest of his family at Swinemunde, a resort on the north-east German coast. Stateless and homeless, the Culbertsons banded together in times of crisis. Ely was convinced that war was going to break out and pressed his father to sell his four per cent Russian Imperial Bonds, but Almon, for whom these bonds symbolized his own personal achievement, re-fused, prophesying, accurately enough, that they would last as long as the Russian Empire. Almon's decision was to have a profound effect on all their lives.

On 28 July war was declared and the family had to decide quickly what to do and where to go. In Swinemunde they were already under suspicion of being Russian spies, as they could be heard speaking Russian at meal-times! It took a great deal of explaining before the local police were convinced they were American. In the end the Cul-bertsons opted for neutral territory and went to join other displaced persons in Switzerland. They settled in Geneva, at the Hôtel des Bergues, by the lake.

In Geneva, Ely had his second encounter with Auction bridge. He met a young American girl there who was at finishing-school. She was a devoted bridge-player, mainly for fashionable reasons. Ely was more interested in her than the game, and for her sake joined in, but when he did he started asking so many detailed questions about the whys and wherefores of the game that the other players were soon put off. Nevertheless his critical attitude towards cards was beginning to manifest itself.

Another short-lived affair was with a young German woman who had come to study psychoanalysis. To Ely's chagrin she switched her affections to a much older man. Perhaps it was not so surprising for, if we are to believe Ely's account of the next episode in his life, his attitude towards women at this stage of his life was distinctly high-handed, though he termed it scientific. He wanted to find the perfect woman, whether as wife or mistress is not clear. He went to Turin, having been reliably informed by a Swiss colleague that this was where the most beautiful women came from. He put an advertisement in the local paper claiming he was an American painter looking for a model ('undress unnecessary', he graciously added). Replies came pouring in, but none matched up to his ideal. He was about to give up when at the last moment a suitable candidate appeared. She was deemed the right material for the newly-evolved Culbertson Pursuit System – first arouse curiosity, then work on her capacity for admiration and finally open up her imagination to the untold wonders ahead. But fate, or rather the Turin police, intervened. The police had seen his advertisement, frankly disbelieved his motives and told him to leave town forthwith. It was not to be his last attempt to achieve a Galatea.

He returned to Paris after a two-year absence. Despite his twenty-four years he was in no hurry to discover his métier. He preferred to go on treating life as an experiment, and remain a student, albeit, in his eyes, of a rather superior kind.

Like many of his contemporaries, he held a strong belief in the power of ideas, abstract concepts that would, in some brave new world, change the nature of society and bring about a new role for the masses. He read extensively in this field, particularly the works of Gustave Le Bon, the author of *Psychologie des Foules*. This was a description of how crowds could be manipulated through the power of the word (slogans) and through the forcefulness of the leader. It owed much to Machiavelli's *The Prince* – another of Ely's favourite authors. Georges Sorel was another influential writer at this time and his book *Réflexions sur la Violence* carried almost as much weight as Le Bon's.

Paris offered the best of both worlds – excellent university facilities for the continuation of his intellectual pursuits and unrestricted opportunities to enjoy a hedonistic approach to life. Ely adopted the cult of the sophisticated but world-weary sybarite. He wanted to be knowledgeable, well-read, conversant in several languages, adept at cards and witty conversation. He studied the texts mentioned above to equip himself for the time when he might be a leader. In the pre-Fascist era such ambitions were thought laudable and in keeping with a modernist viewpoint. He was simply preparing and biding time. He was fortunate enough to be part of the moneyed, leisured class who could afford to wait and whose serious pretensions were often a pretext for not knowing what they should really do.

Paris during the first years of the First World War led a strange existence. The enemy was almost literally at the gates, yet life went on much as normal. The threat of war seemed to make people cling even more strongly to their peacetime occupations, with a spirit of almost deliberate defiance. In the café Ely used to frequent, the boom of Big Bertha bombarding Paris could be heard at one time every twenty minutes. At first the regulars would follow each boom by a period of tense, almost reverential silence but a week went by and then no one paid attention any more and went on with their cards and arguments as if nothing was happening. Ely's own response was not dissimilar. He and many of his fellow students acted as if the war did not exist. They tried to turn normal life upside down. Here the key text was Huysmans' *A Rebours* in which the hero des Esseintes overcomes boredom by the refinement and unusualness of his tastes and sensations.

A typical day for Ely at this stage would consist of getting up at six o'clock in the evening to have a breakfast of Turkish coffee, pomegranates and coarse bread, each item chosen with aesthetic care. After breakfast, dressed in casual, elegant style (in a suit ordered from one of the best English tailors with lapels and buttons discreetly altered), wearing a floppy black tie with a dark-coloured shirt, he would saunter to his favourite café. The time was now about eight in the evening. With his fellow dilettantes, he would sit for hours drinking and discussing, vying with each other in the exactitude, or languor, with which they discussed books, women, and the unspeakable vulgarity of modern life.

Lunch would normally be consumed, or drunk, at around ten o'clock in the evening. As midnight approached, the group would move to a subterranean *café chantant* to listen to songs evoking the Belle Epoque, in an atmosphere of increasing alcoholic and intellectual vapour. Towards three or four in the morning, their last port of call would be Les Halles, the fruit and vegetable market, where, ignoring the traditional onion soup, they would drink more Armagnac and sing ribald songs. As dawn broke, Ely would make his way back to the apartment he had rented near the Luxembourg Gardens (it belonged to a French officer who had gone to the front). Here, in a Proust-like atmosphere, where thick curtains and blinds kept out any semblance of the natural world, he settled down for a good day's sleep.

Cards, too, played a part in their lives. They were a necessary part of the sophisticate's equipment. Poker or *écarté* were preferred but Ely and one or two others frequented the Café de la Péronne where a game of Auction bridge was usually in progress. Now that he was settled in Paris he had taken up this game, and liked it for its intellectual challenge. But there was something mechanical about it and, characteristically, he was on the look-out for ways of improving it, though it was many years before his system emerged from this embryonic state. He also needed card-playing to supplement his income. The aesthete's life was expensive. The wartime exchange rate helped, but he had to rely increasingly on his skill at cards to pay his bills. It was not just the inebriated state of his companions that accounted for his winnings. He discovered that he had a real talent for card-playing that had lain unused all these years. He began to play regularly.

In April 1917, the USA entered the war and Ely volunteered as an interpreter. To his amazement he was turned down on the grounds that his English was not good enough! However fluent his other languages, his interviewers felt that his English lacked 'idiomatic flexibility' and was a mixture of hobo and intellectual terms. Both Sasha and Eugene were involved in the war, Sasha playing concerts in front of the troops, while Eugene had joined the French Foreign Legion the year before. Ely saw him in Paris on his way to the Battle of the Somme, where he suffered injuries that marked him for life.

Ely's pride was hurt by this rejection. Rather than look elsewhere he plunged into the Parisian *demi-monde*. He started to drink more heavily and frequented a milieu that was closer to drugs-trafficking and prostitution than the aesthete's more selective pleasures. De Quincey's *Confessions of an Opium-eater* and Baudelaire's *Fleurs du Mal* became required reading. Women up till now had played a small part in his life as an aesthete. They were only admitted to the inner sanctum of the aesthete's life if they had some mysterious allure, as a *femme fatale* or as an unsuspecting *fille du peuple*.

But now he turned to women more and more. They at least offered sympathy and, in spite of his rapidly dwindling income, he sought to regale them in whatever way he could. One of them stood out from the rest. This was Elvira, whom he had known for some time as she had been on the fringes of his group. She too had come to Paris in search of a better life but had ended up as an artist's model and part-time prostitute. They were drawn to each other. She decided that Ely was her man and clung tenaciously to him. In his more lucid moments he hoped to reform her and wean her from her drug addiction. At first he had been unaware she was a drug addict. She took cocaine, which mixed imperceptibly with alcohol, and Ely at first assumed her excesses were alcoholic. But then she would disappear for days on end and come back distraught and incoherent. Ely patiently tried talking to her and settling her down, but it was not much use.

It was a far cry from redeeming humanity, but in the haze of his Parisian life, his perspective had altered. Then one day the police came to their door and took her away to St Lazare prison. She was charged with robbing a rich American tourist of several thousand francs. She had committed this offence in her craving for dope, and was given a three-year prison sentence.

Ely was now at the bottom of his pit of despair. He felt a complete failure. News came through of the Bolshevik annexation of the Caucasian oilfields, and with that the bulk of the Culbertson family income was gone. He had very few pounds left anyway. For a while he flirted with the idea of joining an unlikely mix of Russian emigrés he knew in Paris, some remnants of the Social Revolutionary Party, others Monarchists, whose aim was to join forces with a counter-insurgency group in Riga rumoured to be launching an attack against the Bolsheviks. For a while Ely was tempted to go with them.

Then another of the curious twists of fate in his life occurred. Culbertson's own account of it has to be relied on for its veracity. He had gone to one of his regular haunts, a gambling club on the rue Volney, not far from the Café de la Paix. He had on him no more than twenty francs – a small enough amount. He watched the roulette game for a while, and then decided to place all his twenty francs on an even chance.

As he stood back from the table, he trod on the foot of a Romanian bystander, whom he vaguely knew and from whom he had once won money. An argument ensued and they went outside to settle their dispute. Mission accomplished, Ely went back inside the club and discovered a great commotion near the roulette table. M. Vardell, the manager of the club, had been summoned and the croupier was calling out, '*Messieurs! Messieurs! A qui est cet argent? Enlevez-le donc.*' On the table stood a pile of thousand-franc, mother-of-pearl chips. Ely went to the table, realized it was his and claimed it. While he had been outside, his winnings had remained on the table and accumulated with every spin of the wheel. He had won something approaching 40,000 francs, an astronomical sum. He worked out later that he must have had a run of eleven consecutive winning throws – not an unheard-of sequence, but rare enough and likely to happen at the most once a week. But it was extremely unusual for someone to run up winnings in this way and Ely noted ironically that had he stayed inside the club, he would undoubtedly have withdrawn his money long before the eleventh round.

This sudden windfall was almost an embarrassment to Ely. He tried to get rid of it as quickly as possible, sending some to his father in Geneva, some to Elvira's lawyer for her court case, buying some new suits and shoes for himself, and giving it away to total strangers, waitresses in restaurants and beggars. But having money again made him feel better, a great deal better, and it gave him a new lease of life. He was released from his debased existence, where his self-esteem had plummeted to an all-time low, keeping almost exact pace with the disappearance of his funds. Now he was on the up again, back into the old familiar world of affluence and stylish living.

By now the war had ended, not that it had made much impression on Ely's life. He had been too taken up with his personal life, his descent into hell, to give it sufficient attention.

To celebrate his winnings he went to London and stayed at the Hyde Park Hotel. In Paris he had got to know some English Auction bridge players at the Café de la Péronne and they had invited him to look them up in London. But after a while he tired of what he described as 'the soporific climate of English society life, with its inane weekends, five o'clock teas, chit-chat cocktail parties, and the thick fog of English respectability'. He went to Germany instead, and stayed in Berlin where the atmosphere was tense and exciting. Post-war Berlin was anything but soporific in the first days of the Weimar Republic. From there he went on to Danzig and the Port of Riga, still full of White Russian exiles plotting to overthrow the Communist regime. He found their company uncongenial and headed for Brussels instead, where he hoped to carry out a plan he had thought up.

He had recently read Milton C. Work's *Auction Bridge Complete*, which made it clear that in America plenty of men and women were making a good living out of being bridge teachers. So why not try it here in Europe? He thought of Brussels as being new territory and his best bet, he told himself, was to put an advertisement in the local newspaper, offering his services as bridge teacher. It met with a less than encouraging response but two days later two official-looking gentlemen presented themselves at his door and asked him to accompany them to the prefecture. He was taken in to see the police chief.

'You put an advertisement in the paper offering to teach people how to win at cards?'

'Yes.'

'You're a professional card player, then?'

'If you mean by "professional player" someone who cheats at cards, then certainly not.'

'But you make your living from cards?'

'No. I was only offering to teach bridge, an intellectual game.'

'Cards are cards,' the police chief said emphatically.

In the previous twenty-four hours they had checked up on Ely's background and found out about his political revolutionary past and his expulsion from Spain. His record as it stood did not look good and the Belgian police feared he might even be a Bolshevist. Ely protested but the police chief warned him that he had better be careful. The then Belgian Minister of Justice, M. Van de Velde, was a socialist with an equal detestation of Bolshevism and cards. Ely was given forty-eight hours to leave the country.

'But what is the charge?' Ely insisted.

'There is no formal charge. The informal charge is that you are a bridge teacher.'

Clearly the lights had gone out all over Europe for Ely, and he decided it was time to return to America. From Brussels he went to Antwerp and spoke to the American consul there. How was he to get back to his homeland, America? He had practically no money left. The consul suggested he went down to the port to see Captain Darling of the ss *Brookline*, a passenger ship about to sail for New York. There was just a chance he might be able to work his passage. There was not time to put Ely's nautical skills to the test, and Captain Darling was short of crew in any event, so he was signed on as an able-bodied seaman bound for New York.

CHAPTER 4

JOSEPHINE

As the New York skyline came into view, Ely Culbertson moved to
the ship's rail along with the other passengers. Many of them were
first-time immigrants jostling for a sight of the land of opportunity
and weeping with tears of joy at the sight of Bartholdi's famous Statue
of Liberty Lighting the World. As always, it had an enormous impact
on the immigrants. They knew they were the lucky ones, as the Dil-
lingham Immigration Restriction Act had just been passed by Congress in May 1921, curbing their number. In the xenophobic mood
that grew up after America's excursion into Europe during the First
World War there was now a fear that there might be political outcasts,
reds, anarchists or other subversive types seeking to infiltrate their
way into America. Gone were the days when the White Star Line
paid the Austro-Hungarian government a handsome annual stipend
to deliver up to twenty thousand emigrants to continental ports each
year. Indeed Culbertson could consider himself lucky that he already
had his own American passport. His past political activities were such
as the authorities might not have welcomed.

In contrast to his last visit in 1908, about to enter Yale and full of
the heady and arrogant enthusiasm of affluent studenthood, here he
was, a penniless refugee from Europe, uncertain of his future, and
lacking even the optimism of the immigrants standing beside him at
the ship's rail.

Before disembarking he went to say goodbye to Captain Darling
and collect his wages. He had grown to like this genial man whose
watery eyes spoke volumes of his regular tussles with the Atlantic.
Once ashore Ely headed for the apartment on West 75th Street where
his father and Sasha had been installed for just over a year. Sasha had
come across to America on a transport ship shortly after the Armistice,
and his father had followed a few months later. Sasha was still con-
valescing from a bout of typhoid he had contracted in France and it
would be some months before he could play in public again. His
father had come to America partly to be with Sasha and also to be
better placed to pursue his claim for compensation against the Russian
government who had nationalized the Caucasian oilfields in 1918. By

the time Culbertson got there he had already filed his claim in Washington, said to be the highest for an individual claimant.

Culbertson had not warned them of his arrival but they were used to him turning up unexpectedly from the other side of the world. Never entirely comfortable in his father's presence, he knew he ought to justify his recent existence to him. It was like reporting to the chairman, only this time the balance-sheet did not look too healthy. Here he was, thirty years old, his university career still incomplete, with very little money and even fewer prospects of getting any. What, his father asked, was he going to do next? He had vaguely thought of becoming a writer or a teacher of languages; in Europe he had heard there might be openings in the movie industry that had just started up. His father listened to him patiently. He told Culbertson not to worry and with typical generosity that he himself had never earned any money to speak of until he was over forty.

Once again the family was having to take stock. They had moved their centre of operations from war-torn Europe to America and had reassembled – apart from Eugene who was still in France suffering from his war injuries – in order to plan their next phase. They were not exactly destitute but they would need to go out to work. Sasha, when he was better, expected to make his debut at Carnegie Hall and Culbertson had outlined his ideas for a job for himself. But it galled him to see his father having to contemplate going out to work. He was over sixty-five now and had been hoping to live out his remaining years in comfortable retirement, watching his sons progress and prosper in their chosen fields. The sudden take-over by the Bolsheviks had thrown all his calculations into disarray. There was still a chance that this new government in Russia might be overthrown or might collapse through inexperience. Certainly some of the major oil companies seemed to think so – Standard Oil, for instance, had been buying up fresh plots in the Caucasus and had even taken over some of the Nobels' holdings there, an indication surely of their confidence in the situation reverting to what it had been before. But their judgement proved to be wrong and this 'refusal of Communism to die' was a costly lesson to them.

The removal of their financial security was to be the crucial catalyst in the Culbertsons' lives, for it meant, quite simply, that Culbertson himself had to go out to work and be responsible for the other members of his family. After ten years of philandering his hand was now being forced. He would, at long last, have to do something.

The only skill he felt confident of using was card-playing – however much his father might disapprove of the 'devil's tickets', as he called them. In any event an ordinary job, he reckoned, would not provide enough for all of them. He started going to Frank Marshall's Chess Club in Greenwich Village. Frank Marshall was a champion chess player and his club was principally a meeting place for chess devotees. He also ran an Auction bridge game there, where the stakes were half a cent a point. Culbertson set aside a special gambling fund of $30, which he calculated should be enough to cover all fluctuations in his fortunes. The regulars at the Auction game welcomed him when he asked if he could cut in. They had seen him around the club before, but only playing chess. At first he kept a low profile until he felt he had got the measure of the other players. Then a few evenings later, he became involved in a game that eventually lasted all night. One of the players, Janowsky, the chess grand master, hit a losing run and wanted to double the stakes. Culbertson and the others agreed and the game went on until the early hours of the morning. By the time they stopped, Culbertson was a clear winner and ended up nearly $100 to the good. Most of this was owed by Janowsky, who promised to pay later that same day. Elated, Culbertson left the club and hurried home. Next evening he went round to the club to collect his winnings. Gloomy faces met him everywhere. Janowsky had died that very same morning and with him his debts had vanished!

He treated it as a temporary setback. His strategy was long-term. The point of having a fixed gambling fund was that it enabled him to adjust to and weather winning and losing runs. These were an inescapable part of a card player's life. At times his fund sank down to as little as $10 but he resisted the temptation to chase his losses. Every evening he set himself a losing limit for the evening and stuck to it. If he lost that amount early on, he would return home and be met by quizzical looks from his father and Sasha, who by now were following his fortunes closely. Tactfully they would make no comment but hope for better things on the morrow.

But the fact was, the most he was able to win at Frank Marshall's, even during a good run, was $40 or $50 a week. It was not really enough to live on and he felt it was time to move on to higher things. The best game in town was to be found at the Knickerbocker Whist Club on West 43rd Street. This club had been founded in 1893 and was famous for its high-stake game on the third floor.

Culbertson's entrée to this club was effected, like so many other things in his life, by a woman. The lady in question was Mrs Lucella Shelton, a prominent bridge teacher with a studio at the Vanderbilt Hotel. Culbertson had seen a picture of her in the newspapers and had gone round to see her, offering to become her assistant. He felt he had gone far enough in developing his own methods of playing Auction bridge to risk giving them a public try out. His experiences at Frank Marshall's showed that his system worked well enough. He was already following, or rather experimenting with, the rudiments of his Approach System, encouraging partners to be more exploratory in their bidding, avoiding the precipitate rush into no trumps. He made much of 'mental play'. Most Auction players counted up their top tricks and left it at that. Culbertson even started emphasizing distribution and the balance of a hand as key factors. It was all 'mathematical', his favourite phrase.

He was convinced that if he could join up with a well-known bridge personality like Mrs Shelton, he might get somewhere. He explained his views and methods of bridge to her, and she was suitably impressed. They agreed to go into partnership and enter one of the Thursday night duplicate games at the Knickerbocker Whist Club. Confident of success, they were prepared to back their judgement. The Thursday night game was open to outsiders and a stranger appearing with a woman partner was given little chance. Culbertson was able to strike up some fairly sizeable bets on their behalf before the evening's tournament started. He knew what he was doing. He had a sound and well-tried system, a partner who now understood him and the inestimable advantage of surprise – no one knew him or what his game was like. They did even better than expected, and not only came out top but won a few hundred dollars into the bargain.

Encouraged by this, Culbertson applied to join the Knickerbocker Whist Club. He started out on the penny-table, feeling his way and slightly in awe of the big names he found himself associating with – Wilbur Whitehead, Milton Work, E.V. Shepard, Sidney Lenz, R.F. Foster and others. Soon he moved on to the two-cent game which was of a higher standard and where some of the experts usually played. He watched them closely and studied their method of playing. He was struck by the mechanical way they bid their cards with little feeling for distribution and a seemingly blind faith in the value of quick tricks. However crude his own system still was, he felt it gave him an edge when compared to theirs.

Soon he felt he could confidently join the five-cent game where the real money was to be made. It was a risk, but one he did not shirk. This table usually comprised top experts and wealthy men who were keen to play against the best talent available and willing to pay for the privilege. Culbertson's winnings now began to mount up and once or twice reached one thousand dollars a month. On the strength of this, he moved to a small apartment of his own round the corner from the Knickerbocker Whist Club and began to play there every day from five in the afternoon to one or two o'clock the following morning. He was soon to achieve an even greater coup.

The third floor of the Knickerbocker Whist Club was reserved for the leading bridge experts of the time. Whitehead presided over it. Other regular players were Sidney Lenz, E.V. Shepard, George Reith, Gratz Scott, Commander W. Liggett and P. Hal Sims. Women players were not normally admitted, except on Duplicate nights, unless they were outstanding. Among those who were, the undisputed queen was Mrs Josephine Dillon, still only in her early twenties, but able to play on level terms with the best men players.

Josephine Dillon was born Josephine Murphy on 2 February 1898, at Bayside, New York. Her father Edward Murphy was a civil engineer. She went to Morris High School in the Bronx and then took a business course at a convent school, St Joseph's. Entering the business world, she became secretary to Pat Powers, the six-day bicycle-race impresario, an unusual step and an indication of her wish to break away from her background. Later she became secretary to Wilbur Whitehead, and for a time his mistress. But she was secretive by nature and rarely talked about her early upbringing. Whitehead taught her bridge. 'Mr Whitehead used me as his guinea-pig', she once said. 'He didn't see why women shouldn't play bridge as well as men, even though at that time they restricted their play to "social bridge".' Through Whitehead she became acquainted with the Knickerbocker circle of bridge players and was something of a favourite among them. They all tried to help her along with her game and teach her, Sidney Lenz in particular. Then, in 1919, she had met James Dillon, a Princeton graduate who had just returned from the war in Europe. He was rather wild, but good-looking and seemed to promise a more glamorous way of life than she had known previously. She was young and impressionable, she wanted to get away from home and they were soon married. But despite the superficial glamour, he was unstable. He drank and took drugs and after only a few months of marriage he committed suicide. It was a shattering blow. Josephine withdrew into herself and would not talk about it. People were left to speculate about the causes of his suicide – and even to this day the exact causes remain unclear. She was still marked by the scars of her disastrous marriage when she came across Ely Culbertson.

They met for the first time one night in March 1922. He had gone for the evening to the Knickerbocker Whist Club and ran into Whitehead downstairs who told him they were looking for a fourth player for a game on the third floor. Whitehead and he went upstairs together, and he was introduced to the two other players – Ralph Leibenderfer, a lawyer, and Josephine Dillon. He had already heard about the legendary Mrs Dillon, and was immediately attracted by her. She was quite tall, slender, with large Irish eyes, a slightly upturned nose and an engaging smile. He noticed her hands particularly - long, narrow and sensitive. She seemed to have an air of relaxed, unhurried calm about her. He sensed she had taken note of him too but was not going to reveal what she felt. They cut for partners and Culbertson drew Liebenderfer. As the cards were being shuffled, Jo turned to Culbertson.

'I hear you're a very lucky player and that you have invented a system. Well, I'm sure it's not all luck. There must be a little skill in it as well.'

It was a promising start. It meant she had heard of him as well. The men played for five cents a point while Jo settled for one cent, which was her limit. The game proceeded as slowly as the traffic on Fifth Avenue outside, largely because Whitehead insisted on lengthy post-mortems after every deal. For him the bridge-table was like a dissecting-slab for the anatomy of quick tricks. While analysing the hand, he liked to pontificate. Jo and Leibenderfer seemed unperturbed by this and were obviously used to it. Culbertson was in no hurry, either, captivated by the presence of Jo. His normally astute bridge defences must have slipped for he soon found himself in a trap of her making. She had twice bid a suit in which she held a void. Culbertson cannot have been listening too closely and doubled; she switched to her real suit, he doubled again, she quickly redoubled and made the contract with a trick to spare. Culbertson had been completely taken in and groaned ruefully.

'I never imagined a woman capable of such a triple-cross.'

'It's the only chance we women have,' Jo replied dryly.

Culbertson silently chalked up the humiliation in his 'someday-I'll-show-you' column. He now understood what Leibenderfer meant when he said she had a man's mind.

But for all her man's mind, she had, in Culbertson's eyes, another inestimable quality - charm. This emanated from her overall presence, her gestures and dignity and her quiet restraint. For Culbertson she was a challenge - the sort of woman he felt he had to live up to, in order to earn her respect. He also felt that there was something, a sort of unspoken intimacy, between them.

When the game ended, he stayed on at the club, talking to Whitehead, who was a resident at the club, listening to his bridge arguments, but his mind was elsewhere. He longed to hear more about Jo. Perhaps Whitehead might even give him some fatherly advice, but he was entirely preoccupied with the game that had just taken place. Culbertson went home but, try as he might, he found his thoughts coming back time and again to Jo. She was his type all right, but he knew he would have to tread carefully. She was still feeling the effects of her marriage to one glamorous personality and would be wary of another.

He decided upon a waiting-game. Instead of pressing his suit, his tactic was to avoid seeing her altogether for the next two weeks. When invited to join a third-floor game at the Knickerbocker Whist Club, he declined, making an excuse that he had a previous engagement. It was the Culbertson Pursuit System, New-York-style. No doubt there was a degree of insecurity in it as well. Beneath his outward conceit and brashness, he still could not quite bring himself to believe that an exceptional woman like Jo Dillon would find him attractive on his own account. Jo seemed to have a host of admirers and he could see that, for her, it had not been a case of love at first sight.

Culbertson took stock. How could he make the Pursuit System really effective? It all revolved around three basic precepts: emotion, reason and imagination. He sat in his room at night working it out, sketching out his plan on to bits of paper filled with notes and diagrams. The first two were linked. First arouse her sympathy, and then lull her suspicions and quieten her fears. At their next meeting he would seek to present himself in a favourable light, display his sincerity and genuineness. Then he would establish intellectual mastery over her. His card system would do that, paving the way for admiration. On to the third stage, then, when her imagination would be opened up as she envisaged the endless possibilities of their triumphs and shared life together. Well, of course it did not work out like that – the human heart failing to be as biddable as a deck of cards. Jo soon came to personify a sort of prize between Whitehead representing the old order and himself representing the new.

He continued going to the Knickerbocker Whist Club where he was viewed as something of a brash upstart. His ideas on bridge seemed so strange that no one took them particularly seriously – yet he still came out a regular winner. He had evolved his system as a reaction against the old methods he encountered – they were rigid and nothing like as flexible as his new scientific approach with its readiness to analyse every nuance of the cards and its step by step bidding. The old guard remained self-satisfied and saw no need to change. They glorified the 'rules' of bidding and would rather score 200 points by following those rules than 300 by abandoning them. Culbertson kept a 'crime sheet' in which he analysed their bids and plays as well as his own and he could prove that they actually threw away thousands of points when they thought they had played perfectly. He imagined that Jo, too, viewed his theories with faint derision. This was his chance. If he could get to work on her and make her see that his system was perfectly sound and probably superior to others, and she had been wrong in her original assessment, then stage three of the Pursuit System was on.

Next time he was invited to the thrd floor, he accepted unhesitatingly. The other two players with Jo were top Auction players and Culbertson at first suspected he had been invited out of curiosity. He was right. The other two players had been keen to meet him and see him with their very own eyes. Every time he made an unusual bid he noticed them exchanging meaningful glances and barely suppressed laughter behind a polite smile. Jo remained cool and friendly throughout, amused rather than critical. Culbertson went away pleased with their second encounter.

Culbertson made a few converts to his system, though he had to admit they were mostly losers in search of a miracle cure. His main ally and partner was Julio Aceves. They played together at the Tuesday night Duplicate games and won a number of substantial bets, struck against them by fellow members who were convinced Culbertson's luck must sooner or later run out. But his winnings put him ahead on the club's championship board by what was then the widest margin in the club's history. Second came Sidney Lenz – a source perhaps of their later rivalry.

Jo still resisted his theories; she remained a Whitehead follower. One evening after dinner at the club, Culbertson ran into her and tried to persuade her to switch her system. 'You've got a false sense of loyalty. If my methods are correct, that will only help Whitehead. I'll hand them over to him as I haven't the slightest intention of becoming a bridge writer!'

But Jo was not only thinking of his system of cards. 'It isn't your ideas or your so-called system that makes you win,' she told him.

'What is it then?'

'It's your knowledge of human nature and your card experience. You'd win with any system.'

This was encouraging. She must have been watching him more closely than he imagined. At last he got her to try out his system, not at the club, but at home. She said she would give it a try and for two weeks, almost every evening, he went to her apartment and they dealt out hands together, bid them first according to traditional Auction methods and scored the results, and then bid them again according to the Culbertson System.

In the end, Jo was convinced, and converted to his methods. They also became fast friends, and moved on to first name terms.

Jo was living at the time in a studio apartment which she also used for her bridge teaching. After her teaching sessions, a group of her friends used to foregather, Culbertson among them. They would have cocktails and then usually go to the Beaux Arts restaurant next door. This was a legendary speak-easy run by the equally legendary Texas Guinan ('Where the hell would I be without Prohibition?') and it was to be the setting for much of their courtship. Speak-easies, following the advent of Prohibition in 1920, were in their heyday. Usually detectable only by the tell-tale line of limousines and taxicabs parked outside, they required an elaborate procedure to gain admission, involving the use of passwords or special latchkeys. So plentiful were they that many New Yorkers seldom ventured elsewhere – even to the extent of measuring distances, like John O'Hara heroines, by the taxi-fares between speak-easies.

Their romance was not exactly aided by the rather sour-tasting Californian champagne that arrived under a French label, and as time went by they gradually withdrew from the noisier crowd, preferring to be on their own. At other times they would go to a small Italian restaurant nearby that had home-made pasta and Italian wines. In such a European setting, Culbertson would regale Jo with stories of his youthful escapades. As spring came and it was warm enough to sit outdoors they would go and sit on a bench in the little park at the back of the New York Public Library on 42nd Street. Jo still could not make Culbertson out. He was such a mixture, open and generous at one moment, secretive and dogmatic at the next. Did he really mean what he was saying or was it all done for effect? She knew he was a calculating type, always seeking the best way to play the hand, as it were; that much she could recognize. But there was another side to him that gradually became more apparent, an inner loneliness that seemed to be tied up with his Russian background and his feeling that somehow he didn't belong in America. She began to see more of that side of his nature when he took her to a Russian restaurant, the haunt of emigrés attempting to re-create the atmosphere of St Petersburg. Jo would listen for hours as he told her about his early experiences in Russia. Another time he took her to listen to Chaliapin in *Boris Godunov* at the Metropolitan Opera. As he talked about Russia, she began to understand how much this had shaped his personality and was responsible for many of its contradictions. It was as if the Russian side, his dreamy visionary self, had not fused with the more practical, business-like American side.

As they spent more time together, they drew closer and closer. Culbertson, impulsive and hasty, ignoring the principles of his Pursuit System, took this as a sign of a fully-established relationship. He was rash enough to show her his diary, partly no doubt to gain her approval, and partly to impress her with the depths of his 'soul'. It was a classic mistake and had the opposite effect from what he had intended. It only filled her with misgivings and confirmed her hidden fears that at heart he was not the marrying kind, but a restless, nomadic individual. Her fear was that if they married and set up home together, some day or other he would go away. For her, this fear was far greater than that of infidelity. Culbertson had failed to notice how fragile Jo was beneath her restrained exterior. The scars of her first marriage were still with her. Once she had read the diaries, she felt she had to speak to him.

'You're too proud, Ely, too full of strange ideas,' she told him. 'You simply refuse to be like anyone else. How can you expect me to build a home on such pride?'

She accused him of being a 'nomad at heart' who viewed women as little more than details in his life. Clearly she feared she might end up the same way. Jo had already been the loser in one marriage and was not keen to risk another disaster. To her Culbertson seemed to be ruled by ideas more than by his heart. How, she wondered, could she rely on someone like that? Set against this was her obvious attraction to him. He was a kindred spirit – determined, not afraid to go it alone. But for the moment she was overwhelmed by her mistrust of him.

Culbertson was taken aback by her perspicacious comments. At first he tried to laugh it off and joke with her. What was marriage after all but a piece of paper? This only infuriated her the more and she threatened to call the whole thing off.

'I want to forget all about you. Please take me home.'

Culbertson shrugged his shoulders and without a word did as she said. It looked like the end.

He went back to his apartment and tried hard to rationalize himself out of it. 'She's not the woman for me,' he told himself. 'My ideal woman must follow me everywhere, regardless of consequences.'

It was the first time he had gone so far as to ask anyone to marry him, and he had been turned down. He tried thinking of her as just another American girl – spoiled, like the rest of them. He plunged into playing bridge all night, and for much of the next day. In the evening he went to the Knickerbocker Whist Club, half hoping to meet her but she did not show up. He telephoned her at home, and her mother answered, telling him she had gone to Saratoga for the races and would not be back for some time.

Crestfallen, he returned home and had dinner with his father. He knew he had not seen much of him recently and now he could, at least, try to make up for it. He tried too to put Jo out of his mind, but she kept returning. Give it another week, he told himself, and it will all have blown over. But another week passed and it only became worse. Without her his life was empty. He became fearful of losing her altogether but his pride still held him back and prevented him from getting in touch with her.

He weighed up the pros and cons. At one level he knew that much of what she had said was right. He should give up his wasteful life and settle down and earn a proper living. By marrying Jo there was every chance they could be happy, have children, and he would end up doing something useful with his life. He had only to look at her to see that she was good-looking, practical, had good business sense, and might even be prepared to look after him – what more could he ask for? If the cost was merely that he had to give up some of his philandering and his obsession with nebulous political ideals, surely that was a reasonable price to pay?

Jo had gone to stay with Connie Percy and her husband in Saratoga. Connie had been a friend of Culbertson's too, so he rang her house the next morning. He learned from her, reading between the lines, that Jo had been unhappy these past few days. He asked if he could come up and stay and was thrilled when she said he could.

The first night he and Jo went out for dinner to a roadhouse, where in a suitably noisy and impersonal atmosphere they talked things over. Culbertson asked Jo whether she forgave him. He admitted his approach had been arrogant and stupid, and apologized for it. He wanted to assure her of his genuine love for her. Had she changed her mind about their getting married? She would not commit herself, saying she needed time to convince herself that he too was really different.

'Am I on probation, then?' Culbertson asked.

'There you go again, proud as always. I thought you said you had learnt a new humility.'

The week at Saratoga sped by. They managed to avoid going to the racetrack altogether, but they did play bridge one evening against Hal Sims and Charlie Downs who had come up for the races. It was during the course of this game that Culbertson first glimpsed the possibilities of himself and Jo becoming a celebrated bridge partnership. Not only did their respective temperaments seem to complement each other at the bridge-table but they already had that essential ingredient to partnership success, a sixth sense or intuitive understanding of each other's bidding and play.

When they returned to New York, they thought they would put it to the test. Culbertson had run into Percy Gregg, a well-known stockbroker and bridge player from Philadelphia. Gregg liked challenge matches, and, fortuitously, also played with a woman partner; he assumed his opponents would consider him to be at a disadvantage for this reason. But the challengers, often over-confident, would be beaten and some hefty side-bets would go Gregg's way. Here then was just the sort of opportunity Culbertson was looking for.

The next time he saw Gregg at the Knickerbocker Whist Club they arranged a match together – one hundred rubbers over ten sessions, stakes to be one cent a point for the ladies and ninety-nine cents for the men. Culbertson did not flinch at this. He was confident of his partnership with Jo. They went into training, practising for hours on end to perfect their technique. They knew that because of the high stakes (a dollar a point was extremely high in those days, usually reserved for only a few multi-millionaires) news of this game was bound to get around, and if they won their reputation would be made.

Gregg's partner was Mrs Lillian Peck (later to play in the American Women's team at Budapest in June 1937) at whose home the match was to take place. They began on a Sunday afternoon and the contrasting styles of the two sets of players soon became apparent. Gregg was a quick, incisive player and Mrs Peck, despite her nonchalant air, played a very strong game also. Jo and Culbertson, on the other hand, played slowly and deliberately, relying on their well-tried technique to see them through. It was the old story of professionals against amateurs, of the steady but sure against the brilliant but unco-ordinated. Gregg and his partner were bold in places and then unnecessarily cautious in others.

At the end of the first session Jo and Culbertson were ahead. But, true to their new professionalism, they set to work as soon as the session had ended, analysing the day's hands and seeing if they could have played or bid them better, trying always to assess the percentage of luck and of skill. By the end of the sixth session, they were several thousand dollars up and looked all set to win more. The partnership of Percy Gregg and Mrs Peck was cracking up. In desperation Gregg tried to 'buy' his way out of trouble and resorted to more and more psychic bids ('that form of legitimate dishonesty' as S.J. Simon was later to term them), in the belief that he stood a better chance of fooling two opponents than one partner. But it was not to be. Matters reached a head when Mrs Peck found herself in a high redoubled spades contract looking at a dummy with minimal values in the suits bid. Rather than play the hand, she quit there and then, and the match was over.

But the other match that Culbertson wanted to win above all still eluded him. Throughout that winter, Jo kept him at arm's length. The more he pressed his attentions on her the more she resisted. She still could not be sure of him, sure that she could really trust him.

Then in the middle of April 1923 he had to go into hospital for an operation. It was his stomach ulcers playing up, an indication of the nervous strain he had really been under. Jo came to visit him. The shock of seeing him ill and vulnerable and his obvious sincerity in talking to her changed her view of him. As he convalesced in hospital after his operation, she began to understand him better and see that many of his traits, his contrariness and obstinacy, concealed a kinder, gentler side, and many of her fears were removed.

She finally relented and agreed to marry him. They went to see Father Duffy of the Holy Cross Church on West 42nd Street (Jo was a Roman Catholic) and asked him to perform the ceremony. On the night before their wedding they worked out that all they had to start married life with was $50, but in some strange way, they relished the challenge of having it all to make. Neither of them would have welcomed a helping hand. They too were linked to the American Dream.

They were married on 11 June 1923, by Father Duffy, with Culbertson's father as best man. The only others present were Jo's parents and Connie Percy. They had not sent out invitations as they wanted a quiet family affair. After the service they went back to Jo's home for a brief celebration and on the way there in their taxi, Culbertson, having to avail himself of the limited opportunities for romantic display, gave Jo a small jewelled box and told her, 'Jo-jotte, some day I'll make you the happiest woman in the world.' Their honeymoon was twenty-four hours at a hotel at Long Beach – all they could afford as the Gregg match winnings had by now been used up.

Many of Jo's old friends were shocked to hear of her marriage. Culbertson was still an outsider to most of them, and something of an unknown quantity. Few of them could make him out and they were sure the marriage would not last. Whitehead and his Knickerbocker circle were sorry to see her go. They had grown used to her presence, they thought of her as one of them. But just as few knew what Culbertson was like, few probably appreciated the unconventional streak in Jo. From an early age she had struck out on her own. Rather than stick to the traditional areas of work for women, she had taken up competitive bridge, very much a male-dominated world. It was this side of her that was attracted to Culbertson. She sensed in him another unusual, unconventional personality, with whom she could continue along the same path.

But however promising the future, they still had to earn a living. They discussed it together. Jo planned to go on with her bridge teaching for which she had built up quite a clientele and the reputation of being one of New York's best teachers. Jo was keen for Culbertson to write a book putting his bridge ideas into print. After all, he had always claimed and wanted to be a writer. But for the moment he thought he could rely on his gambling to earn them a living. They were young and there seemed to be no hurry.

Rather than confine himself to the five-cents game at the Knickerbocker, Culbertson with his eye for the main chance decided to look for something bigger. Through the offices of Walbridge Taft, the son of former President Taft, whom he had known in Paris, he got a letter of introduction to the Whist Club on East 39th Street and was elected a member. This was a very exclusive club, the haunt of bankers, Wall Street brokers and other wealthy businessmen. It was here that he first got to know Charles M. Schwab, President of Bethlehem Steel Corporation, who was later to play an important role in his bridge life. Joseph Elwell had been a member there too before his mysterious murder in 1920. The stakes were high, usually fifty cents a point, or even higher. Wins and losses could run into several thousand dollars a night. But the members enjoyed their bridge in much the same way as they enjoyed bringing off a successful coup at business. They were mostly rugged individualists, who had little time for systems but preferred to rely on their formidable bargaining powers as they strove to reach an optimum contract. It was bridge all right, but of a sort that even Culbertson had not encountered before – full of inconsistencies, brilliant and inspired one moment, calamitous the next.

Like many wealthy men, the members often welcomed the chance to play with an expert, and were happy to pay for the facility. They all knew bridge was Culbertson's sole source of income, while he, in return, repaid them by explaining what he saw as some of the finer points of the game. It was not long before he notched up big winnings as his own methods and his reliance on the early formulations of his Approach System began to pay off. He was able to sail along, as he put it, 'with all sails unfurled in a stiff distributional breeze'. Indeed a bridge colleague and well-known writer on bridge, R.F. Foster, wrote a series of articles for *Vanity Fair* at this time describing some of his 'magnificent plays' and giving him the title of Mr Culbertson Gettritzki!

In July 1923 he and Jo rented a big, sprawling house on the shores of Lake Mount Arab in the Adirondacks. It was a delayed honeymoon and they were blissfully happy swimming in the lake and walking through the woods. His father came up to stay with them and they had a black cook who was keen on the violin. One day she took fright at the strange animal noises coming from the woods and only agreed to stay on when Almon guaranteed to give her violin lessons.

In September they returned to New York and rented a small apartment on West 55th Street, opposite the Gotham Hotel. The furnishing of this new apartment, their first home together, depended mainly on Culbertson's fluctuating winnings at bridge. But now that they were married they were content to lead an easy-going, relaxed life. Culbertson devoted some of his time to helping Sasha who had recently married a former pupil of his, Helen Hamilton, and had signed to give his debut concert at Carnegie Hall. On the day of the concert, his father took his place among the standees and was able to relive for a few brief hours the excitement of Sasha's concert tours in Europe. The hall was full and Sasha played with much of his old virtuosity, but there seemed to be something holding him back, as though he were afraid to let himself go. He had developed a block. Perhaps, in the long run, his father's constant supervision and driving had had a negative effect. After the concert Sasha felt discouraged and resolved to return to Europe to perfect his technique and support himself by teaching others to play the violin. It was not until some twelve years later, in 1936, that he was to perform again in public in America, also at Carnegie Hall in a concert arranged and promoted by Culbertson.

Then Culbertson encountered one of those prolonged runs of bad luck at cards that are an inseparable part of a gambler's life. It seemed never to go away and they even had to pawn some of their valuables and borrow money from friends to keep going. He was forced to leave the high-stake game at the Whist Club and go back to the five-cent tables at the Knickerbocker Whist Club. It was the second winter of their marriage and life became difficult. In the spring of 1925 this culminated in a physical collapse. Culbertson's stomach ulcers were playing up again. They could not afford proper medical treatment or advice. Culbertson was determined to go on playing but it soon became apparent to both of them that what someone of his highly-strung temperament needed was complete rest.

At that point his luck turned and on one day he won $350. It was enough for them to put the furniture into store, pay off the back rent – Jo's own earnings helped here – and leave New York. They made sure Almon had enough money to see him through the summer and set off. Their destination was Mount Arab, the spot where they had had such an idyllic summer two years ago. This time they decided to rent a small log cabin for $40 per month.

They planned to spend three months there and calculated that they had $200 to buy food, pay for medical expenses and whatever else they might need for day-to-day living. The cabin was by no means luxurious, but it suited their purpose. It had two beds in it, an oil-stove, a stable and a bench, but the roof leaked. While they were there they celebrated their second wedding anniversary. All they could muster were some wild flowers plus two volumes of Dostoevsky and Anatole France, two of his favourite authors, that he had bought in a second-hand bookshop in New York.

The remoteness and seclusion of Mount Arab gave Ely plenty of time to reflect. He would sit for hours on the porch turning over things in his mind. He knew he had been forcing the pace too much, spending too long at the card-table, to the exclusion of all else. He would lapse into deep reverie. Jo would do her best to snap him out of these moods.

Reassured by Jo's faith in him, Culbertson pronounced that he would become the agent of his own cure. He had devised a Culbertson System of Self-Cure. This entailed changing direction – not so much in their way of life but by what he termed 'psychic rest', exchanging the humdrum, day-to-day worries of making a living playing cards for other, more intellectual preoccupations with what he saw as the destiny of America and the mysterious forces arising in Europe.

By September he felt well again, his stomach pains had virtually ceased and he felt refreshed and mentally invigorated. It was Jo's turn to fall ill. She had borne the main burden of his illness all through the summer and now found herself with an excruciating abdominal pain. At first she laughed it off and claimed that they were sympathetic pains, trying to share some of his illness. But on the evening of Labour Day, Jo suddenly collapsed while washing dishes. She passed out for a full ten to fifteen minutes and when she regained consciousness, it was clear she was in considerable pain. Culbertson was in a panic. There was no telephone in the house, so he had no choice but to leave Jo and paddle across the lake to their nearest neighbour's house, where fortunately there was a telephone and a doctor could be summoned within minutes.

The doctor made a quick examination of her and recommended that she go straightaway to New York to see a specialist – there was a train leaving in an hour that they could catch. Jo was feeling very weak so they rigged up a stretcher to take her to the train. Meanwhile Culbertson had got in touch with Connie Percy to contact her gynaecologist and prepare for her arrival.

Doctors had told Jo before they were married that it would be difficult for her to have children, but she had wanted to try all the same. It was a fifty-fifty chance, and to her mind that was 'as good as a finesse'. But this time it had not come off. She had had a miscarriage. When they got to the Roosevelt Hospital in New York, the doctors told Culbertson her condition was very serious. She would have to have an immediate operation and the result of it would not be known until she came out of the anaesthetic later that evening. In the meantime the doctor told Culbertson he would only be in the way if he stayed. He went straight to the Knickerbocker Whist Club. The other players were glad to see him and commented on his fine tan.

'You want to play?'

'That's what I'm here for.' His only thought was of the hospital expenses.

He played all that afternoon, had his dinner brought on a tray alongside the table, and continued into the night. He played as hard and as effectively as he had ever played. From time to time he went to the telephone to enquire how Jo was. The hospital told him she would not be coming round until after midnight. He went on playing, and won. He could not help feeling that that afternoon had been the low point of Jo's and his life and now the tide was turning.

When he rang the hospital after midnight and learnt that she was all right, he knew his presentiment had been correct.

It had been a salutary lesson for Ely. Here was his wife prepared to risk her life on their behalf and all he was doing was living in the vague expectancy that one day he might become a writer or an expert on social systems in line with his student days in Paris. So far he had failed to give her the stability and way of life he had originally promised.

For the first time he really began to look hard at what a card player's life was really about – particularly now that he could see it through another person's eyes. Its constant ups and downs, hopes and illusions, were hardly the basis for a constructive future. He should listen more to Jo, remember what she said about giving up gambling, and become a bridge teacher like her. Then he could make a decent living, and give her the security and happiness she deserved.

But the pull of the gambler was still strong, at times it dominated all else, and somewhere at the back of his mind there remained his long-held resistance to a bourgeois existence. He decided to give himself another six months of professional card-playing and see if he could accumulate some capital. At the same time he set about becoming a teacher of Auction bridge, getting a business card printed: Mr Ely Culbertson, Bridge Instructor. He deliberately omitted his address on 55th Street, as the area was full of speak-easies and had acquired a slightly unsavoury reputation.

In bridge circles, his plan was to set himself up as a sort of *éminence grise*, with a view to building up a behind-the-scenes reputation. It was a long-term strategy that, if it worked well, could provide them with financial security. He collaborated with George Reith, Chairman of the Card Committee of the Knickerbocker Whist Club on his book

The Art of Successful Bidding. Reith was much taken with Culbertson's Approach System and the book, which was published under George Reith's name, caused quite a stir.

All this was beginning to have its effect. Rumours began to spread about the mysterious Culbertson who was responsible for new and promising developments in bridge. Close associates of his and Jo's pressed him to write a book himself, and capitalize on his growing reputation. But he wanted to wait. Putting out a book there and then would simply make it one among many others, all competing for the same narrow market, whereas if he waited for the moment when a bridge-confused public really needed a definitive text he stood a greater chance of success.

Initially he had developed his system mostly for his and Jo's use in their own competitive bridge games. Now he thought of how to make it appeal to the average club or social player. A learner can only take in so much at a time. It needed clear step-by-step presentation and simplified rules.

The next step was to establish Jo and himself as top tournament players. Without tournament success, no one was going to take his system seriously. Jo and he began to enter for pairs events, and even take on challenge matches, but the real test for both him and his system would be in a team-of-four tournament.

CHAPTER 5

CONTRACT BRIDGE

Culbertson had a habit throughout his life of getting hold of highly talented people to work for him or be associated with him. A glance at the staff who worked at *Bridge World* or contributed articles to it bears this out. When looking for members for his tournament team Culbertson was equally fortunate in being able to recruit Theodore Lightner and Waldemar von Zedtwitz.

Theodore Lightner was born in 1893. After graduating from Yale and the Harvard Law School, he became a member of the New York Stock Exchange, where he could be seen – an unusual characteristic in these surroundings – standing alone in a corner, muttering furiously to himself and viewing the world over rimless pince-nez. His indecision meant that he was never able to pick up a stock market bid quickly enough. As Culbertson wrote, in a slightly tongue-in-cheek portrait, he was 'gloomy and pessimistic, easily discouraged at first; but if things went from bad to worse he then became a man of indomitable will, for then, having lost all hope, he started to fight out of sheer spite!' He became an invaluable member of the Culbertson team, a close friend of Culbertson and a regular contributor to *Bridge World*, best known now for his invention of the Lightner double. He died in 1981 at the age of eighty-eight.

Waldemar von Zedtwitz was born in Berlin in 1896, the son of a German Baron from Saxony to whose title he succeeded when his father died a few months after birth, and of an American mother, one of the wealthy Caldwells from Kentucky. This gave him dual nationality but after the First World War he relinquished his title and adopted US citizenship. He spent much of his childhood in France, and with his American and German background, was soon trilingual. His facility for and conversancy with many languages, including classical ones, as well as his scholarship in etymology, gave him an international reputation as a linguist and lexicographer. Apart from his time as a member of the Culbertson team, he played regularly in pairs tournaments with Sims and also with Harold Vanderbilt, the latter being a formidable partnership not least because of the renowned slowness of the two players. He had a curious habit of twisting his ear while concentrating at the card-table. A doctor supposedly told him he would get cancer that way, so he immediately switched to twirling his hair! In the 1930s he kept a house at Deal close to the Sims' estate, and was very much part of their entourage. He also had a house near the Vanderbilt mansion at Lantana in Florida, itself a rendezvous for bridge weeks during the winter months. Otherwise he was based in New York where he lived in a penthouse on Park Avenue. In 1948 he played a crucial role in stabilizing the American Contract Bridge League, the governing body for North American bridge activities, and was nominated its President. Then in 1970, at the age of seventy-four, he won the World Olympiad Mixed Pairs tournament. In recent years he lived in Hawaii, where he died in 1984. In team of four tournaments Lightner usually partnered Culbertson while von Zedtwitz played with Jo.

The first tournament success for a Culbertson team of four at Auction was in Detroit in 1926 when they won the All American Auction team of four Trophy, played at the Detroit Whist Club. The team consisted of Culbertson, Jo, Lightner and Ralph Richards. The same team finished second in the following year for the same competition held this time at Hanover, New Hampshire. In that year, 1927, Culbertson won the men's team of four national championship organized by the American Auction Bridge League but the main tournament successes with Lightner and von Zedtwitz were to come in 1930.

In New York Culbertson still had very few pupils. He thought it over and decided towards the end of 1926 to go to California, where he had good contacts. Jo would join him later once she had got free of her own teaching commitments.

In Los Angeles, things brightened up. He stayed at the Biltmore Hotel and fixed himself up with a small studio for his teaching. Within two weeks twenty people had enrolled, each paying $100 for a course of ten lessons. Bridge, even in those days, was an important social attribute in the movie colony and a number of his clients came from Beverly Hills, while others belonged to the social sets of Los Angeles and Pasadena. Jo joined him there after three months. This enabled him to switch his activities to the California Bridge Club which he helped organize with Roy Sargent. From now on Jo did most of the teaching while Culbertson concentrated on the business and professional side.

Things went very well for them. One of the callers at their bridge studio was Rex Leroy, an old-style Western gambler who operated an ornate casino which was one of the sights of the city. Although his income was derived from roulette, faro and poker, he himself was devoted to Auction bridge. He challenged the Culbertsons to a high-stake game which they won. When Leroy issued another challenge, they could hardly refuse. They won again and ended up six thousand dollars richer.

For the first time since they were married they could look forward to the months ahead without any financial worries. They decided to celebrate: a car for Culbertson and some clothes for Jo. The car was a shining second-hand 1924 Dodge coupé. Culbertson bought it in exactly five minutes. Had he waited another five minutes, he might have saved fifty dollars, but his impatience was made more inexcusable by the fact that he did not know how to drive. He had to ask the salesman to show him. Even so he managed to stall the car on a hill and had to ask a bewildered passer-by to drive it for them, Culbertson mumbling something about only being able to drive on the level. All his life his driving was atrocious, one of the few points on which his friends were unanimous.

The early part of 1927 remained one of the happiest periods in Culbertson and Jo's memory. Culbertson finally mastered the art of driving enough for them to set off on a tour of Southern California. They drove south from Los Angeles through the small townships and rose-perfumed valleys till they reached the fabled and gabled Hotel Coronado by San Diego, where they lingered for a few days. From there they crossed the Mexican border at Tijuana which Culbertson could only remember as the 'meanest, filthiest and most vicious spot' he had ever been to. Back up the Pacific coastline to Los Angeles, they again took up their social life, with weekends in Santa Barbara at the houses of one or other of their pupils.

By now Jo was pregnant, to their great delight. It brought out in Culbertson his more solicitous side, and less of the devil-may-care attitude of former years. His father came to join them from New York, with better news of Eugene's health and encouraging news of Sasha's renewed violin-playing. The hitherto disorganized and fragmented family seemed to have come together and found a unity and cohesion that had been missing for years. Now that Almon had reconciled himself to the irretrievable loss of his money, he became much less stern and irritable, and began to appreciate the smaller pleasures of life.

It was during one of their weekends in Santa Barbara that the Culbertsons first came across Contract bridge. They had been invited to a dinner-party to meet a pair of local champions who then proposed a challenge match at Contract. Rumours of this game with its new slam and vulnerability features had been circulating for some time, and friends in New York had sent Culbertson letters describing how it had caught on among the fashionable crowd once Harold

Vanderbilt of the wealthy railway family had brought it into circulation.

Vanderbilt played a key role in the introduction of Contract bridge. Aside from cards, his defence of the prestigious America's Cup between the years of 1930 and 1937 earned him a permanent place in the annals of yacht-racing history. He was an accomplished sailor, as well as a designer. In some respects this was where his interest too lay in cards. He was intrigued by the 'design possibilities' of any game he played. His innovations, which made Contract bridge into the game we know today, stemmed as much as anything from his wish to streamline the shape of bridge as he then knew it. He was not a natural card player; he started playing cards in his Harvard days, and viewed them more as an intellectual challenge, something that he could master by rigorous application. This approach, slow and painstaking, lasted throughout his life. He played an important part in establishing the Laws of Contract Bridge, serving for many years as Chairman of the National Laws Commission whose meetings were held in the board room of the New York Central Railroad. In spite of his many other interests he never missed a meeting.

He wrote one of the earliest books on the new game, his *Contract Bridge* published in 1929 in which he outlined his Club Convention, the precursor of the present day artificial one-club conventions. With his habitual modesty, he claimed that he had originally intended to have this book privately printed for distribution among 'certain of my card-playing friends'. He dedicated it to three of them, Frederic S. Allen, Francis M. Bacon iii and Dudley L. Pickman Jr 'to whose co-operation is due the evolution of Contract Bridge'. By this he was referring to the historic cruise he took with them in October 1925, from which the new game emerged.

In the late autumn of 1925 Vanderbilt had gone to California on a combined business and golfing trip. Rather than return to New York directly, he took a nine-day cruise with his friends from San Pedro in California to Havana, Cuba on board the ss *Finland*. Vanderbilt was going to use this trip as an opportunity to try out his recent modifications to bridge. Vanderbilt had played Auction and its variant, Plafond, for a number of years. The time had now come to take another step forward in improving the successive games of the whist family, he felt. So, after considerable thought, he compiled in the autumn of 1925 a scoring table for his new game, and gave it the tentative title Contract bridge. He incorporated in it not only the best features of Auction and Plafond, but also a number of new and exciting features, namely premiums for slams bid and made, vulnerability, and the decimal system of scoring. These new features, the increases in trick and game values and in all premiums and penalties were what he wanted to try out on the cruise.

The foursome used to gather in the oak-panelled saloon every evening and most afternoons on board for their game of cards. As the cruise progressed, Vanderbilt discovered that his new scoring-table stood up to all his expectations. Its balance was such that it gave equal opportunity to attacking or defensive play, enabling the player to use his judgement whether to make an aggressive or a sacrifice bid. In Auction the penalties for going down had been so steep that the art of sacrifice was practically unknown. But Vanderbilt was still having trouble finding a good term to describe the situation of being 'game-in' – a key factor in his scoring-table, for this was the point at which slam bonuses and penalties and bonuses for made or failed contracts increased. His friends had not been able to come up with any suggestions. Then, on the night of 31 October, the ss *Finland* reached the Panama Canal but was denied landing facilities and had to drop anchor off Balboa on the Pacific side of the Canal. Because of the lateness of the hour, the captain was not keen to let a boat ashore for passengers wishing to sample the nightlife there. A young woman on board asked if she could join in the game Vanderbilt and his travelling companions were playing. She had watched them playing previously and knew enough about bridge from a recent stay in China where other variations of the game had been played. In the course of play Vanderbilt asked her if she could think of a suitable term to describe 'game-in'. The young woman, whose identity to this day is unknown, hesitated only momentarily before suggesting the word 'vulnerable'.

It was just what Vanderbilt was looking for – the word hinted at a sense of danger and a readiness to take risks, each of which Vanderbilt was trying to get across. The next day, as the ship made its way along the Panama Canal and other passengers lined the rail or sat in deckchairs to watch the rapidly changing scenery, Vanderbilt stayed in his cabin putting the finishing touches to his new game. If there has to be a date when Contract bridge was born, then it would be that day, 1 November 1925.

By the time the ship reached Havana he had written out his version in detail and back in New York he gave typed copies of it for circulation among his friends. It caught on – not least perhaps because of his social standing. Vanderbilt, in his systematic way, then went on to develop his own bidding methods centred on his Club Convention, as published in his book. In 1928 he donated the Vanderbilt Cup to allow the game, which now incorporated his scoring system and other innovations, to be tested at the highest level of competition and, if need be, improved. Time was to show that his original scoring system, with only the minor modification of giving forty points for one no trump in place of thirty-five points and some changes to penalty points, has remained unchanged to this date.

Though this may seem surprising in retrospect, it was some time before the new game became widely popular. Many people preferred to stick to Auction and saw no need to switch. First mention of it in *Auction Bridge* magazine did not occur until February 1927, when a long article entitled 'Has Contract Auction a Future in America?' explained why the magazine had not referred to it before 'believing that the country as a whole would not adopt, or even be interested in, this new form of the game'. In August the magazine was still keeping an open mind. Its editorial under the title, 'Contract Still an Enigma', stated that, while some call it 'the Game of Today', part of the reasons why it had not caught on was that 'it appeals to speculative and not to scientific instincts; that it is too complicated and too difficult for any but the super player; and that should it become generally popular, it would drive seventy-five per cent of the old line of bridge players away from the card-table. The game-for-its-own-sake element does not wish to bother with such complications as the variations in the values of doubles and bonuses. They abhor the vulnerability provision and they do not approve of the theory that a game to be scored must be bid for.'

For the latter part of 1926 and the early part of 1927, Culbertson was on the West Coast in California. Although the game had gained a foothold on the East Coast, among fashionable circles and some members of the Racquet Club where Vanderbilt played, it had yet to make the same impact elsewhere and in Santa Barbara it was quite new.

Culbertson was keen to try it. From the little he knew about it, he could see that it had to be an improvement on Auction. In Auction a partnership aimed to secure the bidding at the lowest possible level since game could be reached without bidding it – all the tricks made over the 'book' of six were scored below the line, so that most hands were played at the one or two level with little or no development of the bidding. Now only those tricks actually bid for and made were to be scored below the line. The Auction scoring-table gave high bonuses to honour or ace holdings, and this often influenced the bidding. Now the greatest benefits were for slam bidding and the actual play of the cards assumed greater importance. Each trick counted. All these distinctions were apparent to the Culbertsons after their introductory game in Santa Barbara. They stuck to their own Approach System to see how it stood up to Contract and were relieved to find that it was broadly applicable. The Culbertsons had always looked for the creative side of card play; their Approach System instigated a dialogue which realized the combined potential of two hands. Here at last was a game that was in tune with their way of thinking. When they returned home that evening both he and Jo were very enthusiastic about the new game. They talked long into the night about its possibilities. Culbertson kept repeating over and over again, 'Jo dearest, Contract will sweep the country! It's our big chance and we must go ahead and take it.'

Confident that he and Contract were made for each other and that he could get in on the ground floor, Culbertson really went to work. He devoted hours of study to it. At certain moments of his life he was always capable of sustained application, and this was one of them. He sat at home for hours dealing out hand after hand and analysing each one, first according to Contract and then comparing it to Auction, to the point where he had what he considered an adequate test sample of over a thousand hands. From this data he began to put together a new system for himself, or rather a modification of his existing Auction system, which stood up remarkably well to the new game.

This became the Approach-Forcing System. The keystone of this was the Approach principle which he had already used in Auction – in other words a slow suit exploration instead of a precipitate excursion into no trumps. Culbertson described it this way: 'In view of the fact that in making an opening bid, the player is venturing into unknown territory, it is wise for him to proceed cautiously, to feel his way and thus, protected by a network of approach suit bids of one, act with care until he learns something about the distribution of honour strength held by both his partner and his adversary.' Opening bids should be in suits rather than no trumps. No trump bids were best used after all the other information had been exchanged. The Forcing side of the system was the new element grafted on for the sake of Contract and advocated, an opening two bid, requiring partner to respond as a prelude to game. In Auction he had used the one-over-one bid as forcing. Hands were valued according to honour tricks – the minimum requirement for an opening bid being two and a half honour tricks. (A fuller description of the Culbertson System is given in Appendix 1 on p. 229.)

Imbued with this new enthusiasm, Culbertson and Jo decided to return to New York to be at the centre of any possible new developments. When they came to leave Los Angeles and had settled their bills they found, not for the first time in their lives, that they were short of cash. All they had was a fine-looking Stutz car and $100. Still, leave they must and to get to New York on $100 meant driving fast. Everything went all right as far as Cleveland, Ohio, but from there on they had to improvise. To pay for more gasoline they started selling the car's accessories – spare tyres, tools, the clock, even the chains! This got them as far as Albany, New York, but that was all. They waited expectantly in the next gas-station for a kind-looking individual to come up. A Cadillac drove in with a party of New Yorkers. Culbertson explained his plight to them. The driver carefully questioned him, looked at his car, at the car licence-plate, at the pregnant Jo who was sitting inside covered in embarrassment, then lent them $10 which Culbertson promised to repay once he got to New York.

Back in New York, they rented an apartment at 125 East 63rd Street and immediately set about organizing a regular evening Contract game. Their first major convert was their team-mate Waldemar von Zedtwitz, whose enthusiasm for the game became as strong as theirs. Then Lightner came over.

At the Knickerbocker Whist Club there was still strong resistance to Contract. Most of the die-hard Auction players thought it just a fad. They saw no fault in Auction and saw no reason to change from it. Contract seemed to them to be a game for experts only, with its highly technical methods of bidding slams and this new feature of vulnerability. But Culbertson, quickly establishing himself as an authority on the game, cajoled some of them into playing, insisting that it was an improvement on Auction. One of the main objections to Contract put forward at the Knickerbocker Whist Club was its unsuitability to Duplicate, but Culbertson soon came up with the idea of vulnerable and non-vulnerable boards – an innovation of his that has remained to this day. Soon the first Duplicate Contract tournament ever was played at the club.

Hal Sims and George Reith, after a little early hesitation, both swung over to the new game and now there were enough players there for Culbertson to run a regular Contract game. He was still careful to call his system the Approach-Forcing one, rather than the Culbertson System. He knew that, in the early stages, to call the system by his own name would only antagonize some players and over-personalize the issue. Better to wait until Contract had caught on properly, then he could introduce his name. Timing, as always, was all-important and he knew he ought to wait.

By now, in late 1927, Jo's pregnancy had reached an advanced stage, but she went on with her bridge teaching as they needed the money. Her pupils started leaving little packages behind of tiny knit-ted sweaters, booties, teething-rings, and, inevitably, dummies.

In December the Culbertsons went to Chicago to participate in the first tournament to be arranged by the newly-formed American Auction Bridge League. This took place on 1-3 December 1927 at the Hotel Sherman. Culbertson won the men's Team-of-Four event in a team captained by Ralph R. Richards, also President of the League, playing with Lightner and von Zedtwitz, while Jo won the Women's Team-of-Four with her team. This was still an Auction tournament; it was only with the introduction of the Vanderbilt Cup the following year that Contract tournaments were to get under way.

At the beginning of the new year Jo went into hospital and on 15 January 1928 gave birth to a baby girl. She was baptized a Catholic, like her mother, by the same Father Duffy who had married them, and given the names Joyce Nadya. Waldemar von Zedtwitz was her godfather and Jo's mother her godmother.

The birth of this first child had a profound effect on Culbertson. He felt a compulsion not to fail his offspring. He would make sure he would provide not just for her but for all the family. In return, his daughter would have to fulfil his fondest hopes. By giving her the second name Nadya, which was the one she was to be known by, he was explicitly pointing her in the direction in which these hopes lay and loading her with a burden of expectation that she would be unable to fulfil. But those days were far away, and for the moment she could bask in her father's adulation.

In April Almon came across from California to see his first grandchild. He was growing old now and wanted to see her before time ran out. It was a warm reunion. Now a father himself, Culbertson felt closer to his own father than at any time he could remember. Almon had mellowed of late; gone were the brooding silences of a few years back. Two years previously, he had married his housekeeper, a Czech woman he had met in America. Soon after his visit to New York he fell ill and died of uraemia on 4 May, to be buried alongside Xenia in Woodlawn Cemetery. In his will he left the famed 1732 Guarneri violin, now valued at $100,000, to Sasha and asked that his Russian Imperial Bonds, said to be worth 400,000 roubles, be shared among his immediate family. They were never to be redeemed, and they were in any case worthless.

CHAPTER 6

BRIDGE WORLD

In the summer of 1929 Culbertson rented a house on the ocean front at Westhampton for Jo and the children. Nadya was eighteen months old, and their son Ely Bruce had been born on 11 April in Miss Lippincott's Sanitorium in New York. The house was large but an architectural monstrosity – indeed, so bizarre was its appearance that the landlord was hard put to find other clients to take it and let the Culbertsons rent it very cheaply. Its garden led right down to the beach, and was crowded with gnomes and gargoyles and other weird creatures. None the less it was peaceful.

Culbertson decided that he ought to stay in New York in their apartment at 53 East 66th Street, to which they had recently moved, and come out to Westhampton for weekends only. One evening he was alone there when he heard a knock on the door. Two unknown gentlemen stood outside, asking to speak to Ely Culbertson. They introduced themselves as Herbert de Bower and Lewis Copeland and said they were looking for someone to write a correspondence course for bridge beginners. They needed an expert and had been to see Whitehead and Work but they had proved too expensive. Culbertson's name had been mentioned, and they had come along to talk to him about it. Copeland was a publisher of educational, mainly self-teaching books, and de Bower was founder of the Alexander Hamilton Institute which specialized in economic forecasting. They, too, had spotted the commercial potential of Contract bridge and wanted to get in at the very beginning.

Culbertson invited them in and as they explained their proposal to him, he could see that for him it would be no more than hack-work, worth at the most a few hundred dollars, so he decided to turn the situation back on them.

'Gentlemen,' he said, 'I'm not interested in small amounts of money. But I'll be glad to buy you lunch at the Ritz.'

The Ritz was a favourite haunt of his. He liked its European atmosphere. It was somewhere he could demonstrate his cosmopolitan manners, and where he could converse fluently in French with the waiters, a move likely to impress many a less-travelled New Yorker.

Now that Copeland and de Bower had appeared out of the blue, he wanted to make the most of the occasion. He saw them as potential backers for his grandiose plans. Rather than reveal his scheme there and then, he invited them to come and have dinner with him the following evening at Westhampton, when he would explain it all in much more detail. He hinted that there might be big money involved, far more than they were likely to get from their correspondence course. The boldness of his approach intrigued them enough to make them accept.

At Westhampton he kept up the momentum. Just as his card-playing was based on a strategy of 'Always attack' so here he knew he had to get in quickly and unsettle their defences, or they would never take his outrageous scheme seriously. The offer, he told them, was of a fifty-fifty partnership with him and the promise of a million dollars eventually! Before they had time to draw breath, he described the partnership as being in 'one of the public idols of our times'.

A brief pause and then, 'Which idol is that?' Copeland ventured.

'Ely Culbertson.'

There was a stunned and baffled silence but Culbertson kept up his attack.

'I don't mean the present-day Ely that you see in front of you. No, I mean Ely the Celebrity. Here, I've got it all written down for you in this memorandum.'

He handed them each a copy and watched as they took in its contents. In it he had outlined his plan of campaign; how he and Jo aimed to exploit this new and rising phenomenon of Contract bridge and imprint themselves on the public's memory as the game's leading personalities. The memorandum drew extensively on his theories of mass psychology. The nub of his argument was that Jo and himself were to be presented as larger-than-life personalities, but still as people the public would wish to identify with – hence the importance of showing up their defects as much as their virtues. He sketched out the picture he had of himself: 'The type of celebrity I have in mind is someone who is tough, a bit cocky, conceited even, but with a touch of kindness and rather eccentric. In fact like me, only blown up large.'

Copeland was beginning to get the drift of Culbertson's idea but de Bower's face wore a mask of deep scepticism. Culbertson saw himself as both hero and villain 'projected across the gigantic screen of the mass mind'. This projection would take place via every means of modern publicity available, from newspapers to radio, magazines, motion pictures even, but the greatest stimulus would result from word-of-mouth publicity.

The 1920s was an era of sudden crazes, from mah-jong and

Ely, Eugene and Sasha, aged six, ten and four respectively.

Ely – the young 'Amerikanetz' revolutionary.

Auction bridge 'Old Guard' on roof of Brunswick Studio Building, New York, 1928: *from left to right* Milton Work, R. F. Foster, E. V. Shepard, Sidney Lenz, Wilbur Whitehead and Gratz Scott.

Edward G. Robinson, star of the 1929 Broadway play *The Kibitzer*, watches the 'New Guard' (winners of the American Auction Bridge Championship): Theodore Lightner, Ely Culbertson, Ralph Richards and Waldemar von Zedtwitz.

Newspapermen assembled at start of Lenz Match. Lieutenant (later General) Gruenther, at extreme right, is the referee. Oswald Jacoby seated at left.

Even the children play – 'Fifi' and 'Frère' imitating their elders, with dummy and kibitzers.

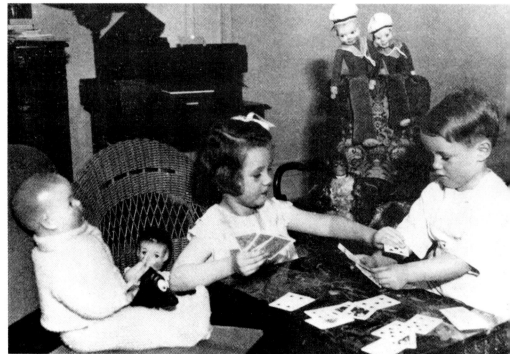

Culbertson and Jo on board the *Bremen*, *en route* to Europe in 1932.

Harold Vanderbilt, third from left, with his team-mates, Willard Karn, Hal Sims and Waldemar von Zedtwitz, winners of the 1932 Vanderbilt Cup.

Signing the agreement for the 1933 Schwab Trophy with Colonel Beasley.

Beasley match in progress at Selfridges. Beasley's partner is Lady Rhodes. Hubert Phillips, seated behind on the left, Colonel Walshe as referee.

crossword-puzzles to flag-pole sitters. This latter craze, popularized by the child stylites of Baltimore, was started by 'Shipwreck Kelly' who wanted to demonstrate the hardiness of the American posterior! A whispering campaign was often what enabled these crazes to catch on. Culbertson had already foreseen this and planned for group leaders to spread the word.

De Bower looked unimpressed and wanted to know why the public should take particular notice of Culbertson. Culbertson still had another card to play. He would add romantic interest by introducing alongside his publicity Adam, a publicity Eve, none other than Jo. She was not only the finest bridge player alive, Culbertson went on, but by nature shy, reticent and peace-loving and would make a perfect foil for Culbertson the 'Celebrity'. In phrasing his programme along these lines Culbertson was consciously using the emotive language of the movie industry, and its emphasis on star quality.

The focal point of his operation would be to launch a bridge magazine, something he had been planning for some time. Every movement, he explained, had to have a base around which its group leaders could rally. They needed to be provided with an organ of information where ideas and publicity could be generated.

Copeland reminded him that there was already a bridge magazine in existence, but Culbertson rightly countered that it was on the way out. He then went on to list his requirements – and this is where his anticipated backers were to come in.

First he needed a small office somewhere in Manhattan, together with sufficient capital for promotional purposes, for instance to build up a mail order scheme. It was all part of the process of softening up the public.

'Then when the public is sufficiently kneaded, we can all make some dough!' Culbertson added, enjoying his own heavy-handed joke.

The essence of his long-term strategy, and where he expected to make some real money, was the series of books he aimed to produce. First would come the *Blue Book*, a name deliberately chosen for its official-sounding connotation. This would be followed by a *Red Book*, then a *Gold Book*, and each of these would be followed up by their own summaries. The main books would be priced at $2 each and the summaries at $1 – an outlay of a mere $9 to learn the complete art of Contract bridge. What, he asked, could be better value than that?

But the more he talked the more he could see the other two becoming less convinced. When he mentioned a figure of $50,000 to put the whole operation into motion, they started back-pedalling fast. It was altogether too far-fetched and grandiose. They got up to leave and he knew they would not back his scheme.

After they had gone, he went to tell Jo about the evening's discussions. He felt downcast, but Jo was still warmly supportive. Her faith in his ability was undiminished. Her role, in this situation as in many others, was to help him through these ups and downs. She knew that his scheme was not as far-fetched as the others thought, and it was her steadfastness and encouragement at this crucial stage that enabled him to go on.

The next day he said he would have one more try with de Bower and Copeland and if that failed he would go it alone and set about publishing the magazine on his own account. Not surprisingly their attitude was unchanged, though Copeland, always the more imaginative and sympathetic of the two, was sufficiently impressed to help in other ways later on.

With hindsight, for anyone to start up a new magazine in October 1929 seems foolhardy. It was the month of the Wall Street crash. But Culbertson, though not impervious to such considerations, had chosen this moment to launch himself on a wider public and had every intention of proceeding. From his point of view, Contract bridge had its own momentum and would continue to become popular regardless of economic circumstances. Indeed, on further analysis, Culbertson concluded that the Wall Street crash might aid rather than hinder its growth, as people tightened their financial belts and turned towards more home-based entertainments, such as bridge. He knew that if he bought when the market was down, the gains later would be much greater. He had been preparing his plan of campaign for some time, and nothing now was going to deter him.

The main problem, though, was capital. All he and Jo had in the world was $3,000, enough perhaps to cover one issue of the magazine. Then came a stroke of luck. In September *Auction Bridge* magazine folded, as he expected it might, and he was able to purchase its subscription list for a nominal sum. This gave him 18,000 names to start with. Adding his own contacts in bridge circles and clubs across the nation, he reckoned that if he could get enough response from the first issue, he would be set up for the other ones.

But first he had to find some office space, some staff, and a printer. The offices he found were three cramped, badly-lit rooms, more like cubby-holes, in a large unprepossessing building at 45 West 45th Street – but that was the point. The office number and the street number were easy to remember and would be certain to imprint themselves on the public's memory. The staff of Ely and Jo and two stenographers were soon installed, and just before the first issue came out, William Huske joined them.

Bill Huske was to play an important role in the development of the magazine. He had first met Culbertson at the beginning of 1928 in Cleveland at an Auction match. Culbertson's team was playing against a team led by Carl T. Robertson, associate editor of the *Cleveland Plain Dealer*. Huske worked for the *Plain Dealer* and was the only newspaper reporter to cover the match. Consequently he got to know the players well. Culbertson he remembered particularly for his habit of coming across to see him to make sure he had copied down a particular bidding sequence or play accurately. Huske was intrigued by this tall, wiry individual who took his bridge so seriously and was already so publicity-conscious. He could not make him out, though, as in spite of his heavy foreign accent he kept insisting he was of venerable American stock. This match for the Eberhard Faber Trophy was one of the first Culbertson won with his team-of-four – Jo, Lightner and von Zedtwitz. It was something of a needle-match, the Clevelanders' system against the new Culbertson Approach-Forcing System (recently outlined in an eight-page pamphlet entitled *Modern Methods of Bidding and Play*).

After the match, Huske did not expect to hear any more from Culbertson, but later in the year he moved to New York, invited by Shepard Barclay, editor of *Auction Bridge* magazine, to become its managing editor. Barclay had made the mistake of trying to make his magazine both a society and a bridge one; in the end it fell between the two stools. Huske arrived in New York the day after Thanksgiving 1928. When *Auction Bridge* magazine foundered in the summer of 1929, Huske welcomed the offer to move across to 45 West 45th Street and he arrived just as they were in the throes of getting out the first issue of *Bridge World*.

At first he had an unspecified role as a general assistant to Culbertson, who was editor-in-chief. Huske had valuable experience as a magazine editor and Culbertson looked to him for his professional expertise and judgement, though often this meant approving unquestioningly what the editor-in-chief had written! But Huske was instrumental in finding a printer for *Bridge World*. This was Cyrus F. Fleck of the Mack Printing Company, Easton, Pennsylvania who was duly invited along to the offices at West 45th Street and taken out for lunch at the Japanese Garden of the Ritz. Culbertson produced his spiel and Fleck agreed to take them on. He had no cause to regret it, and remained with them for years.

The first issue soon expanded from its original thirty-two pages to forty-eight as Culbertson tinkered with the text. Never a 'natural' writer – he later hired a highly-skilled and literate team of contributing editors – he delayed more and more before sending the magazine off to the printers. He wanted to make sure his thinly-veiled attacks on his main adversaries, Whitehead and Work (in an article written by 'A Bewildered Reader') were just right. Here he was following an age-old technique to launch a new magazine – stir up some controversy, the more personal the better, on the principle that no one pays much attention to two dogs trotting down the street together, but if they get into a fight, the whole world watches.

Nevertheless, for a first issue it was a very professional and competent production. Its distinctive orange front cover had the head of Edmund Hoyle emblazoned on it, while the back initiated a regular feature called 'Who's Who Among Our Contributors' with short biographical sketches and a quick résumé of the individual's strongest and weakest points! For Madeleine Kerwin this was 'Strongest point: soundness. Weakest point: excess of soundness'! and even Whitehead was given a mention – 'Strongest point: giving the cards a chance to speak for themselves. Weakest point: disastrous spells of sleepiness'! Its list of contributing editors was impressive: Lenz, Lightner, Reith, Shepard, Madeleine Kerwin to name but a few. It stated unequivocally what its aims were: 'The *Bridge World* tells you how to win. It gives you a cross-section of the minds of the masters who do not lose. It gives you their reasoning. It gives you best methods.' But the main target was the new subscribers. A subscription form was prominently displayed on the opening page with an easy-to-cut-out application form offering various rates of subscription – $1 for three months, $2 for six months and $3.50 for the whole year.

It certainly caught on. The first printing of 20,000 copies was quickly sold out and a strategic reserve of 5,000 had to used up, leaving an unmet demand for a further 3,000 copies from subscribers who sent in the application form after the publication date. Culbertson felt that he was vindicated. It was the right time to start a bridge magazine.

As an office manager Culbertson was less expert. The November issue was even later than the October one. Huske, as an old newspaper hand, knew that the preparations for the next issue should be well under way by the time the preceding issue was out, but towards the end of October there had been no move to set up the second issue. Indeed Culbertson came to see Huske only days before it was due out to ask what he thought they should put in it. It finally appeared on 11 November, over a week late. It took up the cudgels against Whitehead and Work for the second month running, 'From Mr Whitehead's pasture fields we hear distant rumblings ...' and it carried news of the recent sensational Bennett murder story when a Kansas City housewife shot her husband dead as he hid in the bathroom after failing to make a rashly-bid four spade contract. *Bridge World* entered the fray by opining that Bennett could have saved his life had he only followed the correct Culbertson procedure of opening with a minimum of two and a half quick tricks. Had he played the hand better, he might also have saved his life. But Bennett paid the penalty and 'flirted with death as people so frequently do when they fail to have a plan either in the game of bridge or the game of life'.

Now that *Bridge World* had been successfully launched, Jo and Lewis Copeland, now an adviser to Culbertson, pressed him to go ahead and launch his own book on the Culbertson System; they were convinced the time was right and he could make at least $5,000 out of it. No sooner had the battle between Auction and Contract seemed to have been won than another battle between rival Contract systems emerged. Their view was that with such an abundance of competing systems, with all the main experts – Work, Whitehead, Lenz, Shepard, Reith and a score of minor luminaries – wanting to get in on the act, Culbertson ought to act quickly. But his instinct was to hold on, to let what he termed 'this Tower of Babel' die down and choose a moment when the confused and bridge-hungry public would really take notice of what he had to say. He decided to postpone the idea of a book for another six months. At the same time he kept his name before the public eye by advocating strongly the standardization of bidding methods and conventions at Contract under the Culbertson banner. In *Bridge World* he repeatedly claimed that his system was the only one that was both acceptable to experts but simple enough to be understood by a beginner.

Bridge World was running into its first set of difficulties. Culbertson had fallen out with Huske. He expected him to be on call in the office whenever he might need him, but Huske felt that when his work for the day was done he was free to go. He was summarily fired, earning himself the dubious distinction of being the first in a long line of Culbertson employees to be fired. His place was taken by Robert Brannon, who arrived in time for the February 1930 issue.

The strain of being responsible for his new publication and having to keep up a busy tournament schedule (the Culbertsons' team-of-four played in the American Bridge League tournament in Chicago in November and in the Vanderbilt Cup in New York the same month) was beginning to tell on Culbertson. His health, never too strong, was showing signs of wear and he was forced to cancel his projected lecture tour of the States – although he did make a brief visit to Indianapolis on 10 February. He regretted this as such tours were an intrinsic component in his strategy to increase 'word-of-mouth publicity'. Now that his magazine was just beginning to get known, lecture tours were an important follow-up. Also, as so often in his life, he needed the money.

The girls in the office were complaining of overwork. Matters came to a head one Saturday morning in February when he suddenly realized he did not have enough ready cash to meet the weekly pay-roll. Indeed, all he seemed to be able to get hold of was $50 and he needed another $150 to pay the staff. He called them together, ex-plained the situation and gave them the stark choice of staying on at their own risk or leaving there and then. A little to his surprise, he found that they were willing to stay. So he headed off to his bridge club to embark on a marathon bridge session lasting from Saturday lunchtime till Sunday evening. His persistence was rewarded and he won not only the $150 he needed but an extra $200 on top. Back in the office on Monday he gave the girls their money and with it an immediate raise. From then on Wednesdays and Thursdays became known in the office as 'pay-roll' days and the staff waited with bated breath on Friday mornings to know whether they were going to be paid or not. Miss Purdue, his new secretary, had her pay raised from $25 a week at the end of February to $45 by the end of March. But, alas, by mid-April it was down to $25 again.

Having missed his lecture tour, Culbertson had to think of other ways of generating publicity for himself. But first he did a puzzling thing. Either it was a move of great tactical shrewdness, or he had suddenly lost heart. He went to visit Whitehead and Work and offered to collaborate with them. In the case of Whitehead he even went so far as to offer to suppress his own name and simply become his assistant. Furthermore, he would let him have the fruits of his many years of research and analysis of bridge hands. In return they would operate on a fifty-fifty basis, signing a contract for ten years. Culbert-son would be the front man, running the organization which would carry Whitehead's name.

Whitehead was stunned by this. He simply could not believe that Culbertson was prepared to suppress his name, Culbertson of all people. However much Culbertson tried to assure him that his motive for doing it was to try to ensure a stable future for his wife and children, Whitehead could not take it in, and refused to go along with it, concluding that Culbertson was a much stranger individual than he had hitherto thought.

Next Culbertson went along to see Milton Work and made the same proposal to him. Work reacted nore gruffly, pointing out that he already had an established name, with plentiful royalties from his books, syndicates, lecture tours and so on, whereas Culbertson up till now had nothing, or precious little. So where was the gain for him?

He even looked rather aggrieved and Culbertson felt he should apologize for hurting his feelings. 'I only wanted to avoid unnecessary risk to both of us,' he told him somewhat enigmatically.

He had tested the opposition, had given them their chance, and he subsequently felt free to launch out on his own. He could now concentrate all his energies on promoting his own campaign.

First he set about recruiting his teachers, or group leaders as he called them. He used whatever method he could, writing articles in magazines, broadcasting free on the radio, speaking at lunches all over New York – in fact button-holing all and sundry, and explaining to them the merits of the Culbertson System. And it worked.

Next he set a date for his *Blue Book* – he would write it in July and publish it in the autumn. That gave him just four months to maximize the pre-publication publicity for it. He kept to his original formula – word-of-mouth publicity – so that at every opportunity, or speech he made, he mentioned the book, building up what he termed 'symphonic publicity, a gradual crescendo of discussion, punctuated by criticism and doubt and reaffirmation' which would finally lead to a 'swelling chorus of acclamation'. What undoubtedly helped the book's impact and the Culbertson System in general, was the fortuitous intervention of Lieutenant-Colonel Walter Buller.

Buller was a bluff, hail-fellow-well-met Englishman born in 1886. He had joined the Royal Army Service Corps in 1907 and was active throughout the First World War, first in France and then as a staff officer at the War Office. He retired from the army in 1923 and lived in London, quickly establishing a reputation as a bridge player and commentator through a weekly column in the *Star*. He had his own inimitable style, terse and boisterous. At heart he was a showman, given to exaggeration, charming one moment, infuriating the next. His articles in the *Star* were designed to arouse controversy. 'Must do something to stir them up,' was his working guide and only minimal deference was paid to logic or the finer feelings of others.

In 1929 he published a book entitled *Reflections of a Bridge Player*, written in the same staccato style, in which, among other things, he described the introduction of Contract bridge in England in 1927, at the St James's Club by Lord Lascelles and Mr Jimmie Rothschild. 'At first I held out against it and "ragged" its sponsors. We greeted Mr Rothschild with shouts of "Author!" whenever he entered the room. Soon its merit was recognized and partly as a result of my advocacy it was taken up by the Portland Club.' But he also spent much of the book decrying the American influence on bridge and came out with the confident assertion that he would lay heavy odds on an English team, 'a good four', beating any American team 'sky-high'.

Culbertson jumped at this. It was just the sort of controversial publicity that he relished. In the April issue of *Bridge World* he delivered a challenge to Buller, inviting a team selected by him to participate in a Duplicate team-of-four contest over three hundred deals and agreeing to abide by the Portland Club rules. The Portland Club, besides being the most prestigious bridge club in Britain, was also the law-giving body so far as bridge was concerned. It had come into existence in 1824 when a previous club, the Stratford Club, had wanted to expel an extremely unpopular whist player and found that the only means to do so was to change the club's name to Portland, keeping the same members as before with the single exception of the miscreant.

Culbertson stated that he would bring his team over to England at his own expense and would be willing to play for whatever stakes Buller suggested. Culbertson also made sure that his challenge, in all its details, was communicated to English newspapers at the same time. On 22 April Buller cabled Culbertson accepting the challenge. He said he would prefer two hundred hands but Culbertson insisted on three hundred to reduce the element of luck and announced his team as likely to be Jo, Theodore Lightner, George Reith, Waldeman von Zedtwitz and himself. In the event George Reith dropped out. Thus the stage was set and the date of the match was agreed as Monday, 15 September at Almack's Club, Upper Grosvenor Street, London.

As soon as the news of the match was finally confirmed, Culbertson raced to tell Jo about it. She was furious.

'Ely, how could you do such a thing! Here you are announcing before the whole world that you'll play those Englishmen for any stakes they choose, and we haven't even got $100.' It was true, their reserves were at a low ebb.

Culbertson had to brazen this out. 'I have formed a syndicate that will back us up to $5 per point. You and I will have to stick to a betting limit of $2,000. In fact what we need is $5,000 – $2,000 to bet with, $2,000 for travelling expences, $1,000 to keep the office and home running while we're away. Incidentally, Waldy and Teddy are going to pay their own expenses.'

'That's all very well, but where's the money coming from?'

'From the *Blue Book*.'

Jo needed to exercise all her self-control before replying. 'But you haven't written a word of it yet. Even if you do, it still can't possibly come out before September at the earliest and that's after we've left for the match.'

'Now listen a minute. I have an idea. It might sound crazy but here it is. Bridge teachers and players everywhere are clamouring for a book on the Culbertson System. I'll get a loan from them.'

'How?'

'Let's say the *Blue Book* sells for $2 a copy. In the next issue of *Bridge World* in May I'll put an ad in offering the book at the bargain price of $1.50. I'll make this a specially autographed first edition for subscribers only. That way they'll get the book sooner and also save fifty cents each.'

'But suppose you don't write it in time?'

'Then I'll go to jail.'

But write it he did. In the May issue of *Bridge World* he inserted a full-page advertisement for the book based on the slogan that it was 'Simple Enough for a Child, Deep Enough for a Master Player' and added a typically aggressive piece of salesmanship: 'Advance requests for *Contract Bridge Blue Book* indicate that this Subscribers' Special Edition will be sold out practically immediately.' In fact this was the first public notification that such a book was going to be available.

Next he had to find a publisher for the *Blue Book*. Not for him the orthodox method of taking the book to the publisher but instead he requested the publisher come to him. He rang Lewis Copeland who by this time had a small publishing business with just enough spare capacity to suit Culbertson's purpose.

'Lewis,' he asked him. 'How would you like to work for me in your spare time?'

Somewhat taken aback, Copeland asked him to elaborate.

'I'd like to engage you as my publisher, and give you the royalties!'

Copeland had never before heard of anyone suggesting this reversal of the time-honoured publisher-author relationship, but he knew that Culbertson liked to go about things in his own idiosyncratic way. He warned Culbertson that it was hard enough distributing and selling a book, let alone setting up a publishing company from scratch. But Culbertson was undeterred. He was more than confident that if he could produce the book the public wanted, book-stores and salesmen would soon get to find out his name and from where the book could be ordered. But about one thing he was adamant. He was determined to have his own publishing company and, a typically Culbertson stroke, be the person to reap the profits of both author and publisher.

He told Copeland he was going ahead with the scheme anyhow, whether he joined him or not, so Copeland, after not much thought, agreed, and the *Bridge World* Publishing Company came into existence. Culbertson offered to pay Copeland a weekly wage of $75 to be set against the royalty he received on each published book. But Copeland asked that his wage be increased to $100 per week, if he accepted two cents less royalty, to which Culbertson agreed. This small reduction, Culbertson was later to remark, eventually cost Copeland over $10,000 in lost income.

When Copeland asked to glance at the manuscript Culbertson admitted he had not yet written a word. Copeland was astounded and threatened to pull out of the deal. He was amazed at Culbertson's nerve in setting up the England match, advertising the *Blue Book* and now recruiting a publisher, all before a word had been written! It was quite unheard of.

Characteristically Culbertson took full command of his publishing company. He spent hours fussing over what logo and jacket design to use, what typography and how the hands should be laid out. So engrossed was he in the technical details and minutiae of the book that he almost forgot to write it. By July he had yet to put pen to paper.

Then there were other distractions. In the middle of March he had got himself involved in a prolonged pairs match that took place every Friday evening at the Knickerbocker Whist Club. He and Jo were playing George Reith and Howard Schenken. There were to be four hundred deals in all, spread over nine evening sessions. By mid-April Culbertson's team were 3,800 points ahead, but then Reith's team began to win back points, and by the time the match ended, Reith's team were ahead by the narrow margin of 495 points. The result was duly reported in the June *Bridge World*, a demonstration that Culbertson did not shirk from including adverse publicity in his magazine. He was determined to give it a broad base, so that its readership would be drawn from all persuasions. He was a believer in the motto that all publicity is good publicity. A few years later a story, possibly apocryphal, circulated that an assistant came into his office holding a magazine.

'Mr Culbertson, they have published this very damaging article about you.'

'Did they spell my name right?'

'Yes.'

'Forget it.'

Another curious episode in the summer of 1930 was Culbertson's involvement with the French Line. According to Robert Brannon, then editor of *Bridge World*, the story went as follows. In March, a young man, unknown to Culbertson but bubbling with confidence, came into the office and proposed that Culbertson should back bridge tournaments on the French Line. He had a contract with that company already drawn up, conditional on having Culbertson appear as a sponsor. Culbertson immediately liked the idea, could see its possibilities and agreed. Next month *Bridge World* came out with this:

BRIDGE ON SHIPS

French Line Officially Inaugurates 'Bridge Service' on Board its Famous Ships

A complete Bridge Club Including Duplicate Tournaments under Guidance of Many Well-known Bridge Authorities Will Be a Regular Feature

Sponsored by the *Bridge World* Magazine and its Staff of Experts

Culbertson arranged to supply hosts and hostesses from his *Bridge World* organization to oversee these tournaments, and give lessons when required on each sailing from New York to Le Havre or Cherbourg, in return for their free passages. The French Line, aware of the growing popularity of Contract bridge, was eager to be the first among its rivals to offer organized bridge as part of its service. Other shipping lines had their stockbroker offices on board but none had taken up Contract bridge in this way.

Card-playing, of course, had long taken place on board ocean liners. Most of it was of the harmless variety and among friends. Ostensibly every ship had a company rule forbidding gambling; warnings about the activities of professional gamblers were displayed prominently in the smoking room and elsewhere. But a six-day crossing provided an ideal opportunity for those professionals 'playing the tubs'. It was just long enough to effect a coup and short enough to allay suspicion. In his informative and entertaining book *The Only Way to Cross* (Macmillan, 1972) John Maxtone-Graham describes the activities of some of these professionals whom he terms the most sophisticated con-artists in the business. Immaculately dressed, so as to be able to mix easily with the rich people who were their prey, their aim was to induce the mark or target into a private card game in a cabin. A team of three associates was needed for this. Shortly after the ship left harbour a well-heeled passenger would suddenly discover the loss of his wallet. Alarmed, he would hurry down to the purser's office and a short while later be informed that it had miraculously been found on deck, its contents intact. Ever grateful the passenger would seek out his benefactor and find him in the middle of a three-handed game of bridge in his rather large and comfortable cabin. He could thus hardly turn down the invitation to make up a fourth. He would be allowed to win, often quite large sums of money. Of course, he had no idea that his new-found friend sitting opposite him was the man who had lifted his wallet in the crush on the rail on departure day.

Once the ship had docked at Southampton or Cherbourg, the four-some would agree to a last game sharing a compartment on the boat train to London (or Paris). Just as the train reached the outskirts of the town the rubber would draw to a close and a quick game of Red Dog was suggested. The mark, his pockets stuffed full of winnings, could hardly refuse. In five minutes dealing from a stacked deck, the team could take all his winnings and up to twenty thousand dollars more. The victim would be asked to pay the balance by cheque or banker's draft. This was duly cashed within minutes of the train arriving, long before the bewildered sucker had time to work out what had befallen him.

Sometimes the dénouement would take place in a hotel. On another occasion a mark was offered a lift to Paris from Cherbourg in a car belonging to one of his shipboard acquaintances. The car broke down conveniently outside Bayeux. During the overnight stay in the hotel the inevitable 'clean-up' game took place. Gamblers always kept their final act of deception as far as possible away from the ship's public rooms, in case the ship's staff (who were their real enemy) might spot and unmask them. Many victims preferred to keep quiet and absorb the financial and emotional loss privately. No one liked to admit they had been taken for such a ride. Some did complain and, if still at sea, went to see the captain. Maxtone-Graham describes how Captain Rostron of the *Mauretania* became so familiar with one 'crooked' bridge hand that he memorized it. When the victim appeared in front of him and poured out his tale of woe, he would ask him if it contained the ace, king, queen, jack, ten, nine of hearts (presumably Mississippi Heart Hand) and the incredulous passenger would be forced to nod.

Another ploy that he describes was the routine whereby the gam-bler, having pocketed the cheque or bank-draft from his victim, would appear to relent, and suggest, in the name of their new-found friend-ship, that he would settle for whatever cash the other had on him at the moment. As soon as the money was paid over, the cheque would be produced, torn into pieces and thrown away. Or that was how it seemed. The little bits of paper that fluttered down to the water were quite blank. The original cheque was still safely in one of the gam-bler's four waistcoat pockets, each of which contained a cheque in one of the colours of the leading banks. Few victims ever bothered to stop payment on a cheque they had seen destroyed with their very own eyes!

Culbertson's motives for embarking on shipboard card-playing were of the purest by comparison with the card-sharps. The only gain he had in mind was the increase in popularity of his system, more pub-licity for himself and a few free tickets for himself and his family. The first crossing to have a Culbertson representative aboard was the *Île de France* on 15 April 1930, and a specially engraved cup was awarded to the winning pair of the Culbertson tournament during the crossing.

There was no shortage of Culbertson representatives offering to go on these crossings. Most were recruited by *Bridge World* from among their teachers. They got free first-class return passages to Le Havre and back, a three-week stay in Paris, and the right to keep whatever money they made out of teaching on the crossing for an outlay of $250 – which, naturally enough, they had to pay to the Culbertson coffers at *Bridge World*. They were happy, though. A first-class passage to Europe and back would have cost well over $500. Culbertson claimed that the $250 was to cover overheads and the cost of publicity. But the net effect was to provide him with an income of some $1,000 per month for as long as the arrangement with the French Line lasted.

Meanwhile the original expounder of the scheme, having himself cashed in on two or three free crossings, approached the cashier of the French Line in Cherbourg and got him to cash a draft for $500 on *Bridge World* – and was never seen again. Minus one to Culbertson!

After a while the French Line, too, became less enchanted with the scheme. They felt it was becoming too much an exercise in Culbertson propaganda and decided to close down the *Bridge World* bridge club on board. But Culbertson was not to be put off so easily. He referred them to the contract they had signed which still had some years to run. They offered a lump sum to curtail the agreement. Culbertson resisted this, and ended up not only with a sum of money but a number of 'open' first-class passages on any ship of the French Line extending over the following three years.

July came and the preparations for the Buller match got under way. Thomas Cook and Son, the travel agents, pricked up their ears at the news of the match and sent a directive to their branches telling them to 'interview all bridge-builders, prominent steel-men, architects and other allied industries and arrange transportation for the forthcoming international bridge congress in London'. Wrong sort of bridge!

The July issue of *Bridge World*, maintaining an emphasis on bridge as a game for married couples, ran an article entitled 'Does Bridge Playing Break or Make the Happy Home?' It purported to be the fruits of a discussion Jo Culbertson had had with Harold Webster, the noted cartoonist, during a lunch together at the Hotel Pierre. Webster, whose wry humour missed nothing at the bridge-table, asserted, 'Murder's just an anti-climax after some of the bridge fights I have witnessed.' Bridge highlighted the everyday drama of family life. Players, he was convinced, were drawn to the game as much for the pleasure they got out of a 'decidedly unhealthy exhibitionism in the matter of family quarrelling than for any particular liking for the game'. He gave the example of 'Old Henpeck being sat upon twice as hard by his wife. If she's the worse player, she makes him suffer and if she's the better, she flays him alive.'

Jo, on the other hand, saw the game quite differently. For her, bridge should be an occasion where behaviour could be improved rather than worsened. A partnership should aim to achieve a sense of decorum and self-control as they went about their business. 'Mr Culbertson and I have made it a rule never to discuss bidding or plays while the game is on,' she averred. Family disputes had to be carefully monitored because bridge was like a 'lightning-rod, a safety-valve that releases pressure and brings out all the ill-feeling that has gathered in the irritations of family life'.

Webster was a dedicated bridge player and undoubtedly the finest cartoonist and humorous commentator on the game. His regular cartoons in the *New York Herald Tribune* and *New York World* (he also collaborated in 1932 with Culbertson in a book *The Culbertson Webster Contract System*) stand out for their subtle wit and depiction of the obsessive nature of the game – the battleground for marital strife that it represents. Jo, on the other hand, needed to present the game as a respectable family pastime. The Culbertson plan of campaign was centered round this viewpoint. They had to keep the game on the level.

Jo also drew attention to the influence that women had on the game. Bridge was a great leveller of the sexes; nothing counted but skill. 'I really think that bridge has done more for feminism than the Women's Party or all the suffrage movements. It has taught men and women the practical experience of thinking and playing on equal terms and they like it.' Culbertson echoed these views, for he very much hoped that women would spearhead the spread of bridge under the Culbertson banner.

But to judge by newspaper reports, Webster's arguments won the day. In Seattle on 20 May readers learnt that William Ellis was now a single man because he trumped his wife's ace during a bridge game. He told the divorce court, 'My wife completely lost her temper when I spoiled her play. She threw an alarm clock at me and knocked out one of my teeth. Then she packed my clothes and ordered me out of the house!' Harry Meacham, of Wilkesboro, North Carolina, got so tired of holding bad hands that he threatened to shoot the next person who dealt him a bad hand. On his own next deal, he picked up a hand without a court card. He kept his word!

In London, Mrs Grace Lapham, the head of the Child Training Institute, let it be known that more than twenty per cent of the requests she received for governesses insisted that they should play bridge. She quoted a satisfied parent commenting on the educative values of bridge for her child. 'By respecting his bids, you teach him to respect yours and a child who gets intelligent and interesting answers to his bridge questions will be more likely to come to his parents with his more important problems.'

The Culbertsons found time in mid July to play in the first ever Asbury Park Tournament. Culbertson wanted to win this to prove that his team was justified in being chosen to represent America in the forthcoming international match. His team won, beating a team captained by Hal Sims, whose wife had sculpted the bronze statue of a winged goddess presented to the winners. Culbertson had promised Sims to have his name inscribed on the buttocks of the goddess if his team won. Sims felt his wife's artistic talents deserved better recognition than that.

The date for the Culbertsons' departure for England was rapidly approaching. They were due to leave on the liner *France* on 5 September, which meant there were exactly three weeks left. In desperation Jo rented a cottage at Shippan Point, near Stamford, Connecticut. There they could seclude themselves without any distractions and get the *Blue Book* completed. Culbertson had not written one word so far.

Culbertson's preferred method of writing was to dictate his books, believing that this achieved a better rhythm. Accordingly, he set to work with a relay of three secretaries, working by rotation for up to eighteen hours a day. Soon the first chapter was completed. But then disaster struck. Culbertson was taken ill and had to be rushed off to hospital for an operation. It was a recurrence of his old stomach ulcer problem. He went back to New York and entered the French Hospital where he was treated by the surgeon, Dr F. C. Yeomans. His first words, allegedly, on coming out of the anaesthetic were, 'Never pass a forcing bid.' He continued his dictating in hospital, where he had to convalesce for a further ten days. Dr Yeomans wanted him to stay longer, since by now he had lost twelve pounds in weight but his schedule was so tight that he discharged himself and went back to the New York apartment.

A week remained prior to their departure. Under Jo's supervision, they established a non-stop working routine. Culbertson would dictate to a secretary who would type up the pages, pass them to Jo for editing, then she would hand them over to Bill Huske (now back in harness at *Bridge World*, at Whitehead's instigation) for checking, before being sent to Lewis Copeland who transmitted the text to the Mack Printing Company at Easton, Pennsylvania. The proofs then came back to the *Bridge World* offices for Jo to do a final check on them. Her role in this, once again, was crucial.

By Thursday 4 September, the day before they were due to sail, the book still was not finished. Culbertson continued dictating on the morning and throughout lunch on the Friday and even in the taxi-cab on the way down to the pier. Copeland came to see them off. As they leant over the ship's rail to wave goodbye, he called out, 'How about the dedication?'

Culbertson with Jo alongside him shouted back, 'Dedicate it to my wife and favourite partner!'

The final proofs came through while the team was in London. Huske checked them through and found he had only to alter two paragraphs out of 300-odd pages – a fine testimony to the teamwork involved. As with so many Culbertson books, rumours abounded that this one had been written by someone else. In this case we have Huske's word for it that Culbertson wrote all but the two paragraphs Huske had to change. A glance at its rather dogmatic style seems to confirm this.

Copeland had agreed with Culbertson a first printing of 6,000 copies. They had 4,000 advance orders for the special edition as advertised in *Bridge World*, and they anticipated another 2,000 possible buyers. But they were in for a surprise.

CHAPTER 7

CULBERTSON v BULLER

The Culbertsons arrived at Southampton on 11 September, ready, as the *Daily Mail* put it, 'to beard the English lion in his den'. The match had caught the English public's imagination. Bridge was new as an international sport, and it came at a time of great contests between America and Great Britain, the Davis Cup at tennis, the Ryder Cup at golf and the America's Cup in which Harold Vanderbilt's *Enterprise* had beaten Sir Thomas Lipton's *Shamrock V*. Bridge looked all set to join the ranks of these other sports and, because of this, there was a whole host of newspapermen waiting on the quay.

The American team duly gave an interview to the press before they boarded the train for London. At Waterloo Station they were greeted by Lieutenant-Colonel Buller and Frank England of the *Evening Standard*, who was to be one of the referees for the match, and were taken to their hotel, the Carlton in Pall Mall. Buller told them that a press reception had been arranged for noon the next day at their hotel.

Next morning at breakfast, when he read the newspaper reports of their arrival at Southampton, Culbertson was furious. Clearly the pressmen had sought to portray them as classic Yankees on their first trip to Europe, full of trite Americanisms such as 'Gee whiz', 'Gosh' and so forth. Culbertson was determined to get his own back on them at the forthcoming press reception. If they wanted Americanisms then he would give them a bellyful.

'Mr Culbertson, in your opinion, who is the best player in the world?'

'Me.'

A moment's silence.

'And the second-best player?'

'Me, too.'

Polite laughter.

'And the third?'

'Me. You see,' Culbertson explained blandly, 'I am all three – the first, second and third best player in the world. After that there's a gulf, and then come the other players.'

'How about your team-mates?'

'They're the same way. Each of us is the first, second and third best player in the world . . . we're all like that in America.'

The reporters began to look a bit suspicious.

'In your opinion, Mr Culbertson, what chance of winning has the British team?'

'Not a chance in the world.'

'Not a chance?'

'Nope! They're *lousy* players.'

'Lousy?' The word then was still raw and unprintable and the reporters looked uneasy. Culbertson drove the point home.

'Yes, lousy! Gee whiz! Don't you guys know what the word lousy means? It means just what it says – lousy.'

The newspapermen got the point.

The American team were much fêted before the match. A luncheon was given for them at the Ritz, organized by A.E. Manning Foster, editor of *Bridge Magazine*, and by other leading bridge personalities. Some fifty people attended and many speeches were made, including one by Emmanuel Lasker, the German chess champion who was covering the match for Austrian and German newspapers. Lasker had fallen on hard times and came to see Culbertson in the hope of being nominated as a European correspondent for *Bridge World*.

The luncheon gave Culbertson the first opportunity to size up his opponents. He had met Buller already and liked his bluff but sportsmanlike manner. Now he came across Mrs Gordon Evers, white-haired and strikingly handsome, who had lived for several years in America and toured there as an actress with Sir Herbert Tree's company. Then there was Dr Nelson Wood-Hill with his air of urbane detachment, a Fellow of the Royal College of Surgeons, whose play was as delicate as a surgical operation. Lastly there was Cedric Kehoe, at twenty-five the youngest member of the team, a lieutenant in the Royal Navy, serious-looking but apparently an astute card player.

In the meantime Buller was writing his daily articles in the *Star* and *Daily Telegraph* which continued to attack Culbertson and vaunt the English approach to bridge. Culbertson did not mind this at all. As he freely admitted, Buller was his best publicity-agent in England!

The opening night of the match was something of a gala occasion. Spectators arrived in evening dress to make their way up the wide staircase to the thickly-carpeted room on the first floor of Almack's Club where a single bridge-table had been roped off by a square of crimson cord in the middle of the room. Liveried servants had placed chairs around the ringside before the contestants came in. There was a buzz of excitement as the ladies entered first, Mrs Evers and Mrs Culbertson both immaculately clad, Jo making quite an impression with her American-style short hair. Then the men, Culbertson, lean, assured, highly strung, Waldemar von Zedtwitz with his inscrutable face and his habit of brushing away an imagined speck of dust on his sleeve, Theodore Lightner looking aloof and slightly puzzled, and then the English team led by Buller.

Before they could start, a problem arose over the Duplicate boards. Culbertson had brought a set with him, specially donated by the United States Playing Card Company. But Duplicate was still new in England and the English objected to them. Instead, each hand had to be first dealt in one room, recorded, duplicated behind a screen by four officials, then passed in separate envelopes to the next room. This inevitably led to delays and what had been intended as a five-day match had to be extended to seven – even though the Americans now agreed to reduce the number of hands from three hundred to two hundred.

Just before the first hand was dealt, Culbertson gave a quick run-through of his system for the benefit of the English players. They, under Buller's guidance, were going to play 'common sense' methods.

The first session went well for the home side. The English, playing with dash and enterprise, managed to achieve a short-lived advantage and were ahead by 960 points at the conclusion of the day. But the second day told a different story. It became known as the Black Tuesday of British bridge and the main reason was this hand, 'the Colonel's Zero Hour':

Both sides vulnerable
Dealer East

Jo
♠ Q 10 7 6
♡ Q J 3 2
◇ A 9 7 6 5
♣ —

Buller
♠ A K 4 3 2
♡ —
◇ 10 2
♣ A 8 7 6 4 2

Evers
♠ J 9 8
♡ K 10 9 8
◇ Q J 3
♣ 10 9 3

von Zedtwitz
♠ 5
♡ A 7 6 5 4
◇ K 8 4
♣ K Q J 5

The bidding:

South	West	North	East
1 ♡	1 ♠	4 ♡	Pass
Pass	5 ♣	Pass	Pass
Double			

That was four down doubled and vulnerable, and cost the home side 1,400 points (the second undertrick was then scored at 400 points). Culbertson likened the Colonel's gallant dash under enemy guns to the Charge of the Light Brigade. Certainly as a game-saving ploy it was a risky undertaking. Buller subsequently tried to justify his bid by stating that his side had just had a run of eleven bad hands in quick succession, on which they had played poorly, and he was trying to recoup by blocking what he thought was a certain game in hearts for the Americans.

Nothing went well for the English that day and they ended up 4,445 points behind, a massive swing of nearly 4,000 points to the Americans. Wednesday was a rest day and on Thursday the English struck back to 2,770 points behind. Culbertson and Lightner at one point had missed bidding a grand slam. This upsurge in English fortunes led to increased public interest in the match and the press even entertained hopes of an English victory, but by Friday evening the Americans were in the lead again by 5,610 points.

Attendance at the match grew all week. In contrast to America spectators were allowed in to watch the match, provided they kept a respectful distance and stayed in only one room. Jo and von Zedtwitz had been apprehensive about this before the match had begun, aware of the antics of some kibitzers back home, but they were so impressed by the civility of their English hosts that this passed off without incident.

On Saturday the English spectators had something to feel pleased about as they witnessed the English pair, Wood-Hill and Kehoe, making a grand slam in no trumps, lacking the heart ace, but not long afterwards they were treated to the sorrier sight of them going down six tricks in a contract of two no trumps.

On Monday, the final day, the American lead at one point reached 6,700 but eventually, thanks to some spirited slam bidding by the English, was reduced to 4,845 points.

Why did the Americans win? The short answer is that they had better teamwork and more tournament experience and were playing to a system whereas the English relied primarily on 'common sense' methods. There were deeper reasons as well. Culbertson was determined to win. For him this match was crucial; he had staked out a claim for his team as the true representatives of bridge-playing Ameri-

ca, and his Approach-Forcing System was being given a prolonged
trial under the full glare of publicity. Defeat for him would have
meant more than just the loss of the international match; it would
have entailed the collapse of all that he had striven so hard to build
up over the past few years. In its way it was a huge gamble and much
of his credibility in England, and more importantly back home, rested
on it.

Buller, on the other hand, gambled in a different way. He felt that
it was unsporting to use a systematic, or so-called scientific approach;
somehow the game should be allowed to stand up for itself. Much of
this attitude goes back to the public school tradition of glorified amateur versus professional, expressed in Newbolt's often recited tag,
'Play up, play up and play the game.' It was a tradition that discouraged serious preparation for a sporting encounter and relied on
the Corinthian principle of a group of like-minded individuals going
out to play the game at a moment's notice. In his original challenge
offered to the Americans, Buller as good as said, 'We'll show these
Americans with their new-fangled ideas how to play the game of
bridge.' But however willing the spirit, the technique was sadly lacking. When Buller went down that calamitous 1,400 points on hand
twenty-eight, he claimed what he was doing was trying to fool and
deceive the Americans when he felt they were too much on top and
needed 'pulling up'! Even at the end of the match he found it hard to
reconcile himself to defeat. 'I would go so far to say that in fifty per
cent of the hands we played, the result was due solely to luck.'

Hubert Phillips, later to found *British Bridge World* and to become
a well-known radio personality, expressed his views in the *Manchester
Guardian*

> The Forcing System was definitely vindicated. The contest showed that
> 'card sense', intelligent guesswork fortified by experience, cannot stand up
> against a methodical system of conveying information also fortified by
> card sense. Colonel Buller's error in his sweeping criticisms of American
> methods, which led to the American challenge, was the assumption that
> card sense and systems are mutually exclusive. Unfortunately for his ar-
> gument, the Americans have as much card sense as we have. They have
> also thought out – what we in this country have failed to do – how to
> give it scope.

The upshot of the match was that there were a number of Culbertson converts in England. Many who had come in a sceptical
frame of mind 'stayed to take notes' and became converted. After the
match a banquet for the players was held at Almack's, presided over
by Sir Harold Reckitts, chairman of the club. The American team

praised the camaraderie and sportsmanship of the English team and the match ended with expressions of good feeling on both sides.

There was nevertheless a feeling in English bridge circles that perhaps they had not fielded their strongest team. A group of players from Crockford's Club got together to form a team to challenge the Culbertson team once the Buller match was over. The challenge was accepted, needlessly perhaps, since Culbertson risking losing the prestige gained from the Buller match for comparatively little reward. But nothing ventured, nothing gained.

The Crockford's team was composed of Colonel H.M. Beasley, Sir Guy Domville, George Morris and Captain Hogg (the nucleus of the team that played Culbertson for the Schwab Trophy in 1933). The match was over two hundred boards at Duplicate – this time the English team agreed to the use of Duplicate boards – and lasted from 29 September until 4 October. Again the Americans won, by a not dissimilar margin of 4,905 points. Two days later, they even found time to play a 'cock and hen' match against another Crockford's team – (Mrs Cavendish Bentinck, Miss Ethel Thomas, Mr F. Lyon and Mr Ivor Birts) – over seventy boards which they also won by 6,000 points.

However enervating their schedule, the Culbertsons were instantly buoyed up by the news they received when they got back to their hotel on Thursday evening, 18 September. They found this cable waiting for them from New York:

> BLUE BOOK OUT NO STOP FIRST EDITION SOLD OUT
> TWENTY FOUR HOURS NO STOP SECOND THIRD EDITIONS
> NOW PRINTING ALSO SOLD OUT SUCCESS ENORMOUS
> NO STOP YOU ARE RICH

It had exceeded their wildest expectations. Success was now assured, the Buller match had triggered it off. Once the reports of the Culbertson team's successful endeavours in England had filtered back to America, allied to their earlier successes at the Asbury Park tournament and at the Knickerbocker Whist Club, the public really began to take notice and were clamouring to be let in on the secrets of this winning Approach-Forcing System. The *Blue Book*, long delayed but now delivered at exactly the right psychological moment, gave them the answers they were waiting for.

At last Culbertson could relax a little. It had been an exhausting time for him and, in characteristic fashion, he had driven himself hard throughout his stay in England. Now, as he surveyed his achievements – the *Blue Book* selling by the thousands (it was to run through seventeen impressions by mid-1931), his *Bridge World* organization firmly established, the circulation of the magazine constantly expanding, teachers flocking in to be registered as Culbertson teachers, and now this new venture in England bringing countless Culbertson adherents – he felt his long and patient strategy had been justified. Jo and he deserved a holiday, and where better to go than Paris? They booked on the Golden Arrow to leave the next day for a week's visit.

Before leaving England, Jo was interviewed by a reporter from the *Daily Express* and asked about the respective merits of men and women players. She maintained that the average woman player was better than the average man.

'Why? Simply because a man is all vanity. He knows so much that he will not bother to learn or study. He takes things for granted, and there is next to nothing that you can take for granted at the bridge-table.' Bridge, she felt, enabled women to level the score with men and this accounted for much of its popularity in America. It was also a powerful antidote to gambling and she hoped this would be recognized more fully in England. In America people took bridge more seriously and credited it with teaching patience, fortitude, courage of thought and the ability to make decisions quickly and accurately!

In Paris, while Jo relaxed and visited the fashion shops in the Faubourg St Honoré, Culbertson had a special mission to fulfil. He took a chauffeur-driven limousine to Le Vésinet, near St-Germain-en-Laye, a suburb about fifteen kilometres to the west of Paris. He was going to see Eugene, whom he had not seen for ten years. As he approached the town, he told his chauffeur to wait and continued on foot, feeling his arrival would otherwise be much too conspicuous. Eugene was living at the Hotel du Centre. The *patronne* of the hotel told him his brother was upstairs in his room. Culbertson asked whether he was happy. Of course he was happy, she told him. When he went upstairs he knew what she meant. His worst fears were confirmed; Eugene's unkempt condition and ragged clothes meant that he was drinking steadily. They went downstairs to the restaurant and talked. Culbertson ordered some lunch but Eugene wanted only wine and a little cheese. The effects of his war injuries were still troubling him. His left arm was still paralysed and his movements were slow and painful at times.

Culbertson tried to persuade him to come and stay with him in Paris for a few days and then come over to America, but Eugene refused. He was happy where he was, the local people liked him and he had his religion. He had now become a devout Catholic, and had just come back from a pilgrimage to Lourdes. As Culbertson rose to leave, Eugene handed him two small religious medals as a parting gift. Chastened and somewhat saddened by this encounter, Culbertson returned to Paris. Two days later, they sailed for America.

As they walked down the gangplank of the *Île de France* in New York on 22 October, it felt as if they were coming back to a different America from the one they had left. Now they were famous. The *Blue Book* was selling at the phenomenal rate of 2,000 copies per day, giving Culbertson an income of approximately $2,000 per day since he was both its author and publisher. When he went into his office the next morning, he discovered that he had been inundated with requests to attend this or that function, to answer a mass of enquiries from readers of *Bridge World*, in short to put himself in the limelight. This was what he had coveted more than anything, but he knew he had to be careful. His moment of success was also his moment of greatest worry.

How was he to make sure his success lasted and was not just a temporary manifestation? He was deeply conscious of the experience of his father who had been riding on the crest of the wave one moment and then lost everything in the aftermath of the Russian Revolution. What he needed to do was to plan ahead, not just one year, but five and ten. It all hinged, he felt, on establishing his name as a household word – whenever Contract bridge was mentioned, the name of Culbertson would be mentioned too. From his years of studying mass psychology, he knew how short-lived and ephemeral the public's memory was. He might be famous today, but his fame was only on the surface of the mass mind and would quickly be forgotten. How then to make sure it became embedded in the depths of their consciousness? A lot depended on the value and efficacy of his system. If the public really took to that, then they would see him as an authority on bridge – the man with all the answers. More and more people were turning to bridge. It had become an acceptable social pastime, indeed it had become more than that, and in certain circles it carried a social stigma not to play bridge. Culbertson's aim was to get hold of the public's attention and hold on to it. His system was such that beginners could learn bridge in a matter of days or weeks rather than months. 'Simple enough for a child, deep enough for a master,' was the catchphrase he used. He understood the need to provide a complete service for them, so that once their allegiance, or 'brand loyalty', had been established, it would never be lost. Two things made him successful – his application of up-to-date marketing techniques to what had previously been thought of as an intellectual pastime and his recognition that the mass media was his ally. He was among the first to use radio and newspapers as a vehicle for self-advertisement and free publicity, and in an age which idolized film stars, he realized that the public needed larger-than-life figures with whom to identify.

But there were practical steps to take as well. Ely set up a bridge laboratory at the *Bridge World* offices; he deliberately chose the term for its scientific ring. A team of analysts were enlisted to sift through hundreds of bridge hands from past tournaments and score them according to the Culbertson System and other systems. He gave them the benefit of his compilations made up over the years from his own tournament and rubber bridge play. From these 'laboratory technicians' would come both validation of his own system and suggestions for any future improvements. He urged them to smooth out any possible defects, warning them that to leave in a bid that was defective 'by half a trick on a lead which might lose one trick in every ten hands could cost Culbertson followers, throughout the USA, several million dollars each year, even playing for nominal stakes!' No doubt the bridge laboratory did produce useful suggestions and certainly its existence looked impressive to the public.

The laboratory technicians, newly-recruited members of the expanding *Bridge World* organization, were also set to work answering in detail the readers' letters that poured in. For Culbertson this was a key part of his campaign. A mass following would only come about if the average bridge player, right across the nation, felt that the magazine spoke to him or her as much as to the club player.

It was his bridge teachers he counted on most to spread the word. For these he formed the Culbertson National Studios with its headquarters at 33 East 48th Street. These were his front-line troops, proselytizers who were going to go out and convert the needy masses. They were mostly intelligent, progressive women, wives of doctors, lawyers, businessmen and prominent in their local community, for whom the advent of Contract bridge had been a godsend, allowing them to extend their range of activities and social life in a way that was considered both self-improving and respectable. Culbertson realized that it was essential to give his teachers a clearly defined role. It was not enough just to be part of a loose association. He organized them on a regional basis, with their own group leaders, and instituted on their behalf monthly teachers' conventions as a rallying-point and a means of disseminating information. Here too they could acquire status as certified Culbertson teachers by passing qualifying exams. They were given embossed certificates, as if they had acquired a degree. The first Teachers Convention was held in the ballroom of the Chatham Hotel at the end of November and consisted of a three-day course, attended by some two hundred people. Both Whitehead and Work lectured on this occasion. Culbertson set out to ensure that attendance at these conventions was mandatory for every self-respecting teacher.

Culbertson still maintained a busy schedule on the tournament circuit. He knew his reputation still relied on his achievements on the 'field of battle'. A month after landing back in New York, he and Jo played a Challenge match resulting from their victory in the Asbury Park Trophy the previous July. Their opponents were the runners-up in the earlier competition, a young team from Columbia University including Johnny Rau, then twenty years old and William Barrett aged eighteen, a partnership noted for its predilection for psychic bidding. The Culbertson team nevertheless beat them by a resounding 5,675 points and were thus able to push their remarkable run to six successive match play triumphs.

The first week in December saw Culbertson line up unexpectedly with Rau and Barrett for the National Contract Team-of-Four Championships, at the American Bridge League tournament at Cleveland, Ohio. Culbertson had gone to the tournament not expecting to play. But Rau and Barrett asked him to make up a team with them. They got hold of an unknown, James Carpenter of Salem, Ohio, to be his partner. Carpenter had never played the Approach-Forcing System before. He was given a quick run-through of it by Culbertson minutes before the match, with these strict instructions: 1. Always bid one in a suit. 2. With a strong hand, jump the bid. 3. If Culbertson jumped, never pass. By some miracle and much to the chagrin of Culbertson's friend and rival Hal Sims who had come with a strong team, they won by half a point. Whether their opponents were defeated by superior skill or the fact that it took Carpenter ages to work out his bid is not recorded. Sims couldn't get over it and spent ages poring over the result sheet to see if he could find a discrepancy, much to Culbertson's huge delight.

From Cleveland Culbertson's schedule took him back to New York where, on 8 December, he co-hosted with Elsa Maxwell a charity bridge tournament at the St Regis Hotel in aid of the women's section of the unemployment fund. This was on the eve of the Vanderbilt Trophy held at the Ritz Towers on 10 December where fifteen of the strongest teams representing the principal New York clubs competed, and which the Culbertson team won.

The New Year brought with it news that the circulation of *Bridge World* now stood at forty thousand. It was also estimated that there were now twenty million bridge players in the USA. Culbertson had a survey carried out on *Bridge World's* behalf by a market research organization to see what percentage of players favoured the Culbertson System becoming standard. Gratifyingly, they came back with the answer of eighty-four per cent. It seemed like a good moment to bring out the promised summary of the Culbertson System of Contract bridge, *Contract Bridge at a Glance*. This was priced at $1 and had forty-eight pages of text. It proved to be the biggest money spinner of all. The first two impressions totalling 40,000 copies were sold before publication – by 1937, sales had reached 713,000 copies.

During most of the first half of 1931, Culbertson was on the road, conducting a non-stop lecture tour that started at the beginning of March at the Hotel Soreno in St Petersburg, Florida, then went via Atlanta, New Orleans, Dallas, Austin and San Antonio before going up to Boston at the end of the month. In between lectures he gave countless interviews to reporters – one of his favourite adages was 'Every gentleman of the press is my friend'. From Boston, at the beginning of April, he went to East Orange, New Jersey before flying across to the West Coast to lecture in San Francisco and at the Hotel Biltmore in Los Angeles. In all he gave sixty lectures and he was literally reeling when he returned to New York in mid May.

Culbertson was a first-rate lecturer. His impromptu speech giving all those years ago in Russia had taught him how to speak without notes and be aware of each particular audience. He had an unmistakable presence and his Russian accent only added to the impact he made on his audiences. These were mostly women and he knew how to play up the full suggestive nuances of his system. First he would hint at the 'splashes of romance' in it, then move on to the more direct: 'Take forcing bids, for instance. Partner is held by the throat and willy-nilly must obey your sovereign commands. At last you can satisfy your inferiority complex through the thrill of an inexorable command' – usually over the tired businessman husband, returning home to be coralled into a bridge game by his socially aspiring wife.

People travelled some distance to hear him lecture. Once in Dallas, he thought he was giving a particularly impressive lecture and was gratified to see a woman listener in an aisle seat busily taking notes throughout. As he passed by her chair on his way out of the hall, he looked over to see what she had written and found only the words 'Never pass!' underlined several times over. So much for lecturing skill.

The main body of his lectures was a detailed run-through of the Approach-Forcing System – this was what he was trying to promote after all. At another lecture he explained his theory. 'When I speak of Culbertson I speak impersonally. I am just a shadow. Culbertson is a nationally advertised product like Coca Cola, chewing gum or Camel cigarettes.' Sometimes Jo accompanied him and he would invariably introduce her in the warmest fashion – 'Jo, to whom I owe everything, who owes me nothing, my ever-patient and favourite partner in bridge and life' was one such introduction. Culbertson encouraged questions from his audience and usually managed to include one or two enlivening personal anecdotes into the proceedings.

CHAPTER 8

CULBERTSON v LENZ

The effect of the Culbertsons' success on the tournament field (as sweeping in its way as Bobby Jones's record at golf), the increasing sale of his books and the acceptance of his system by the bridge-playing public, caused the other bridge authorities to band together to oppose him. After a series of meetings at the Hotel Delmonico they agreed to merge their individual systems into a collective one and call it the Official System. This formidable group gave themselves the title Bridge Headquarters and consisted of Milton Work, Wilbur White-head, Sidney Lenz, George Reith, E. V. Shepard, Commander Liggett and Shepard Barclay from New York; Charles Adams from Chicago, Walter Wyman from Boston and Edward Wolfe and Henry Jaeger from Cleveland. The upshot was the beginning of the systemic war that was to dominate the bridge scene from July 1931 until February 1932.

The warning shot across the bows was fired by F. Dudley Courtenay at the beginning of June. Courtenay, from South Dennis, Massachusetts, was only a middle-range bridge player but he had high hopes of becoming a bridge impresario. Nowadays he is remembered for his invention of metal Duplicate boards and of the losing trick count. Having got himself appointed as the representative and business manager of Bridge Headquarters, he decided to pay a call on Culbertson at the *Bridge World* offices.

He tried to brow-beat Culbertson into joining the group; pointing out that there were now twelve eminent bridge authorities against him, so why didn't he join them rather than take them on alone? But this argument cut little ice with Culbertson for two reasons. Firstly he now had enough evidence to show that the American bridge-playing public liked his system and would go on buying it – the survey he had had carried out showed that eighty-four per cent of the public were pro-Culbertson. Secondly, his books were selling at a fast rate whereas those of the others were not, and there seemed no reason why they should not go on doing so. What had he to gain by joining the others?

Privately he welcomed the rivalry. A systemic war was bound to engender a great deal of publicity. Handled right, it should work in his favour, though it all depended on the way he presented his case. Culbertson was gifted with a shrewd understanding of what the public wanted. He had his finger on the pulse. It was the era of the New Deal, and the old order was being challenged. The public were likely to side with him as the upstart trying to raise his voice against the entrenched authorities. He would depict himself as the David challenging the Goliath of the bridge establishment, a pioneering figure from American folklore, the lone fighter who pits himself against the mighty giants of authority and government.

Knowing that Culbertson was not going to join them, Bridge Headquarters went into attack in mid June with a nationwide press release entitled 'The Biggest Story That Bridge has ever Produced'. The twelve authorities had banded together 'in the best interests of the American public' in order to standardize Contract bridge on an 'official' basis and to promulgate a new system that would be understood by all or, as the *New York Journal* wrote, would enable 'Africans and New York clubmen to speak the same language...' A printed version of their Official System was promised within two weeks. To Culbertson's annoyance they had got hold of two ex-Culbertson employees to write it; one of them, Robert Brannon, had been until recently editor of *Bridge World*.

When it came out, the Official System was seen to be a hotchpotch of different systems, some sound, some less so. Its main component was the one-two-three sequence of opening bids: 'If you have a small hand, bid one. For an intermediate hand, requiring help from partner, bid two. For a sure game, bid three,' as George Reith summed it up. It included a 4-3-2-1 point count (a contribution from Milton Work) and an artificial two-club bid.

As he looked at a copy of the new system with Jo, Culbertson had to admit that it presented a bigger threat than he had at first anticipated. The public were bound to be impressed by it. It looked official and had an authoritative ring to it. 'We knew,' he later wrote, 'the time had come for the biggest fight of our lives. To all appearances we were on top of the world; only Jo and I realized how shaky our position really was. We were still ephemeral little bridge gods, playthings of public fancy to be pulled down tomorrow and forgotten the day after tomorrow. We had made our bid – and it was a forcing bid – but arrayed against us were the most formidable and most intelligent bridge authorities, who had been in the field for years. Even Jo's first teacher, Sidney Lenz, was in the enemy camp.'

But Culbertson was a fighter and before long he had thought up a plan to give them the advantage. 'Always attack' had been his policy at the card-table and, as he was wont to say, in life. Now was his chance to do so. If he waited too long, the odds might go against him, anything might happen and the other side were much more powerful than him. He had to act fast and decisively. His plan, both simple and audacious, was to challenge the other side to a challenge match, each side, of course, playing its own system. By doing this he was robbing them of the initiative, turning them into the hunted and making himself the hunter.

He quickly put an announcement to this effect in the *Herald Tribune* on 24 June:

BRIDGE EXPERT SUPPORTS CHALLENGE WITH $10,000
Culbertson Offers to Meet Group
That Has New Bidding System

Ely Culbertson, bridge expert, pitted agaist twelve other masters of the game who have merged to found a uniform system of bidding, announced yesterday that he had placed $10,000 in a bank to cover a challenge made by him to the other group to play two hundred rubbers of bridge. He and Mrs Culbertson challenge any four members of the other group to a bridge match, the losings and winnings to go as a donation to the New York Infirmary. Culbertson's $10,000 would be pitted against only $1,000 of the group, according to the terms. If only two members of the group wished to play, the odds will be only $5,000 to $1,000.

Now he could sit back and wait for their reply. He guessed it would catch them on the hop as they could not have been expecting a move like this so soon. His 'challenge' was met by a deafening silence. Time now for his second line-of-attack, a specific challenge to Sidney Lenz, their leading player. He broadcast this on NBC's Station WJZ. Lenz, he said, could choose whoever he wanted as partner. Behind this seemingly open-handed and generous offer lay a well thought-out stratagem. He knew that Lenz was likely to turn down the challenge if it stipulated that he had to play with another member of the Bridge Headquarters as his partner. By widening the choice to anyone, he was pre-empting this and making it very hard for him to refuse. He repeated the terms of the match, two hundred rubbers for a stake of his $5,000 to their $1,000, the winnings to go to the New York Infirmary for Women and Children.

Culbertson waited to see what sort of reply this would elicit. Meanwhile, having *Bridge World* at his disposal, he thought he would indulge in a little gentle humour at Bridge Headquarters' expense. The July issue included a section entitled 'From the War Front' with these 'Decoded Telegrams from our Intelligence Department':

BROOKSVILLE, PENNA

BRIDGE HEADQUARTERS
NEW YORK, NY   PAID

SHIP AT ONCE ONE GROSS BRIDGE PENCILS EMBOSSED IN GOLD
OFFICIAL   SYSTEM   WON   SIXTY-NINE   DOLLARS   VERSUS
CULBERTSON SYSTEM
(SIGNED) A. DUBB

BROOKSVILLE, PENNA

BRIDGE HEADQUARTERS
NEW YORK, NY   COLLECT

PLAYED AGAIN – CANCEL ORDER
(SIGNED) A. DUBB

Culbertson used practically every opportunity to have a dig at the group. On the radio, Station WJZ again where he had an estimated one million listeners, he compared the Official System to a cooking recipe as follows:

Put five pages Work's common sense in a pan. Add thirty-five cents' worth advice to dubs and stir well. Add seventeen pages of Lenz' *ein, zwei, drei* after mixing with Reith's one-under-one forcing. Season with Shepard's mathematical formula. Boil down gently. When finished serve in small portions.

For all its corniness this method worked. It was all part of his plan to get the public on his side. By using his radio talks to confide in them, and depict the other side as old fogies, he could infiltrate himself into their homes.

Being a bridge doctor (which incidentally is a dog's life) I am often awakened by long-distance calls from my suffering bridge patients who get a violent attack of slamitis or a vulnerable rash. Perhaps the depression has something to do with it – for all my answers are free. The only thing I ask of my listeners or readers is please to limit their questions to bridge. Only the other day for instance I received a letter addressed 'Air Mail, Special Delivery, Urgent, Personal Attention Mr Ely Culbertson'. With some trepidation I opened the letter. I read the following: 'Dear Mr Culbertson, I am the fiancée of a young Prince Charming who is perfect in all respects except one. Yesterday, while playing bridge against him, I unfortunately revoked. He called a penalty for a revoke. Do you think that under the circumstances I should marry him?' A delicate problem...

Just as the systemic war seemed to be hotting up, Culbertson was forced to leave on his already once postponed trip to Europe. He felt, though, that he had done enough for the moment. The ball was firmly in the other side's court.

It was 30 June by the time the Culbertsons, with their children, sailed on the ss *Bremen*. But just before they sailed, a shadow was cast over the whole proceedings by news of the death of Wilbur Whitehead of a sudden heart-attack in mid-Atlantic. He had been aboard the *Île de France* on his way to visit his wife Parthenia and his daughter in Paris where they were living. Whatever their recent differences, the Culbertsons owed Whitehead a big debt; he had given them both a helping hand in the early years. For Jo this was particularly poignant as Whitehead had been her first mentor at bridge and for a time she had been his mistress before meeting Culbertson.

Bridge World paid Whitehead a handsome tribute. He 'had revolutionized bridge and we owe more to him than to any other analyst. He was probably the principal factor in making Auction and Contract the wonderful intellectual pastimes that they are today.'

Culbertson was looking forward to going to Europe both as a much-needed vacation and to continue, away from the furore of the systemic war, writing the next book in his scheduled series on leads and play (later to become the *Red Book*). But his main purpose in going to Europe was to do something he had always wanted to do – he was going to take Jo back to where he grew up in the Caucasus.

They went first to Paris where they put up at the Hotel George V. Culbertson always stayed there when in Paris, the manager, Max Blouet, being a close personal friend. He wanted to show Jo as much of Europe as he could. After Paris, they left the children with their governess at the house of some friends in Germany, and went to stay at Baveno on Lake Maggiore for a week's complete rest and relaxation before embarking, in typical Culbertson fashion, on a whirlwind tour through southern Italy and across Eastern Europe to Russia. They went to Naples, Capri, Rome, Florence, Venice, Milan, and thence by train to Warsaw; from Warsaw to Kiev, then a change of train to Dnepropetrovsk in the Ukraine where they visited an old friend, Colonel Hugh Cooper, who was in charge of building the massive dam there, and finally on down to Sebastopol and to Yalta on the Black Sea before crossing to Novorossisk. Culbertson was back in his beloved Caucasus for the first time for twenty-five years, and what he saw shocked him. The people were downcast and depressed, ill-shod and poorly-fed. As visitors, he and Jo had the compulsory Intourist guide with them and Culbertson looked forward to conversing with him in

Russian. But to all his questions about social conditions and the visible poverty, he only got routine, party-line answers.

Walking around Krasnodar, formerly Ekaterinodar, was an eerie experience, not just the fact of returning after so many years to such familiar streets and houses but also seeing soldiers on street-corners just as there had been in the days of the Black Hundreds – only this time it was the Cossacks who were the targets and the victims. They found his Aunt Glafira living in the same house, but only in one room of it – the rest had been commandeered by party members. She had aged noticeably, though still retaining much of her former dignity. She told them what had happened to her in the years since the Revolution. Her husband Constantin had been taken away before her very eyes and shot. She herself had been forced to join a washerwoman's union as everyone had to have an occupation. It was a harrowing tale and both Culbertsons were deeply moved on hearing it. Culbertson pressed her to leave Russia. He was sure that if she came to Moscow with them he would be able to use his influence and get her a permit to leave the country, but to his surprise she would have none of it. Russia was her homeland, she told him, here she was among her people, and she could never countenance living elsewhere when her people were still suffering. Only by suffering and paying for their sins would God forgive them and Russia be redeemed. However much Culbertson insisted she still refused.

From the Crimea, the Culbertsons moved on to Moscow. At the Hotel Metropole they received noticeably better food and accommodation than in the impoverished Caucasus, and Jo enjoyed the sightseeing. They had one or two friends to visit in Moscow, among them the newspaper correspondent, Walter Duranty, author of several books on Russia. But Culbertson's main purpose in Moscow was to visit the Russian Card Trust. He had his own five-year plan for the Soviet government to consider. Why not, he told the Director, introduce Contract bridge into Russia? It might take five years to get established, but it could run alongside the current five-year work-plan and it could prove an excellent means of psychological relaxation for the Soviet workers. Culbertson offered to translate his *Blue Book* free of charge, organize teachers where necessary and even do a little inconspicuous sales promotion. The net result for the Russian Card Trust would clearly be a tenfold increase in the sale of playing-cards.

The Director of the Trust looked at him for a few moments and then quietly said, 'Mr Culbertson, you do not seem to understand the purpose of our Card Trust. Our aim is not to sell as many cards as possible, but as few as we can. Cards remind our workers of the old days of kings and queens and bourgeois society. All the people you see here in this office are trying to restrict the sale of playing-cards, not increase them.' Culbertson looked around and had to admit he had never seen a busier office in the Soviet Union. This meant someone must be buying cards. Undaunted, he suggested that, since the Soviet Government objected to kings and queens, the difficulty could be overcome by calling the ace of spades 'Lenin'. But by then the Director was gently ushering him out of the door.

By 18 September 1931 the Culbertsons were back in New York, and back into the intricacies of the systemic war with Bridge Headquarters. Asked by reporters on the quayside for his comments on the Official System, Ely categorized it as 'eighty per cent Culbertson, twelve per cent Work and Lenz and eight per cent rubbish'. Courtenay, on hearing this, commented, 'Any system that is only eight per cent bunk must be a highly efficient one.'

Culbertson embarked on a major office move. The old offices on West 45th Street had become far too cramped for the present scale of operations and before he left for Europe he had located new premises on the twelfth floor of the General Electric Building at 570 Lexington Avenue and 51st Street. This Art Deco building was better situated, close to most of the bridge clubs on the East Side, and spacious enough to house the steadily expanding staff of the *Bridge World* organization. Each executive could have his own private office and secretary. Lewis Copeland, his adviser since the first days of *Bridge World*, became the new business manager of the publication and Lilian Brunesen was appointed to the important post of office manager.

Culbertson was itching to get back into the struggle with Bridge Headquarters. There had been no reply from Lenz to the challenge he had issued before leaving in the summer. He got one instead from Damon Runyon who chipped in and offered to play him with a team of Broadwayites for $5 a point, but on closer inspection it looked like the outcome of a late night at Mindy's. To keep the ball rolling, Culbertson summoned newspaper reporters and told them, 'They call me a gigolo; they treat me like a suspicious Russian; but when I issue a challenge, for the benefit of a charity, no one says a word ... Moreover Mr Lenz probably will not accept the challenge, and if he does, the match will probably never take place. Mr Lenz's reputation is only based on tops in whist, and articles written by him in which he is the hero.'

The more pressure he put on Lenz, the harder it would be for him to back down. Culbertson knew that he had to 'get Lenz's goat', needle him to the point where it became a question of honour for him to accept. Lenz was a rich man who played cards for enjoyment and interest rather than monetary gain. He once turned down an offer of $1,000 for a single bridge lesson saying he had not got time. In fact he had already made it widely known that he refused to play card-games for high stakes. This was because of his special skill as a magician and his famed ability to deal seconds. He did not want the opposition to suspect he had an unfair advantage. He was the first amateur to be elected an honorary member of the American Society of Magicians. Houdini, a close friend, often stated how relieved he was that Lenz never turned professional.

Sidney Lenz was born in Chicago in 1873 but brought up in Vienna, from where his family originally came. Returning to the USA as a young man he entered the timber business in Michigan and was so successful in pulling off a series of spectacular coups that by the age of twenty-seven he was rich enough to retire. He decided to take a trip around the world and spent a year in India studying Hindu magic, oriental philosophy and, presumably, the Indian rope-trick. Back in the United States, he became a man of leisure and devoted himself mainly to sport, at which he excelled. He played tennis against 'Little Bill' Johnston to an almost equal standard, he was a scratch golfer who later 'shot his age' at sixty-nine. At bowls he once held the national record of an average of 244 points for twenty-one consecutive games. He was a table-tennis champion and he regularly played chess with José Capablanca.

But it was cards that really interested him and many considered him the finest Auction bridge player of his era. He came into national prominence in 1910 when he won the Minneapolis Trophy for bridge whist for the third year running. By the mid-1930s he had won so many trophies, cups and medals that he had a special cabinet built in his bachelor apartment at 240 West End Avenue in New York to display them. He was a prolific writer, noted for his classic book, *Lenz on Bridge* (1926). He contributed short stories to *Liberty* and to the humorous weekly *Judge* magazine, of which he was part-owner. He was a wit and well-known raconteur, though this was not always apparent in his dealings with Culbertson. He introduced the term 'squeeze' into bridge, borrowing it from baseball, and many of the better-known plays at bridge, which have since become standard technique, were introduced by him, though none bears his name. In later years he became known as the 'Grand Old Man of Bridge' and was often asked to act as honorary referee at tournament matches. He lived, like so many other bridge 'greats', to a ripe old age, dying in 1960 at the age of eighty-seven.

The Culbertsons were well aware of his versatility. Lenz had been one of Jo's first teachers. Because he was such a skilled player the match was bound to be a true test of systems. Culbertson's confidence in their ability to win was greater than Jo's. She wondered whether they had not taken on too much. He sought to convince her by a 'scientific' argument based on his reading of the laws of probability. He brought out sheets of paper covered with his calculations. He had gone through a series of hands, scoring them according to the Official System and the Culbertson System. Supposing the average rubber was 1,000 points, his calculations showed that the Culbertson System was seven per cent better than the Official one. That was seventy points per rubber. Jo rightly pointed out that they might get a run of bad cards. But Culbertson had taken that into account as well. The variation of luck in cards worked out at about four per cent over a lengthy period, such as the 150 rubbers they were now intending to play. That still gave them a margin of three per cent in their favour – enough to be a winning one. In point of fact, when the match was played Culbertson's predictions on the run of the cards were right and both sides had more or less equal holdings of good cards.

A great deal depended on this match. It was make or break. Either they would be ruined and fade into obscurity, or they would triumph and be recognized as the number one team of Contract bridge and be able to control the development of Contract bridge from then on.

On 19 October news came through that Lenz had at last accepted the challenge, 'with all the reluctance of a small boy whose parents have told him not to fight unless he has to', as one newspaperman put it. He hated being 'used' by Culbertson. He deposited a cheque for $1,000 with his publishers, Simon and Schuster, and nominated as his playing partner Oswald Jacoby. Here then were a trio of men each with a European background, and an American woman, about to embark on the 'Battle of the Century'.

Oswald Jacoby was a relative newcomer. Then aged twenty-nine, a Brooklyner by birth, he had been to high school at Erasmus Hall in the old Flatbush part of Brooklyn. At the age of fifteen he was already showing signs of his prodigious memory for figures – he was captain of both the chess team and the maths club. After school he went to Columbia University but quit after two years to become an actuary. He joined Metropolitan Life and became, at twenty-two, the youngest actuary to qualify. Indeed so well did he do out of his actuarial business that he was able to retire six years later in 1928, thinking he had enough money to last him the rest of his life. But the Wall Street Crash put paid to that and he was forced back into work.

He first got into serious bridge in 1926 when he went to play at the

Knickerbocker Whist Club with Dr William Lamb, the principal of Brooklyn High School in the Thursday night Duplicate game. It was the first time he had played Duplicate, but despite the presence of some of the Auction bridge 'greats', such as Whitehead, Lenz and so on, they won. He went back again the next week with a lawyer friend, Fred Payne. They found themselves playing in a different section, among unfamiliar faces. Jacoby asked the tournament director George Reith why they were not playing in the first section again since they had won last week. Reith told him this *was* the first section. At the tables were Culbertson, Sims, von Zedtwitz and so on. Jacoby recalled that Sims watched him play a series of hands in this tournament and, when a group of them went out to eat afterwards, told him that he was the best natural player he had ever seen. It was the beginning of a long friendship and Jacoby was indebted to Sims for the way he helped him to better his game in the early stages.

Jacoby first played Contract in 1928 when he was in Palm Beach. He was invited to the house of Jules Bache, a well-known stockbroker, whose daughter insisted on playing the new game of Contract. From that moment on Jacoby was taken by the possibilities of the game. His first introduction to tournament Contract came in 1929 through George Reith, who rang him up and asked him to be his partner for the first Goldman Pairs event held at the Eastern Championships, of which Reith was in charge. They won and from then on Jacoby's reputation grew.

Lenz and Jacoby had never played in a tournament together but they had practised in private. When their partnership was announced, Culbertson immediately warned his *Bridge World* readers that Jacoby suffered from a 'chronic weakness for the so-called psychic bid'. It was an essential part of Jacoby's armoury, as he himself admitted. Culbertson called the psychic the 'boomerang' of bridge: 'Thrown accurately at the enemy, it produces havoc in their ranks, but, should it go wide of the mark, it returns, frequently causing even more damage to one's own side.' Lenz was to understand the full import of this remark during the match in which Jacoby made thirteen psychic bids in all, one or two leading to severe partnership misunderstanding at crucial points.

The term 'psychic' had been invented by Dorothy Sims back in 1923. One day she was playing in a duplicate tournament at the Knickerbocker Whist Club and dealt herself a hand containing five spades to the ace-king, and five hearts to the ace-king. Not knowing which of the two suits to bid (in Auction duplicate the combined honours were an important factor), she opened a club, and her partner responded in hearts, with the result that they ended up with the best score on the board. Writing up the hand for the *Auction Bridge* magazine afterwards, she had wanted to describe her bid as a psychological bid but her spelling failed her and the word came out as 'sycic' and from then on the term, in its more orthodox spelling, came into general use.

The terms of the agreement for the match were drawn up and signed by Culbertson and Lenz on 14 November with some of the razzmatazz normally reserved for champion boxers. Each of the main contestants must play at least seventy-five of the one hundred and fifty rubbers with their principal partner – Culbertson with Jo, Lenz with Jacoby. Play was to start on Monday 7 December and thereafter four sessions per week were to be played preferably on Monday, Tuesday, Thursday and Saturday nights. Eash session was of eight rubbers, starting at eight p.m. and the last rubber to be commenced before twelve-thirty a.m. The match would begin at the Chatham Hotel on 48th Street, where the Culbertsons had their apartment, and continue at the Waldorf-Astoria. Lenz nominated Fred Rogan as official referee, Culbertson nominated Ralph Leibenderfrer as his and Lieutenant Alfred Gruenther was agreed as the third official referee and was, in fact, to become the acting referee.

Gruenther was then aged thirty-two and on the teaching staff at West Point. He had to be on parade at eight o'clock each morning following the bridge session which seldom ended before one o'clock. His wife drove him back while he slept on the back seat. He was a first-rate tournament director, his firmness and tact were qualities that underlay his subsequent distinguished career as a General during the Second World War. He became a close friend of General Eisenhower. Indeed it was rumoured they played bridge together on the night of the North African landings. After the war as Chief of Staff at NATO and then Supreme Allied Commander of SHAPE, he kept up his bridge interests via the ACBL and the Laws Commission. He was the author of several books on bridge notably *Duplicate Bridge Simplified* (1931) and *Duplicate Bridge Complete* (1933).

As soon as the agreement was signed Culbertson posted his cheque for $5,000 destined, if he lost, for the Unemployment Relief Fund (Lenz's nominated charity). If he won, the New York Infirmary for Women and Children would be $1,000 the richer. He now started orchestrating his publicity campaign. The agreement had foreseen extensive coverage by the press and radio. Culbertson already had many contacts in this field, notably Deac Aylesworth, President of NBC, and he sought to capitalize on these. Through Aylesworth, he went to see Jack Wheeler, President of the Bell newspaper syndicate to discuss their coverage of the match. Discovering that Wheeler himself was not a bridge player but might like to learn the game, Culbertson suggested that he got together with a group of his friends and associates and Culbertson would teach them himself. Flattered at this offer from the 'master', Wheeler rounded up a small group of extremely influential media personalities – Bruce Barton, of the Batten, Barton, Durstine and Osborne advertising agency; Frank Crowninshield, editor of *Vanity Fair*; Kent Cooper, general manager of Associated Press; Grantland Rice, newspaper columnist; Sumner Blossom, editor of *American Magazine*; and Deac Aylesworth. They played a regular weekly bridge game at different venues, usually at the home of one of the participants, with Culbertson there as mentor. Their various reporters and other representatives can hardly have failed to notice the boss's friendship with Culbertson!

His pre-match publicity campaign concentrated on the same themes as before – Jo and he were depicted as the young couple taking on the forces of parental oppression in the guise of the twelve jealous elders of Bridge Headquarters. It was, he claimed, a grudge match – the two giants of bridge locked in gladiatorial combat. Out of all this the public stood to gain by being able eventually to choose their 'winning' system.

Soon, the match was a topic of conversation at most bridge-tables and many non-bridge dinner-tables besides – long before it actually took place. An atmosphere of tense expectancy had been created. Three weeks before the date set, Culbertson knew the match had generated enough interest to be 'one of the biggest publicity tidal-waves in the history of sport'.

Wires and cables for newspapers all over the world were laid right into their apartment. Associated Press assigned two of their first-rank men to the match, and prepared for a play-by-play coverage. Later Western Union and Postal Telegraph each took over one of the spare rooms for their exclusive use. They had six employees on practically twenty-four-hour duty whose function was to relay a blow-by-blow account of the match to the waiting world outside, via the twenty-four lines of cables they had leading from the apartment.

Culbertson took as much trouble over the arrangements within the Chatham Hotel as he did outside. The apartment, on the tenth floor, had ten rooms leading off a long central corridor. The decor was appropriately rose-coloured, and every room was to be used for the match with one exception – this was the children's bedroom where 'Fifi' and 'Frère' (or 'Jump-Bid' as a Culbertson friend Bill Tolcott had called him in commemoration of the current fashion for such bids) slept. At night while the match was in progress a notice was hung on their door 'Children Sleeping and Dreaming' – an unmistakably Culbertson touch.

The night before the match started Jo suddenly became apprehensive. She wondered how Culbertson would stand up to the terrific strain of playing the hardest match of his life as well as doing all the other things he had contracted to do – writing his article, annotating the hands after play and giving the stream of interviews and talks on the radio that were to go with it. 'Don't worry,' Culbertson told her. 'I'm at my best like this.' He was right. Like many whose temperament swings between elation and despondency, Culbertson, once he had set his mind to something, was unstoppable and thrived on bouts of intense activity.

Culbertson did not stint on his hospitality – at the best of times he was a lavish spender with little regard for money, as his creditors and most of his office employees discovered – and he was always punctilious paying his gambling debts. Oswald Jacoby recalled how he had bet him in 1936 that Roosevelt would be returned with a landslide majority in the election and was surprised to find his cheque waiting for him the next morning. The Russian in Culbertson liked to display largesse and as a host he was effusive and flamboyant. He also knew that nothing sharpened the quills of visiting pressmen more than the sight of attractive food and drink. The press were given their own room by the entrance of the apartment.

Play was to take place in the main room of their apartment – the large drawing-room at the end of the corridor. Guarding the entrance, like Cerberus as someone commented, was Lewis Copeland. Visitors were by invitation only and absolute silence had to be maintained in the playing area. About fifteen spectators at a time could enter the room and sit on chairs on one side. Then in turn they would get up to peek at the play. Culbertson had erected two large leather screens in the middle of the room with inch-wide cracks in them. Through these, spectators could get a glimpse of the actual play. Not much could be seen, but Culbertson knew exactly what he was doing. The fact that only four spectators could see through the screens at any one time and that no spectator could remain in the end room longer than fifteen minutes only stimulated interest and the sense of exclusivity. The queues to get into the room were continuous, pausing briefly to sample the rival attractions of the corridor buffet-table. Eminent visitors to the match included such dignitaries as Charles Schwab, Judges Freschi and Corrigan, Henry Taft, the Grand Duchess Marie of Russia, Chico Marx, Mr and Mrs Marshall Field III, Mrs Vincent Astor, Franklin P. Adams, as well as sundry presidents of banks, generals, bishops even, movie-stars and society figures. It became, to use Culbertson's term, 'the Greatest Peep-show in History'.

The preliminaries before the match on the Monday evening were hectic. Five hours before the first hand was dealt the Culbertson drawing-room was a seething mass of cameras, radio microphones, Kleig lights, sound-newsreel apparatus, photographers, reporters and the usual uninvited kibitzers. Cameramen were trying to photograph the players in groups and individually. Culbertson and Lenz were asked to pose under the glare of lights, first to smile at each other and then to scowl. Next a microphone was thrust in front of them. They had to wish each other the best of luck, and then to hope that the other would hold nothing but Yarboroughs throughout the match.

The match was to be preceded by a dinner. At seven p.m., Culbertson finally made his appearance, having kept everyone waiting for an hour – not for the only time in the match! Lenz had meanwhile sat down to a game of cut-throat with Frank Crowninshield and Bruce Barton. The bidding over, it was Lenz's turn to play. He put down what seemed at first to be the ten of spades but it changed right in front of the players to the ace. Barton jumped up from the table, threw down a $10 bill and said, 'That's enough for me.' Eventually the players, referees and about forty distinguished guests, all in formal attire, sat down to a sumptuous eight-course dinner, interrupted at regular intervals by radio interviews. During one of these, Culbertson recited a little doggerel he had made up about 'All the Lenz aces and all the Lenz kings'. Lenz, a vegetarian, looked on and took another swallow of spinach. The Culbertson babies, 'Fifi' Joyce and 'Jump-Bid' Bruce, emerged unexpectedly from their adjacent room clad in blue satin nighties and had to be led back to bed. Jo, wearing a blue taffeta evening-gown with an elaborate corsage of orchids, then had her say on the radio. She felt her selection as her husband's partner was a 'direct compliment to the millions of women bridge players', and the many thousands of women listeners immediately took her side; Culbertson's central strategy in holding this match in his home was paying off. Other married couples would identify and side with his and Jo's progress.

Finally, two hours late at ten p.m., the players withdrew to the playing area. A notice was hung up above the table proclaiming 'Absolute Silence'. The room was cleared of all extraneous persons and Alfred Gruenther, in his uniform of the United States Military Academy with its gold epaulettes and red stripes, broke out a new deck of cards, spread them on the specially-made table with its inlaid ashtrays, and announced that Hand No. 1, Rubber No. 1, of the historic match was about to be played.

In the press-room, reporters waited with bated breath. The *American Mercury* correspondent described the scene: 'After minutes of unbearable suspense, the first messenger burst forth, panting and breathless, with the world-shaking communiqué: Mr Lenz wins the cut and sits down in the North seat. The first words of the match were spoken by Mrs Culbertson. They are 'Where do you wish to sit, Ely?' Telegraph instruments start flashing this piece of news to the farthest outposts of civilization. Copyists scribbling frantically, distributed copies of the hands to the throngs milling about in the corridors and lobby. In the room set aside for the working press, reporters phoned in the news. Hot upon the heels of the first message came another: Mr Lenz and Mr Jacoby get the contract on the first hand at three no trumps. Pause. They are set one trick. Later the communiqué runs: Flash! Mr Lenz and Mr Jacoby win the first rubber amid some of the most terrible bridge ever played by experts.'

It was true. The effects of the bibulous dinner undoubtedly influenced the first few hands of the contest. Take the fourth hand played:

North–South vulnerable
Dealer West
No score

Lenz
♠ A 6
♡ A Q
♢ A Q 10 9 6 3 2
♣ 9 4

Culbertson
♠ K 9 8 5 4 3
♡ 9 4 3
♢ 5 4
♣ 10 8

Jo
♠ 10 7 2
♡ J 10 8 7 6 5
♢ J
♣ A J 2

Jacoby
♠ Q J
♡ K 2
♢ K 8 7
♣ K Q 7 6 5 3

The bidding

South	West	North	East
	Pass	2 ♢	Pass
3 ♣	Pass	3 NT	Pass
4 NT	Pass	Pass	Pass

As he looked at the dummy, Lenz could see there was an easy slam in diamonds, so he began to play the hand as if that was the contract, leading out the side suits first. He was set two tricks.

'I'm sorry, Jo,' Lenz said. Then, blushing, he realized his error. 'I mean, Ely,' he tried to correct himself. 'I wouldn't be surprised,' said his partner, 'if in the final analysis, when all is said and done, you mean me.' Two days later at a dinner reception for fellow members of the Knickerbocker Whist Club at their new club rooms at 47 East 47th Street, Lenz again referred to this hand and jokingly remarked that he had made a small slam in diamonds, but had been set two tricks at four no trumps! For Jacoby this was an early warning of the difficulties to come, showing Lenz's predilection for no trumps rather than suit bidding. Jacoby had no idea his four no trump bid was going to be left in by Lenz. It was one of the weaknesses of the Official System, that a player was always fearful of the bidding stopping short of game, even after an original two bid, hence the quick exit into no trumps.

Due to the lateness of the start only three rubbers were played on the first night. Lenz and Jacoby, holding first-rate cards but missing a couple of slams, won all of them and were 1,715 points ahead. As the second session started, Culbertson discovered that Jacoby still had not placed any bets on the match. Odds of two to one were immediately offered and Jacoby snapped these up to the tune of $1,000 to $500. Culbertson was just about to repeat the offer when Lenz intervened testily, 'Let's get going.' Culbertson next hung a wishbone over the bridge-lamp. It made little difference. They still ended the session 2,075 points behind. The cards were clearly running Lenz and Jacoby's way.

The following day Culbertson tried another tack. In the midst of play, he ordered a rare broiled porterhouse steak to be brought to the table and began eating it. Jo let him get started, then said, 'Ely, we're playing cards, you know.' Culbertson had to acknowledge that was the case and took another mouthful. Jo now flashed him a last warning and a frown. Lenz joined in and asked him why he could not 'eat at the proper time like the rest of us'. But Culbertson was ready for that, 'My vast public won't let me, Sidney,' he replied. The cards still went with Lenz and Jacoby, and by the end of the fourth session on the Friday they were 5,650 points ahead.

Now it was Jacoby's turn to steal the limelight. He arrived with a finger heavily bandaged and decorated with mercurochrome. He had, it seemed, been behind on his rescue work and had picked up a dog, on his way to the Chatham, that had been knocked over by a car in Park Avenue. The dog, unimpressed by such gallantry, bit him.

But he wasn't the only one to arrive late. Culbertson was constantly behindhand. At the beginning of every session the others were kept waiting. Never once did an apology pass his lips, except for the one occasion he actually arrived five minutes early. He apologized, then pointed out that his watch must be faulty! To Lenz, waiting impatiently and increasingly irked by these late arrivals, the same question was always addressed, 'Well, Sidney, have you changed your system yet?'

The newspapers seized upon all these details and played them up for all they were worth. As welcome was the news that now Jacoby was ordering venison steaks for himself and once munched a whole basket of strawberries while the hand was being dealt. The public reports lapped up on how the experts had fluffed their play, Lenz's famous forgetting he was playing no trumps on hand four and, not long afterwards, Jo leading out of turn allowing Jacoby to call a lead and make a small slam. By the sixth session the Culbertsons had begun to pull back. They won six rubbers in succession and that night were in the lead for the first time by a mere fifteen points. Once they had gained the lead they were never to relinquish it.

Jacques Curley, the wrestling impresario and promoter of Madison Square Gardens, put in an appearance on 15 December, took one look at the assembled throngs, nearly wept when he realized that no admission charges were being made and rushed up to Culbertson to ask him why he had not thought of putting the whole show on at Madison Square Gardens. Curley described how he would have put the players in a big glass enclosure and have had huge scoreboards for the estimated hundreds of paying customers. But Culbertson told him that he saw the match quite differently. His audience was locked away in the privacy of their own homes, listening to the radio, reading the newspapers and watching every move. They were the silent millions who were waiting to see the outcome of the match before committing themselves. What Culbertson stood to gain in this way potentially far exceeded anything he could get from putting on a short-lived spectacle at Madison Square Gardens.

At the end of the seventh session Jo retired to be with her children, and to do her Christmas shopping. Her place was taken by Theodore Lightner who, with his 'angular frame and Michigan drawl' proceeded to hold a sequence of exceptional hands that put the Culbertson side even more firmly in the lead. What helped them was this hand, perhaps the most controversial of the whole match:

Both sides vulnerable
Dealer South

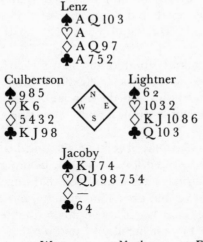

Lenz
♠ A Q 10 3
♡ A
♢ A Q 9 7
♣ A 7 5 2

Culbertson
♠ 9 8 5
♡ K 6
♢ 5 4 3 2
♣ K J 9 8

Lightner
♠ 6 2
♡ 10 3 2
♢ K J 10 8 6
♣ Q 10 3

Jacoby
♠ K J 7 4
♡ Q J 9 8 7 5 4
♢ —
♣ 6 4

The bidding

South	West	North	East
1 ♡	Pass	3 NT	Pass
4 ♡	Pass	4 NT	Pass
5 ♡	Pass	6 NT	Pass
Pass	Double	Pass	Pass
7 ♡	Double	Pass	Pass
Pass			

This bidding sequence was the subject of much subsequent comment. An extremely interesting and informative account of the whole contest, a 438-page book entitled *Famous Hands of the Culbertson – Lenz Match* (*Bridge World*, 1932) was published shortly after the match. All the important hands were analysed from three different viewpoints – those of Culbertson, Jacoby and Gruenther. This hand, for instance, merited especial attention. Culbertson strongly criticized Lenz's obsessive no trump calling, particularly his three no trump call which looks like a shut-out bid. He praises himself for his shrewd 'largely psychological' double of six no trumps, as this forces Jacoby into seven hearts, against which he has a defence.

Gruenther terms this 'one of the most grotesque hands of the match', criticizing Jacoby for his vulnerable opening semi-psychic bid of one heart and Lenz for being blinded by the glitter of 150 Aces. While the race between the two partners, one of them bidding no trump ferociously, the other equally insistent upon hearts was going on, neither noticed that a grand slam in spades was makeable.

Jacoby's defended his opening heart bid as follows: 'Although I did not hold two and a half or even two quick tricks, I was nevertheless prepared to play the hand at four hearts, even if my partner held very little. In fact, I might well have bid four hearts on this hand originally, were it not that my second suit was spades, and I did not want to shut out a possible spade bid by my partner.' Hearts were clearly his 'port in the storm'. He found Lenz's six no trump bid the worst of all.

Whatever the blame, the bidding shows clearly the characteristics of each player – Lenz's lack of flexibility and his Auction bridge obsession with no trumps and the honour value of four aces, Jacoby's propensity for psychic openings, and Culbertson's aggressive 'psychological' doubling.

After Lightner had played for two sessions, his place was taken by von Zedtwitz who played for one session before going off on holiday to his house in Florida. Remarkable too that during this session Lenz, affected no doubt by the prevailing climate, hazarded a psychic bid. Jacoby missed it! That became five down doubled and vulnerable – 1,800 points, the highest penalty of the match. The last session held at the Chatham Hotel was on 22 December at which point seventy-eight rubbers had been completed and the score stood at 10,705 points in the Culbertsons' favour.

After the festive season, the scene shifted to the Waldorf Astoria where Sidney Lenz was host. The lay out there was more or less similar to that at the Chatham, with a twelve-room apartment set aside especially for the match. By now tempers were getting a little frayed.

Culbertson continued to turn up late and just as unforgiveably took ages to play a card. Once, on lead in his own contract of four spades, he spent ten minutes making up his mind. Lenz dozed off. Finally awakened and told it was his turn to play, he put down the Jack of spades. This only confused Culbertson more since this was the first round of trumps. 'Go back to sleep, Sid I have another decision to make,' Culbertson told him. Lenz stormed off into the corridor, flinging back a taunt as he did so, 'Send me a telegram when you are ready!' Soon he was to refer to his opponent as 'That guy Ely.'

Whenever he was dummy, Culbertson never waited to see the hand played but used to leap from his chair and dash from the room, too nervous to watch. Often he would go into the press-room to check on the newspapermen. Lenz would turn to Gruenther after the hand had been played and say, 'Get Ely!' (Lenz was later to remark that these words haunted his sleep in the last days of the match.) In his account, Gruenther had nevertheless high praise for Culbertson, admiring his tremendous energy, his ability to attend to five or six things at once while engaged in playing the most important bridge match of his career. For Gruenther he was both an intellectual genius and a greatshowman – his magnetic personality immediately making him the centre of interest in any gathering.

At times disputes arose about whether each side was sticking to its declared system. Lenz at one point accused Culbertson in a sharp tone of not doing so. Culbertson insisted he was, and quipped, 'Why don't you read my *Blue Book*? Every sucker in the country has read it except you.'

'I haven't', piped up the kibitzing Chico Marx in the tense silence that followed, rapidly changing an awkward incident into a light-hearted one.

When the match was resumed, Culbertson presented each of his opponents with a copy of the self-same *Blue Book* as a Christmas gift. Jacoby thanked him and told him he now needed only two more to make a table in his study stand level. Culbertson asked him if he had seen the inscription inside. It read 'To Ossiebuco'. 'That's stew in Italian', Culbertson reminded him.

Culbertson kept up his frequent excursions to the press-room, usually to hand in his communiqué or bulletin on the hand just played (usually a factual 'Down one' but once or twice more enigmatic such as '*Ah mein gott*, Teddy' referring to a particular act of treachery by his partner). On 30 December, just before play started, he got into an altercation there with Sir Derrick Wernher. Wernher, an Englishman with an Eton and Oxford background, was a well-known figure in bridge circles, unmistakably so because of his massive build (he was over 6 ft 3 ins tall and weighed over 250 pounds). After a misspent youth, Wernher went partly voluntarily, partly at his father's instigation, to live in the USA, where his main interest was bridge and he became a playing partner and close associate of Hal Sims, spending much of his time at Deal, New Jersey. Later he helped introduce the Master Point System. On this occasion, Wernher was sitting in the press-room with, among others, George Reith and the author Louis Vance, analyzing the play when Culbertson walked in. Wernher, choosing an inopportune moment, asked Culbertson what had happened to the challenge he had issued the previous summer. Culbertson was clearly out of sorts, dismissed Wernher in an offhand way, saying he had no time for 'minor shots', and started to walk away. Wernher resented this and called after him, 'You're yellow.' There was a brief scuffle and Culbertson was about to leave when he spotted Lenz who had come in to see what all the fuss was about. Culbertson immediately challenged him: 'Why do you bring your friends in here to insult me? They call me yellow and a coward. Don't you think that's an insult?' Lenz pondered for a few moments and then responded,

'Well, it's certainly not a compliment.' Jo came in and pulled Culbertson away to the playing room, but Culbertson refused to start play until Wernher had left the hotel.

The assembled pressmen drank all of this in and as the words became more heated, they rushed to their typewriters. One young cub reporter watched the whole proceedings with awe and edged over to where Thomas H. O'Neill, the Associated Press representative, was feverishly dictating to an operator. 'You're not going to send anything about this fight to the newspapers surely?' he stammered. 'No, sonny,' replied O'Neill. 'I'm just writing a letter to mother. Run away and play with your blocks!' Some of the *Bridge World* staff at the match feared the effect of such unfavourable publicity, but Culbertson himself was not put out. 'They'll print what they want to print, and it's a good thing for bridge,' he declared. 'I hope they tell the whole story.' With his keen news sense, Culbertson could already visualize the story of the 'fight' across the front page – along, that is, with the figures showing the Culbertson lead had now mounted to 14,525 points.

As the match progressed, visitors became more numerous. Friends of friends of the players and others descended on the Waldorf. A Boston businessman said he had come all the way from the Bay State simply to look at Mr Lenz and Mr Culbertson. A middle-aged couple from Kentucky pleaded for admittance on the grounds that they came from the sticks and wanted to tell their neighbours about the sights of New York.

Now the rift in the partnership between Lenz and Jacoby became more accentuated. There had been occasional 'petty squabbles' and the break finally came after the 103rd rubber. Jacoby subsequently claimed that Lenz's public criticism of his bidding at various stages of the match often had little justification. Their mismatch as partners had become apparent to Jacoby after the fourth hand of the match (when Lenz had misplayed the four no trump contract). Matters finally came to a head in the 102nd rubber when Jacoby interposed a couple of 'psychic' bids, while the Culbertsons, ignoring Jacoby's interventions, bid up to an easily-made game. While the hand was being played, Lenz kept muttering about Jacoby, and afterwards challenged him with 'Why do you make such rotten bids?' Jacoby countered this by asking why Lenz made such stupid defence plays, particularly the one he had made in the second rubber that same evening that had allowed Jo to make a contract of one no trump when she should have been set a trick. Jacoby felt once again the criticism was unjustified and said he was resigning. Gruenther came up to the table and reminded them that, according to the match agreement, they were still due to play another rubber (it was not yet midnight). Jacoby replied, 'Not with me in it' and rose to leave. He was persuaded to play out the rest of the session, but the next day he announced he was withdrawing from the match and issued the following statement:

> Due to last night's misunderstanding quite natural to many bridge matches, I have been unfortunately misquoted in regard to both my partner, Mr Lenz, and my opponent, Mr Culbertson.
>
> I consider Mr Culbertson one of the truly great practical and analytical players in the world, and no list of the first five players of the world can reasonably be made up without including his name. While we all make mistakes, I have learned during this match to respect, even more than before, his subtle and most imaginative game.
>
> As for Mr Lenz, it would be, to say the least, presumptuous on my part not to hold him in highest regard, both as a gentleman and as the Grand Old Man of Bridge, to whom we all owe so much. Our differences are of ideas and methods of treating bridge, not of personal friendship. However, I have now become convinced that these ideas are so radically distinct that it would be unfair to him for me to re-enter the match. I will always remember the high honour that Mr Lenz has done me by selecting me as his partner, and only regret that I could not have done better.

The good-tempered nature of these comments and Jacoby's sportsmanlike decision to retire when he felt the situation between himself and his partner was irreparable gained him many friends. His place was taken by Commander Winfield Liggett Jr, an old friend of Lenz and a former First World War naval commander. Jacoby had played for 103 out of the 150 rubbers and most experts agreed his skill had been fully in evidence during the match. It was he who contracted for all the eight slams bid and made by his side, and four times he selected the only lead to defeat a Culbertson slam contract.

When he left some of the sparkle went from the game. But the fact remains that, as a partnership, Lenz and Jacoby were incompatible. What Lenz probably had in mind when inviting Jacoby to be his partner was the latter's brilliance as a card player. Lenz was hoping to prove that the combination of two outstanding card players would triumph over any 'system'. But partnership requires more than individual brilliance – they were more like, as *Bridge World* put it, 'an express-train and a hansom-cab' harnessed together. Jacoby belonged to the younger generation that welcomed the advent of Contract for the aggressive and imaginative bidding it allowed. He was a strong opening bidder, whereas Lenz was the opposite, favouring light openings as befitted the Auction bridge player that he still remained underneath. Jacoby remained as a friendly observer until the end of the match and can be seen in the post-match photographs. Shortly afterwards he joined the Culbertson camp as secretary of the United States Bridge Association and went on a lecture tour on Culbertson's behalf.

By now it was 29 December and the fifteenth session was due to start. Soon the Culbertson side reached its high-water mark of 20,535 points in the lead. Jo absented herself for the eighteenth and nineteenth sessions, being replaced for the first by Michael Gottlieb and the next by Howard Schenken, both promising players of the young school. But Lenz and Liggett held phenomenally good cards for these sessions, leading Culbertson to comment, 'We weren't playing. We were kibitzing.' His side dropped 8,065 points, and Shencken earned the dubious distinction of losing more points during his session than were lost at any other time during the match.

Jo returned to play for the final and twentieth session on 8 January. As the cards were dealt for the final rubber, Culbertson, with his unassailable lead, refused to pick them up. 'I can't lose now, so I'm not going to bid.' Jo was not going to stand for this. 'Pick them up, Ely.' As it happened they had good cards and even managed to win the rubber. Culbertson played the final hand of the match in a five diamond (his favourite suit) contract and made six! The winning margin was 8,980 points.

The match had truly become the subject of breakfast-table conversation in several million American homes. Listeners to the midnight broadcast of the results of the day's play were estimated at five million. Much of the credit, or the explanation, for this phenomenon must go to Jo. Here was a woman and mother participating in the most important bridge match ever played, competing with ranking bridge-players of the opposite sex. The American public longed to see how she fared. Edwin C. Hill of the *New York Sun* described her thus:

> There in the East seat, eyes veiled by drooping lids – motionless except for a flicker of white fingers as the cards drop or a jeweled cigarette holder cuts an arc – she seems detached, immeasurably removed from bickering and back-biting – gentle, tolerant, forbearing, slightly superior.

Her successful partnership with her husband was probably the decisive factor in the match. Just as Lenz and Jacoby 'lost' the match through their ill-suited partnership, so it was the practised, harmonious partnership of Culbertson and Jo that won the day. A glance at the penalties incurred by either side emphasizes the crucial importance of partnership understanding in this match. The Culbertsons incurred seven penalties of 600 points or more, totalling 5,900 points. Lenz and his partners incurred fourteen, for an aggregate of 11,500 points. Thus, since the winning margin was 8,980 points, well over half, some 5,600 points came from penalties and indicate the Culbertsons' superior accuracy in bidding. The statistics of the match (see Appendix II, page 232) make interesting reading and bear this point out. They also confirm Culbertson's earlier prediction that the distribution of luck in cards was more or less even.

The show was over. Culbertson's comment was, 'We had won millions of new friends. We were world famous. But we were broke.' It had been an expensive undertaking, feeding the endless lines of spectators and the newspapermen. While the match was in progress, the public had stopped buying his books, preferring to wait for its outcome first. Now at least they would start buying again. The bets on the match had gone to charity, as arranged, but the biggest bet of all was for the future control of the bridge industry and Culbertson had won that one.

Predictably the match had taken its toll on Culbertson's health. Jo and he decided that they needed a short break and went off to Havana for a week's holiday. Between a little bridge at the American Club, they relaxed at their hotel and sunned themselves on the beach. Culbertson needed this time to reflect and plan his future and work out his priorities. Foremost in his mind was the over-riding need to provide for his family. He was haunted by the spectre of his father whose failure to think ahead had caused them all such uncertainty. He decided what he needed was a slogan for himself – 'first consolidate, then expand'. Consolidate his system, make his name impregnable and expansion was bound to follow.

Back in New York he found things had got off to a flying start. The *Blue Book* and the recently issued *Summary* (*Contract Bridge at a Glance*) were selling at a phenomenal rate. On one day alone orders had come into *Bridge World* offices for over 5,000 copies of the *Blue Book* and 11,000 copies of the *Summary*.

CHAPTER 9

FAME

It really meant that the Lenz match had had the desired effect and had caught the public's imagination. Just as the momentum of book sales gathered pace, so did the stream of outside requests for his endorsement of bridge-associated products. But Culbertson had to pick and choose carefully. Some of the proposals were very odd. For instance, a man came to see him at his office describing himself as a purveyor of tissue paper – toilet paper for short. Would Culbertson like to endorse his product? The idea was for the Culbertson System, honour tricks and all, to be printed on each individual sheet of paper. His visitor suggested that Culbertson might care to add some useful tips of his own.

'Forcing bids, you mean . . .?'

'Exactly, Mr Culbertson. Excellent.'

'How about minimum response, then?'

'Even better.'

But Culbertson quickly tired of the joke which his visitor had been too obtuse to spot, and sent him on his way.

There were two major endorsements that started at this time that made him a lot of money. The first of these was Wrigley's Chewing Gum. Culbertson related how this came about at a Teachers' Convention at the Waldorf-Astoria on 2 May 1932. In March of that year Allan Ross, vice-president of the Wrigley Chewing Gum Company of Chicago, had approached him with the idea of a series of radio broadcasts on bridge, sponsored by his company. Culbertson told him that he had never chewed gum in his life before and he wasn't keen to be associated with a product that he didn't know personally. The next day a large parcel full of chewing gum packets arrived on his doorstep. Culbertson unwrapped one and tried it out. But, as he told his audience, being of a rather forgetful and nervous disposition, he was soon thinking of something else and before he knew what he had done he had swallowed the gum. He had only just come out of hospital for treatment of his stomach ulcers and he became increasingly anxious about the effects this chewing gum might have on his insides. He had visions of it covering his delicate stomach wound and sticking him to death. A sleepless night followed. But in the morning he woke up none the worse for wear. This convinced him there was no reason not to proceed with Wrigley's and in due course the first broadcast of the series went out on 4 April over the Red network of NBC and continued three times a week for thirteen consecutive weeks. It proved to be a valuable source of income over the next two years.

Chewing gum coincidentally played a key role later on at a tense moment in a 1934 tournament in which Culbertson was playing – this time less to his favour. It was during the final round of the Men's Pairs Championship at New York's Hotel Commodore. Most of the players had finished and stood around the half-dozen games still in play in the centre of the huge smoke-filled grand ballroom. Culbertson and Lightner, in partnership, were playing against David Burnstine and Oswald Jacoby, and the result of the match depended on this hand. Lightner had bid six spades. The lead, as all the other players spectating knew, was all important. Burnstine was on lead. There was never much love lost between Burnstine and Culbertson. So Burnstine prepared to use a little psychology, or subterfuge. He knew that Culbertson was always nervous and fidgety before going down as dummy, waiting impatiently for the opening card to be led before spreading his hand and hurrying away, often without arranging the suits. Burnstine made full use of this. He took his time. Then very deliberately and slowly he reached into his pocket and took out a piece of chewing gum. Even more slowly he unwrapped it, put it into his mouth and gave it a tentative chew. By this time both Lightner and Culbertson were losing patience. But still Burnstine delayed before leading. Suddenly he threw something down on the table. Like a flash Culbertson put down the dummy hand. A second later he realized his mistake and scooped up his cards again, but it was too late. It had been the chewing gum wrapper. Ethical or not, Burnstine had taken a peek and decided his lead accordingly and the contract was defeated.

Chesterfield cigarettes were the other manufacturers to form a long and profitable association with Culbertson. They wanted to produce a small cigarette-pack size booklet on bridge and distribute it free with their name emblazoned all over it. Culbertson let them have a schedule of prices relating to authorship of the booklet. If he alone was to be the author, that would cost $7,500. If it was written by Jo, then $5,000. Co-authored by both of them was $10,000. Going down the scale, if written by one of his associates, $1,000, or $500 by any of his office staff. Given this bewildering choice, Chesterfield opted for Culbertson himself and in the end over three million copies of the booklet were distributed.

Books poured forth after the Lenz match. The Garden City Publishing Co. in New York approached him for a book for their 'Star Dollar Series', one-dollar-books that were distributed through chain stores. Culbertson remembered that a chapter had been put into type for the *Blue Book* but excluded at the last minute as it would make the book bigger than required. Advance royalties of $10,000 were produced and the discarded manuscript was renamed *Contract Bridge for Auction Players* and embellished with some hands from the Lenz match. Thus a 200-page best-selling book was put together in next to no time and Culbertson reaped an easy $10,000.

The *Retail Bookseller* in February 1932 observed that Culbertson was 'once more the individual star of the Best Seller lists'. His victory had nearly doubled the sale of his books. His *Summary* topped all the lists, followed by the *Blue Book*, and these two books led all book sales for the entire year of 1931, overtopping fiction and non-fiction leaders. In March 1932 the second edition of the *Blue Book* was brought out – the reason being that, after an astounding sixty-five consecutive printings for the first edition, the plates, made of hardest steel faced with nickel, were worn out! The word was spreading – 'Culbertson is standard: we play Culbertson' and the demand for his books grew and grew. Teachers of the Culbertson system reported a similar response. Their earnings had tripled since the Lenz match.

The Lenz match also provoked a whole rash of books about bridge – some satirical and humorous like William Ashby's excellent *Slam! A Ga-Ga History of the Lenz Match*, others less literary like the versified *Culbertson for Morons* by Warren J. Lynch, and novels – the two best known being Russell Hertz's *Grand Slam* (in which the central character is a bridge playing Russian refugee) and C. C. Nicolet's thriller *Death of a Bridge Expert*. In the second book, the central character was one Ian Werber, formerly Ivan Boursetski, a thinly-disguised portrait of Culbertson described as 'a tall, thin man, dynamic, nervous, who seemed to radiate attention-calling waves of personality. About his face there was the suggestion of a romantically idealized Satan, a suggestion which he did nothing to discourage. He was dressed with sleek elegance ...' Other recognizable characters were Samuel Kurtz (Sidney Lenz) and Hornsby Farling (Hal Sims). The setting was among New York's bridge community, 'that phenomenon without a counterpart. Sunk in the midst of Manhattan, it is a world by itself. Except for a few colonies in suburban districts, it is bounded by 35th and 75th streets and by Madison and Lexington Avenues. The core of the community is made up of fifty men and women to whom the game of bridge is almost life itself.' Werber, as the title indicates, comes to a sticky end. Life, in this case, refused to imitate fiction.

Meanwhile, Hollywood began to take an interest in bridge. The film *Grand Slam* appeared in 1932 with Loretta Young as the young wife of a fanatic bridge player, acted by Paul Lukas, with 'Culbertson' making a brief appearance as a waiter. Indeed it was only a matter of time before Hollywood and Culbertson came together. They were made for each other.

The first steps towards Hollywood were taken in June 1932 when Deac Aylesworth of NBC got in touch with Culbertson and said that Ned Depinet of RKO was interested in making a series of pictures on bridge that would, as the publicity hand-out stated, 'go beyond the actual playing of the game into the psychological and mental equipment of the players', a typically Hollywood statement meaning they had not got a clue what they were going to make, as Culbertson, the master of ballyhoo, was to find out.

Because of his existing commitments, Culbertson could not go to Hollywood for the time being, so the film company arranged for a film director, a gag-man and scenarist to come across from Hollywood to New York to work on preliminary ideas for the film. The studios were convinced that a new angle on bridge had to be found. The first suggested scenario was one in which three southern ladies were stuck for a fourth at bridge and called up the negro butler to make up their numbers. Hardly had that one been put on one side than they suggested a musical ballet number à la Busby Berkeley with fifty-two shapely girls each dressed as a playing-card. The rhythmic title they had chosen to go with this musical number was 'Ely – you lie – in July'!

These suggestions were clearly preposterous and Culbertson hoped for better when he eventually went to Hollywood in February 1933. But the first thing the film company told him was that they had spent many hours and considerable expense finding people who had no idea how to play bridge since they were convinced this was the only way bridge would come across in a fresh and alive manner! The Culbertsons were amazed and appalled at what lay in store for them. Bridge experts they might be in New York but out here in Hollywood they were just a couple of outsiders caught up in the Hollywood Dream Factory. The first director the RKO studios allocated them was again determined to provide something unusual. He suggested, for a change, that the bidding and dealing should proceed from right to left, rather than the normal way practised by 25,000,000 bridge players. None of this made any sense to Culbertson and he soon called a conference to discuss the whole project. At his insistence, Morris Brock, a bridge player, was appointed producer, and Sam White director.

This seemed to work better and the first short, or 'featurette' as they were called, was produced – a two-reel drama entitled *Murder at the Bridge-table* which had unmistakable echoes of the Bennett murder and showed a woman on trial for having shot her husband as a result of a bridge argument. Culbertson played the role of the expert witness who, when called to testify, demonstrated how the husband twice had a chance to save his life – once during the bidding and once during play. It was hard work making movies. Culbertson did not react well to being directed and there were frequent retakes.

As a diversion Ely and Jo enjoyed spending time with the movie colony and the Beverly Hills set. They ran into the Marx Brothers who were making *Duck Soup* for Paramount. Chico was the keenest bridge player of the brothers (he was the originator of the memorable advice to a partner: 'If you like my lead, don't bother to signal with a high card, just smile and nod your head!') and lived up to his reputation of being prepared to bet on anything by immediately offering a challenge to the Culbertsons for a $5,000 match over either ten or twenty rubbers. But Culbertson resisted the temptation and stuck to his well-established formula that no match was worth taking on or was a fair test of skill unless it was over at least 150 rubbers.

Anyway, the chance to play with Chico and Harpo occurred frequently enough in New York where they were part of the famed Thanatopsis Inside Straight and Literary Club that met regularly at the Algonquin and whose leading bridge light was the playwright, George S. Kaufman of whom Harpo once wrote, 'He had great integrity, George did. You never had to watch him when he was dealing!' Kaufman was a dedicated bridge player and one of the very best amateur players around, a frequent visitor to Crockford's Club and to the Regency. His spontaneous humour at the bridge-table was legendary. At the Regency Club one afternoon he watched a fellow member make a hash of playing the hand. 'All right, George, how would you have played the hand?' the member challenged him. 'Under an assumed name,' was Kaufman's reply. Another time his partner temporarily left the room to go to the men's room. 'That's the only time this afternoon I've known what he's got in his hand,' Kaufman remarked.

Bridge was already a fashionable pursuit among the movie set and the Culbertsons moved easily, as celebrities, in such glamorous surroundings. On the whole the standard of bridge in Hollywood was, according to Culbertson, 'atrocious'. Without a director to tell them what to bid, they were lost! Marion Davies and Bebe Daniels were two exceptions.

At the studios, the script-writers were now finding it difficult to write for the idiosyncratic Culbertson who treated their work as a guideline rather more than finished text. In the end it was felt safer to let Culbertson write his own scripts. He was at work one evening in their hotel apartment on the twelfth floor when suddenly the floor started to shake and the chandelier sway. They were in the middle of an earthquake. Jo was in the bath and she only had time to wrap her prized sable coat around her before rushing down the outside fire-escape to the comparative safety of the street below. It proved to be one of the worst earthquakes in the Los Angeles area for some time, but they had their deadline to meet before shooting the next morning, so they returned to their apartment to complete the script. Faint tremors were still felt the next day and the Kleig lights on the film set blinked ominously. Culbertson subsequently claimed this was why his performance was so shaky! But the simple truth was that he was a bad actor.

In all they made six featurettes: *Murder at the Bridge-table*, *What Not to Do in Bridge*, *Three Knaves and a Queen*, *Transatlantic Bridge Tricks*, *A Forced Response* and *Society Cheaters*. The best one was probably *Murder at the Bridge-table*, and this opened at Radio City Musical Hall in New York on 19 October 1933 to a packed and loudly participating audience. As a reviewer the next morning commented: 'No sooner had the title been flashed on the screen than the audience broke into a machine-gun fire of comments ... when the hands were shown, everyone counted the honour tricks out loud ... when the murder was committed, some husband remarked to his wife that the victim might, but for the grace of God, have been he ... when Mr Culbertson stated the honour trick requirements for an opening bid, some wife said, "See, I told you so." '

But time has been less kind to Culbertson's movie ventures. They faded fairly quickly into deserved obscurity. William Huske, who saw them in preview in Manhattan, remembered the last two or three shorts when Culbertson had taken over the role of director. In the as yet unedited version of the films, Culbertson's voice could be heard loudly declaring, 'Cut, cut.' It was hardly surprising, therefore, that there was a story circulating shortly afterwards that the studios had paid Culbertson a handsome cheque not to make the remaining six featurettes he had been contracted for. Nevertheless, he was paid $270,000 for his work, so he can have had little cause to grumble.

Before he left Hollywood Culbertson attended the annual meeting of Wampas (Western Association of Motion Picture Advertisers). Here image-maker met image-maker. He explained how his own advertising campaign was orchestrated around three basic principles; sex, flattery and fear. All three were targeted towards women. His Approach-Forcing System had unmistakable sexual connotations, it flattered women by making them equal at the bridge-table with their husbands, and played on their fear of missing out, of not being part of the social swim, if they did not play bridge.

The constant motif in his campaign was the image he promoted of himself and his wife Jo. They were there to be identified with – not so much as an idealized figures like movie-stars, but as more down-to-earth, more readily understandable personalities. Their flaws and shortcomings should be as visible as their strengths. Culbertson pointed out that he planned to keep his conceit and cockiness, his unfailing egotism, in the public eye at all times. He hoped the public would remember him as representing the new, young, thrusting generation in its struggle against the old. His brashness was offset by Jo's calm and sophistication, her cool and her touch of class. She was a perfect foil, reflecting the essence of their bridge partnership.

Culbertson was in his element talking to these advertising men. In many ways he was a man before his time, with a keen sense of the advertising angles which are now such a feature of our lives but were then in the 1930s rarely used quite so thoroughly and cynically.

Lecturing in this manner was now very much part of Culbertson's everyday life. He had preceded his visit to Hollywood by giving a series of lectures in San Francisco. One, in the Oakland Auditorium, was attended by an estimated 3,000 people. His theme was the usual one delineating the merits of the Culbertson System but including some advice to his predominantly female audience: 'Beware the man who holds his cards so close to his vest that he does not know what he holds – he'll scrutinize every bill and make your married life miserable!' He reminded them too that bridge fights often cleared the atmosphere. They were 'in the nature of a safety valve and should be hailed with great delight by all players'.

On the domestic front, things were not always so secure. In New York he received a kidnapping threat to his children. He told pressmen that they were being kept under close guard in their New York apartment at the Chatham Hotel, their nurse had been equipped with a police whistle and other precautions taken. Such threats were not to be taken lightly. In the wake of the Lindbergh kidnapping of March 1932, there had been a sudden 'epidemic' of child seizures, crudely known as the 'snatch racket', and so no chances could be taken.

Following the Lenz match Culbertson had launched the first World

Bridge Olympic which took place on 1 April 1932. This idea had been hatched by Culbertson and his associates the previous year. On a chosen day at the same time in whatever part of the world they happened to be, contestants would play a par contest of sixteen hands and the winners declared later when all the score-sheets had been received by *Bridge World* in New York. It was an ingenious and novel idea. More than just a gimmick, it helped to foster Culbertson's avowed aim – to internationalize bridge as much as possible with himself as its spokesman. The starting-time was 8.01 p.m. (New York Standard Time) and at that precise moment game captains (over nine hundred of them) all over the world broke open the sealed and pre-pared hands and delivered them to their contestants.

An immense amount of pre-match publicity was generated, some of a rather dubious kind. Two days before it was due to start the *New York Times* received a copy of all sixteen hands through the post. Word soon got out that they had been leaked by Louis J. Vance, the author and creator of the 'Lone Wolf' series of mystery thrillers, and long-time adversary of Culbertson. When challenged Vance claimed that the hands were being bootlegged around the speak-easies of New York and that was where he had picked them up. How he got hold of them was never made clear. Clearly he hoped that the tournament was going to flop. The *New York Times* treated the whole thing in light-hearted fashion and, aware of its news value, printed the story without disclosing the hands, including Culbertson's offer to bet Vance $1000 to $1 that, even with his prior knowledge, he would not score more than sixty per cent of par on them. Vance declined. Over-night, from being just a bridge matter, the Olympic became head-line news. Vance met a tragic end a year later when he fell asleep in an armchair in his New York apartment with a lighted cigarette in his hand and was burned to death.

For the participants a sense of anticipation was evident wherever a 'game' was due to take place. Every major city in the USA held one, and thirty-two other countries throughout the world participated – as far away as Shanghai in China, Cairo in Egypt and Perth in Aus-tralia. The cost to each entrant was $2 or its equivalent in local currency, half of which went to the local game captain and half to the National Bridge Association, Culbertson's bridge organization that had been set up the year before and was handling the proceedings.

The sixteenth and final hand afforded some amusement. The Com-mittee had included it to add a little 'zest and comic relief after the strain of the first fifteen hands'. It was a Goulash hand (such deals were very popular at that time, especially the 'wilder' variation of passing Goulashes):

East-West vulnerable
Dealer South

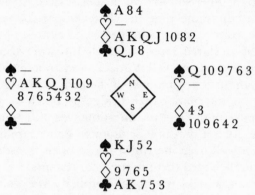

♠ A 8 4
♡ —
♦ A K Q J 10 8 2
♣ Q J 8

♠ —
♡ A K Q J 10 9
　8 7 6 5 4 3 2
♦ —
♣ —

♠ Q 10 9 7 6 3
♡ —
♦ 4 3
♣ 10 9 6 4 2

♠ K J 5 2
♡ —
♦ 9 7 6 5
♣ A K 7 5 3

East-West par: Any score playing the hand at hearts.

North-South par: Seven no trump bid and made in case West overcalls immediately with seven hearts. If West does not bid seven hearts immediately, par for North-South is seven hearts doubled and made by opponents.

At the Cavendish Club in New York, Oswald Jacoby held the West hand. South opened one club and Jacoby favoured a psychic bid of one diamond. North, with his powerful diamond holding, was not to be out-psyched by Jacoby and bid two hearts. Two passes followed round to Jacoby. He passed! North lost all thirteen tricks. Elsewhere the hand led to equally convoluted bidding. Some of the North hands correctly diagnosed West's holding after he immediately leapt to seven hearts and bid the required seven no trumps, but others got into a tangle and sometimes it was South who ended up in seven no trumps – with disastrous consequences. In Oscaloosa, the West player carefully bid up to seven hearts in gradual stages only to find his partner, with a void in the suit and reckoning his only valuable trick-taking card was the queen of spades, took him out to seven no trumps – this was doubled and vulnerable and all thirteen tricks were lost. Had East taken it upon himself to redouble, he could have earned himself the maximum penalty for one hand, down 10,000 points!

The joint winners of this first tournament were not experts but everyday players, Mr and Mrs Byrne Baldwin from East Orange, New Jersey in the North–South seat, and Lewis Frank and Robert Mayer of Detroit for East–West. All this was grist to Culbertson's mill and widened his hold over Contract bridge. They each received one of the much coveted trophies that Culbertson had specially donated, made of platinum and designed by Cartier's, the Fifth Avenue jewellers.

After its first trial run, the Olympic tournament became an annual fixture. There was a brief flurry of protest from Avery Brundage, President of the American Olympic Games Committee, at the use of the word 'Olympic' in connection with bridge, but when Culbertson pointed out that Homer had copyrighted it and that 'the scope of bridge is by far greater than any sporting event in history and consequently the word fits the occasion nicely', Brundage thought it wiser not to pursue the matter.

The high point came in 1934 when over seventy countries participated and 90,000 players took part. Then, in 1938, following the merger of Culbertson's United States Bridge Association (which had incorporated the National Bridge Association) and the American Bridge League to form jointly the American Contract Bridge League, the latter organization took over the running of the World Bridge Olympic. But three years later, with the advent of war and the problems of foreign exchange the contest was abandoned.

In April 1932, Culbertson had another important visit to make – to President Herbert Hoover. Dressed in spats and wearing a black bowler-hat, Culbertson paused on the White House steps to tell the assembled newsmen about their discussion. He had recommended bridge to the President as the 'light beer and wine solution' to the gambling problem and had told him that if he passed a law abolishing kibitzers, he would be certain to be re-elected! Hoover was not a bridge player, nor even a card player – unlike a number of his successors (notably Roosevelt, Truman, a poker-player, and Eisenhower, who, whenever he was in Washington, held a regular 5 p.m. bridge game every Saturday at the White House, usually with General Gruenther as his partner). Roosevelt was both a bridge and poker-player. The story goes that he once went straight from the poker-table to broadcast one of his fireside chats on the radio. Throughout his speech he absent-mindedly clicked his poker chips, obliterating many of his words.

Encouraged by the success of the Olympic tournament organized by the National Bridge Association, Culbertson set about organizing the United States Bridge Association. Culbertson wanted this to be constructed on the same lines as the US Golf and Lawn Tennis Associations, in other words to be the co-ordinating body and spokesman for all American bridge clubs at national and local level. Much of the incentive for doing this was Culbertson's rivalry with the American Bridge League and his personal rivalry with its director, William McKenney.

The ABL had been founded five years earlier in June 1927 at Hanover, New Hampshire. Initially it was known as the American Auction Bridge League in charge of Auction tournaments but when Contract came in and the first Duplicate Contract tournament was played in Cleveland in November 1928, it changed its name to American Bridge League to avoid being identified solely with Auction. The driving force of the new organization was McKenney, himself a local Cleveland man and former Dunlop tyre-dealer. Cleveland was very much a centre for bridge activities in those days. His aim was to try and set up the ABL as *the* authority for all forms of bridge. It was inevitable therefore that sooner or later he would clash with Culbertson. Culbertson had started off by setting up his National Bridge Association in May 1931, linked to *Bridge World*. Then, in July 1932, he converted this into the much grander-sounding United States Bridge Association.

The ABL had very few members – its membership hovered somewhere between 100 and 300 members per year. It was not a grassroots organization and this is where Culbertson sought to outdo them. His aim, all part of the wider objective to control the bridge industry, was to recruit members for his organization from all over the country. He had representatives appointed in all forty-eight states and charged entrance fees of no more than $2 per year for individual members.

He organized an annual Grand National Tournament, a pyramid-structure tournament 'truly national in scope', local city winners progressing up to state, regional, then national level tournaments. It would encourage unknown players to show their skill and make a name for themselves. Lieutenant Gruenther, the referee at the Lenz match, would make a nationwide tour to instruct local tournament directors how to run these tournaments. He named as President of USBA Milton Work, his erstwhile enemy – their truce was commemorated by a Pathé News newsreel showing them talking amicably together and vowing to 'bring order from chaos'. The committee included such dignitaries as Gruenther, Jacoby, Liggett, Lightner and Dudley Courtenay, formerly president of Bridge Headquarters. Culbertson was wasting no time in rounding up his troops for an all-out assault on the ABL. The ABL was caught napping; USBA 'pinched' the February 1933 Eastern Championships (including the important Reisinger and Goldman Trophies) formerly held under the auspices of the ABL. Any incident unfavourable to the ABL was highlighted. *Bridge World* made great play of McKenney's conduct during his running of the ABL's Winter Tournament at Cincinnati in December 1933. His 'inexcusable language' and 'gruff cross-examination' of a young lady player were readily seized upon. It looked for a while as though the USBA was going to sweep the ABL off the board. Then, in

1934, the ABL started up the Master Point System as a register of achievement in tournament play and this saved it from extinction.

The bitterness between the two organizations continued until 1937. At times it was so bad that some players would only participate in tournaments conducted by their particular organization. In 1937, after five years of strife, the two organizations agreed to merge. The prime mover in this was Nate Spingold, vice-President of Columbia Pictures and donor of the Spingold Trophy. He managed to get those two highly-charged personalities Culbertson and McKenney to agree to bury the hatchet. The merger produced a new organization, the ACBL, with Spingold as its first President. To this day, this organization, with its headquarters in Memphis, Tennessee, is the governing body of Contract bridge in the USA.

The Culbertsons spent the summer of 1932 in Europe but by mid September they were back in New York and Culbertson decided to open his own bridge club. Some said unkindly that it was the only way he could be sure of getting into one – unlike Groucho Marx, who once remarked that he would never dream of joining a club that would have him as a member! Culbertson's critics' remarks referred to an incident a year or so back at the Whist Club where he had been involved in a fight with another member, Elmer Campbell, and been barred from playing there.

Culbertson found temporary premises on the fourth floor of the Waldorf-Astoria. He had named his club Crockford's after the famous English nineteenth-century card-club. There was also a Crockford's in London run by Colonel Beasley but there was no formal connection between the two. By October new premises were found at 14 East 62nd Street, a five-storey limestone building that had originally belonged to Charles H. Sabin, chairman of the board of the Morgan Guaranty Trust Company. Culbertson chose it for its central location next to Fifth Avenue and Central Park. He was determined to make it the premier bridge club of New York, its 'temple of bridge'. Its smart address helped and he spent a small fortune, estimated to be in the region of $40,000, on the furnishings and decorations. Luckily it was the sort of New York mansion that was easily adaptable to the needs of a club. A member entered on the ground floor through a high entrance-hall, covered with Flemish tapestries, hanging above black ebony furniture. This led through to a reception-room of Louis XVI chairs and settees in blue and cream tints and then on to the restaurant which, by contrast, was decorated in a startling 1930s decor of brilliant tones of red, black and scarlet. The card floor above was reached via a wide curving staircase. The first room on the right, called the Green Room, held up to thirty-two bridge-tables and was the main card-room. Behind, across a domed foyer, was the smaller English-type Oak Room, with its hand-carved wood panelling, previously the library of the house. This became the favourite room for men bridge players. Culbertson had special leather-upholstered chairs made for the players' use and spent time and effort trying to gauge the size and shape of the average bridge player! On the upper floor were the so-called 'Experts Room', for high-stake games and the twin private salons of the Culbertsons with pastel drawings of some of the country's leading experts on the walls.

Much of the eventual success and prestige of the club were due to the superlative restaurant and bar run there by Raymond Modolo, the *maître d'hôtel*. Modolo, a Venetian by birth, had worked at the Savoy and Ritz Carlton in London before coming to New York as *maître d'hôtel* at the exclusive Meadow Brook restaurant from which Culbertson had enticed him away to Crockford's. Modolo acquired a French chef, Réné Durand, himself a product of the Ritz in Paris. Soon the menu with its house specialities, Poulet Lavaroff, Veal Kidney Crockford's and Crêpes Suzette, became justly renowned.

The opening night on Thursday 3 November 1932 was a gala event attended by many prominent New Yorkers. Culbertson's circle of acquaintance was now quite wide and charter members of the club included such diverse personalities as the bridge-expert playwright George Kaufman, song-writer and lyricist Howard Dietz, the American-born Princess Henry of Reuss (formerly Mrs Anson Wood Burchard of New York), the tennis-star Mrs Molla Mallory, financial leaders such as Jules Bache and Otto H. Kahn and a whole host of prominent socialites, plus a wide sprinkling of bridge personalities. The membership list was limited at first to 200 members. The Committee of the club contained such stalwart figures as Harold Vanderbilt, Walter Beinecke, Harold C. Richard and Joseph Thaw and the club was all set to establish itself in the highest echelons of New York society. Members were given their own shiny key to let themselves in, but, in best English tradition, a stiff-collared butler was usually at the door to admit them.

In charge of the club's bridge and social activities was Mrs T. Charles Farrelly. Culbertson had been as fortunate in his choice of her as he was of Raymond Modolo to run the restaurant. Nina Farrelly, as she was known, was the widow of an Irish general. Italian by birth, she was a tall, dignified woman in her sixties, well-known in New York bridge circles. Prior to coming to Crockford's she had been in charge of a famous Monday afternoon women's bridge club in New York, run jointly with another well-known teacher, Charles Stewart

Street. Indeed, so exclusive was this club that when one member died
she left her seat at the table as a valued item in her will. When Mrs
Farrelly moved over to Crockford's, she brought many of the Monday
afternoon club members with her. She inspired loyalty, as Culbertson
was later to discover to his cost.

On Sunday evenings a buffet supper was provided more as a social
event to enable members to get to know each other. Culbertson would
be much in evidence on these occasions. He was very much its *ani-
mateur* – as this contemporary account in the *American Mercury* shows
'The Master, slim, imperial, magnificently turned out and as cold as
ice, weaves his way among his guests, smiling mechanically, greeting
old friends, making new ones.' Perhaps the smile was not always
so mechanical for there is no denying that Culbertson enjoyed these
early days at Crockford's. To have started up a club of this calibre
was a long-cherished ambition, and it looked to be an outstanding
success.

Women in particular loved Crockford's. They used to meet there
for lunch, followed by an afternoon's gentle bridge. Dorothy Sims was
among them: 'One day, having nothing to do, I dropped into Crockford's. A line of hats and coats preceded mine. Mink predominated,
topped by two sables and a silver fox. I knew the bridge would be
dull. I climbed the stairs. I glanced in the card-room; it was full of
smoke and people...' Indeed Mrs Farrelly was heard to comment
that the quality of the bridge declined severely in the afternoon due
to the excellence of Modolo's cuisine.

By mid-1934 the club was going so well that Culbertson decided to
expand and bought the house next door at 16 East 62nd Street. He
planned to knock the two buildings together and use part of the new
building for the club and the upper two floors as his family's extended
duplex apartment. This new purchase was made in the name of his
company, Culbridge Inc., of which he and Jo were sole proprietors.
This company then leased the building back to him for $6,000 per
year. He then sublet the club premises to Crockford's for $12,000 per
year, thereby netting himself a gain of $6,000 a year.

It was this sort of financial juggling that led eventually to his
difficulties with Mrs Farrelly. At the best of times Culbertson had an
original and idiosyncratic view of financing. His attitude towards
money was quite arbitrary. Some days he could be immensely generous, others quite the opposite. Alfred Sheinwold told the story of
George Beynon, an ex-employee of *Bridge World* whom Culbertson had
fired and who found himself stranded out of town; Culbertson unhesitatingly wired him enough money to get him out of trouble. But
mostly, despite his immense wealth on paper, Culbertson was flat

broke. Jack Korshin, his lawyer and close friend, remembers going with him one morning to get a much-needed loan, at outrageous interest rates, from a finance company in the Empire State Building. They spent all morning negotiating it as the question of collateral was complicated. At lunchtime they had a recess and the two of them went to a restaurant in the Empire State for lunch. Culbertson ordered his usual array of expensive dishes, hardly touching any of them. When the bill came at the end of the meal, he turned towards Korshin, 'Do you have any money, Jack?' Korshin did but saw no reason to pay for the meal. Culbertson then told a waiter to summon the manager. The manager came and Culbertson told him imperiously, 'I'm Ely Culbertson. I want you to cash my cheque.' The manager obliged and Culbertson wrote out a cheque for several hundred dollars. Korshin knew at the time that the cheque would certainly have bounced had not the loan from the finance company come through that afternoon.

On another occasion Korshin went to see Culbertson as he himself was short of money and Culbertson's professional debt to him for his services as lawyer stood at between $4,000 and $5,000 – in those days a fair sum of money. Korshin needed some of it immediately. Culbertson asked him how much. Korshin replied one thousand dollars. Culbertson's extraordinarily generous solution was to say, 'Jack, I'll tell you what I'll do. I will borrow it and I will lend it to you!' Korshin protested that he did not want to be lent the money since he was already owed nearly five thousand dollars. Culbertson saw it quite differently. 'But that's business, Jack. This is personal. I will lend it to you.' In the end of course Korshin simply put the 'loan' against the debt, but the story is an indication of the way Culbertson construed financial matters. Eventually Korshin arranged to take promissory notes from Culbertson and then discount them. Even then Culbertson saw no reason to be left out and, as he was signing them, would suggest to Korshin if the amount due was $750, the note should be made out for $1,500 and he be given back $750!

Likewise with Crockford's – Culbertson considered it *his* club and it was up to him to decide its finances. But Mrs Farrelly had held a twenty-five per cent share in Crockford's from the beginning and was entitled to know the state of affairs. He had not told her about the leasing arrangement, nor did he think to inform her when, in April 1935, he started paying himself a monthly salary of $750 as president of the club. Just as idiosyncratic was his determined effort to elect the proprietor of the *New York Mirror*, Stanley Kolber, to be a member of the club, because Culbertson wanted to write a column for his newspaper. This was done without consulting her or the other members.

But ultimately it was the restaurant, the pride and joy of Crockford's, that was his undoing. Two things coincided. Firstly he took to
wining and dining his family and friends in the bar and restaurant at
the club's expense. Since he was an extravagant host, this put a severe
strain on the club's finances. Raymond Modolo found it impossible to
keep the restaurant in profit. But even more reprehensible was Culbertson's habit of 'borrowing' money from the Crockford's till, which
for a time was his only source of ready money. While he was immersed
in the Kem cards venture (as described in a later chapter), he was
desperately short of funds and looked to Crockford's to keep him
going. When Mrs Farrelly got wind of this in the spring of 1936, she
immediately went to Culbertson to seek an explanation. He became
evasive and offhand. She then talked it over with Walter Malowan,
the club secretary, who advised her to confront Culbertson and tell
him she would have to reconsider her position at Crockford's. Faced
with this and imbued with an arrogance born of successive firings and
re-hirings at *Bridge World*, Culbertson told her in no uncertain terms
that she could 'peddle her papers'. This was his club, he said, and if
she did not like the way it was run, she could go. He never expected
her to do so. In his eyes Crockford's was still riding on the crest of the
wave and was the top club in New York. But leave she did, and what
was, much worse, she took most of the members with her. She and
Malowan, with the assistance of a Crockford's founder-member, Mrs
Hallam Keep, moved a few streets away and opened up a rival club,
the Regency Club on East 67th Street, where it still stands today.

Crockford's never recovered from the body-blow of Mrs Farrelly's
departure. The loss of membership was considerable but the loss of
prestige was even greater. From being the fashionable and smart club
it always used to be, it suddenly became *démodé*. Culbertson had to
resort to desperate measures to try to keep it going. He lowered the
membership fee to $20 per annum and invited visitors from out of
New York to make use of its facilities. Restaurant prices were reduced
and a package including morning lectures on bridge plus lunch for
$2.50 was introduced. The Thursday night Duplicate game was
switched to Monday night so as not to clash with other Duplicate
games elsewhere. But it was to no avail. The club staggered on for
another year or so with shrinking attendance; even Raymond Modolo
was getting disheartened by the scarcity of customers. In May 1938,
Culbertson decided to throw in the towel and he leased the premises
to the Cavendish Club. The Cavendish, founded in 1925 by Whitehead and Gratz Scott and hitherto lodged in rooms in the Mayfair
Hotel on Park Avenue, welcomed the extra space and agreed to take
over the restaurant under Modolo's capable charge. It remained there

until 1950, before moving, via the Ritz Tower Hotel, to its present quarters on Central Park South.

It had all gone wrong, and it was entirely Culbertson's fault. He had, in plain language, blown it. Whatever his success at managing *Bridge World*, here his management skills had gone sadly awry. In fact the termination of Crockford's became a messy business. There was a protracted lawsuit between Mrs Farrelly and Culbertson which came to the courts in June 1938. Mrs Farrelly demanded a proper accounting of Crockford's Inc. during her years there in the belief she might still be owed some money from her share of the profits. She also claimed mismanagement. Culbertson rejected all of this and countersued for conspiracy, claiming she had undermined and diverted the business of the club by attempting to remove some of its membership. He put in a claim for $250,000 damages.

In court, Culbertson stated that he had lost $56,000 of his own money through running the club. Out of an original investment of $100,000 he had only got back $44,000. The judge was unimpressed by this tale of woe and ordered him to submit proper accounts. His court performance seriously alarmed Jack Korshin who was representing him. Korshin had told him to stick to the questions and speak only to matters relating to the lawsuit. But Culbertson's idea of the courtroom was to treat the witness-stand as an opportunity to expand on his views on life in general and his view of contracts in particular. Eventually the judge cut him short but the bad impression had been made. His performance was worse when he was asked about the club's accounting. Korshin's advice had been, 'Don't guess. If you don't remember, say so.' Rather than admit he did not know the answer to a question, Culbertson insisted on giving one which was often factually incorrect. It was the old familiar mixture of vanity and stubbornness, which once again proved his undoing.

Luckily for him, Mrs Farrelly dropped the case. She soon realized that there were no 'hidden assets' or missing profits and that she was unlikely to get a penny more. Besides, she was now busy with the thriving Regency Club and the last thing she wanted was long-drawn-out legislation with Culbertson.

The demise of Crockford's was complete. It had brought out the best and worst in Culbertson. In its heyday, from 1933 until 1936, it had been a stylish, glamorous centre of New York bridge and social life. So well had it done that other affiliated clubs had been opened, in Chicago in 1935 at the Blackstone Hotel, with an equally renowned restaurant, and in Paris in May 1936 on the Champs Elysées, under the direction of the Baron de Nexon. But once Culbertson had started over-playing his hand and begun to think of the club as his exclusive personal domain, the end was never far away.

CHAPTER 10

CULBERTSON v BEASLEY

By the beginning of 1933 Culbertson was ready to turn his attention again to his favourite field – international bridge. He persuaded Charles Schwab, Chairman of the Board of Directors of Bethlehem Steel Corporation and also President of the Whist Club to donate an international trophy. Culbertson had first got to know Schwab in his early Whist Club days. But his name had long been familiar to him even before that. During his youth in the Caucasus, if his father found him playing cards he would be apt to shake his head and say, 'You would never see a great man like Mr Schwab wasting his time playing cards.' Schwab was a fellow Pennsylvanian and the fact that he had made good as a financier and steel magnate was held up to the youthful Ely as an example of the traditional Pennsylvanian virtues of thrift and hard work.

The truth was that Schwab was a very keen bridge player participating regularly in some of the highest-stake bridge games then on record. His genial personality and the fact that he was a good loser who enjoyed the 'gentle joshing back and forth' at the Whist Club ensured his popularity. On Sunday afternoons he would host bridge gatherings at his magnificent residence, modelled after the Château de Chenonceaux, on Riverside Drive. Indeed he told Culbertson that nothing stimulated him more for business than a good game of bridge.

Culbertson hoped the Schwab Trophy would become emblematic of the Contract bridge championship of the world. Such, in any event, was the wording of the letter Schwab wrote to Culbertson on 15 May 1933 addressed to him as President of the United States Bridge Association rather than to him personally. The letter went on to suggest that 'inasmuch as your team organized and won in 1930 the first international match against England, you inaugurate the competition this year by assuming the captaincy of the American team'. This was a neat way of getting round the team selection problem. The new member of his team was Michael Gottlieb, who had played briefly in the Lenz Match as Culbertson's partner. Gottlieb was a Californian by birth and earned a good living as a real estate broker. His film-star good looks attracted admiring glances from many bridge followers on this first trip to Europe. Later he was to captain the all conquering Four Aces team.

The English team they were due to play was captained by Colonel Beasley. Culbertson had played and defeated a Beasley team at the time of the Buller match, and the idea of a return had been in the air for some time.

Before they left for England a reception was given by New York Mayor O'Brien at City Hall, where the splendid Schwab Trophy, commissioned from Cartier's, the Fifth Avenue jewellers, was handed over for safe-keeping to Culbertson to take to England. But Culbertson was in for a shock. The English insisted on a thirty per cent import duty for bringing valuable items such as this trophy into the country. Culbertson learnt about this only at the last minute. The English took the view – logical, if not well-informed – that the trophy might stay in England. Despite vigorous lobbying and urgent protests by cable to England and wires to the State Department, the English customs refused to make an exception. Culbertson, much to his annoyance, was forced to leave the trophy in the USA and take a photograph of it with him to England instead!

The Culbertsons set sail from New York on a Sunday morning, 21 May. The previous night, there had been a gala dinner at Crockford's. It must have been quite a party as many of their dinner guests were later present in the Culbertson suite on board ship the next morning. Culbertson gave his usual press interviews. When asked how Jo would fare as a woman player in the tournament, Culbertson commented: 'Give me the woman player for match play. She never cracks up, no matter how terrific the strain. She may appear to be nervous, excited, upset even, but all the time she maintains her composure and her ability to use her skill to the utmost even when the game is going against her.' Harry Acton from the *New York American* immediately asked him whether this meant he thought Jo a better player. But Culbertson was not going to be drawn on that one. 'On Mondays she's better, on Tuesdays I'm better and so on,' was all he was prepared to divulge.

Arguments always raged as to which was the better player of the two of them. The confusion arose partly from Culbertson's deliberate strategy of putting it about that Jo was the better player as a means of recruiting women players to his system. Later on he credited Jo with the invention of the Grand Slam Force in 1936 known as the 'Josephine' for much the same reasons. So far as playing ability was concerned, Culbertson was undoubtedly the more gifted player, aggressive, prone to make mistakes but able at times to play with real flair. 'I play men, not cards' was one of his maxims. Jo was steady, reliable, with her own quiet determination, and made an ideal partner. This, in fact, was where their strength lay – in the 'personal equation' as Culbertson called it, their partnership understanding, the crucial importance of which Culbertson understood before most of his opponents.

The Culbertsons stopped off first in Paris to play a challenge match against the top French team. He wanted to dominate European bridge in the way he now felt he dominated American bridge after the Lenz match. The French refused to play Contract and insisted on Plafond, then still the most popular version of bridge in France. Culbertson didn't object. His aim was to prove that a systematic approach could be applied and triumph in any version of bridge. So confident was he that he rashly offered the French odds of three to one against their winning. The French team, captained by Pierre Bellanger and consisting of Pierre Albarran, Adrien Aron and Sophocles Venizelos, later to become Greek Prime Minister in 1950, were understandably piqued at Culbertson's low estimate of their chances and flatly refused his offer. An even-money stake of 5,000 francs for the match was put up instead. Plafond's scoring system was similar to Auction and the lack of a vulnerability feature and absence of any advantage in bidding slams initially confused the Americans. They failed to establish any ascendancy. Indeed at the beginning of the third and final day with thirty-six boards to play, the score was almost level. Then came the 101st Board, this innocuous-looking hand.

Dealer West

Albarran
♠ 10 5 4
♡ 10 8 4 3
♢ Q 10 6 4
♣ Q 7

Culbertson
♠ A Q 9
♡ J 5
♢ K 5 3 2
♣ K 4 3 2

Jo
♠ K 8 6 3 2
♡ A 9 6 2
♢ 8
♣ 10 9 8

Venizelos
♠ J 7
♡ K Q 7
♢ A J 9 7
♣ A J 6 5

The bidding was straightforward – three passes to South who bid one no trump, which was passed out. Culbertson went through his usual hesitation, with what the French commentator Le Dentu called 'his air of terrible suffering', before deciding on an opening diamond lead. Venizelos captured East's eight with the jack and returned the seven of diamonds. Culbertson put up the king on which Jo discarded a small heart. Then, as Culbertson himself put it, 'I am famous for my mistakes, but this time I produced one of the brilliant plays of which I am sometimes capable. I played the Ace of spades. My wife signalled with the eight, and we took poor Venizelos for a 300-point ride.' Venizelos had to find three discards on spades and went three down.

But in the moment of triumph and amid all the animated post-mortems going on, the hands were wrongly replaced, and the Americans in the other room were given the same cards. Their East–West pair at the second table reached a contract of two spades, making four for a score of 168 points. The match committee was called upon to adjudicate and argued the matter for two hours before finally announcing a distinctly curious verdict: the deal should stand but the contract bid and made by the Americans at the second table should be credited to the French. But the tension caused by this incident had been too much for all present. The French were too nervous to continue and, after one more hand, the match was brought to a close. The Americans were due to leave for London the next day, in any case. The match was deemed a draw – a face-saving device that did not displease either side.

On Friday 14 July the American team arrived at Victoria Station in London on the boat train from Paris. They were staying at the Savoy Hotel and could look forward to a couple of days' rest before what was to prove an extremely hectic fortnight.

The Beasley match started on the following Monday at Selfridges in Oxford Street. Large department stores had been associated with bridge for some time, and were used regularly for bridge functions and bridge lectures. Now there was an added reason; Gordon Selfridge, the owner of the store, was a well-known gambler and society figure with a strong penchant for the casinos of the South of France – usually in the company of the Dolly sisters. So his store was a natural choice as the venue for a match. He even lent Jo his own personal armchair – in the USA she always insisted on having one to sit on, rather than the hard upright chairs that were more common.

Selfridges' reputation as a smart London store was at its height and crowds flocked to this match both out of genuine interest and a sense of social occasion. Two innovations had been laid on especially, one was a massive electrical scoreboard in the Palm Court area which displayed the cards for all four hands, gave the bidding sequence and followed the play, indicating who was on lead, who had taken the trick and how many tricks had already been won (a forerunner of the present-day Bridgerama).

The other innovation was the periscope. This was placed outside the playing-room and enabled spectators to get a glimpse of the players in action. The idea of using a periscope had been put forward by one of Selfridges' staff – an indication of the keen interest the organizers had in this match. For the contestants such matters were of secondary importance. More to the point was that at the start of the match London was experiencing an unusual heatwave. Selfridges' solution to this was to provide huge blocks of ice at strategic intervals throughout the building.

The American team consisted of the Culbertsons, Theodore Lightner and Mike Gottlieb. The English team was to be drawn from Lieutenant-Colonel H.M. Beasley, their captain, Sir Guy Domville, George Morris, Percy Tabbush, Graham Mathieson and Lady Rhodes.

'Pops' Beasley, as he was known, was born in 1876 in Jhansi, India and entered the army straight after leaving Bedford College, his school. He joined the Royal Artillery and spent his early years abroad in the far-flung outposts of the Empire, in India, Burma and China. He took part in the relief of Peking in 1900 that followed on from the Boxer Rebellion. In the First World War he served for two years with the RA on the staff of the Anzac Corps, was mentioned in dispatches three times and awarded the DSO. He had always been a keen card and bridge player and invented his own one club system. Once back in London he made his home at Crockford's Club of which he was co-founder and later chairman and very much the dominant personality. This brief pen portrait of him by Hubert Phillips describes this well:

Here, at some hours of the day, and almost any hour of the night – never aloof, never unsympathetic, yet never losing his air of half-ironical detachment – 'Pops' presides over the gilded rooms. He will sit down to a rubber at three in the morning as little ruffled as at three in the afternoon. As he plays the hand, a stream of dry, *sotto voce* comments keeps the game on his own detached plane. 'What's that fellow up to now? – have I returned the wrong suit? – looks good to me' and so on. He is not, in conversation, a fluent or pedantic talker; in fact he somewhat resembles, to my mind, the sahib as presented by, say, Kipling:

> But sometimes, in a smoking-room,
> 'mid clouds of 'haws' and 'hums',
> Obliquely and by inference
> illumination comes.

But behind his vague and at times indeterminate 'patter' ('You know what these fellas are') lurks a shrewd intelligence and a very gallant spirit.

Beasley wrote various books about bridge – notably *The Beasley Contract Bridge System* (1935) and for many years he was bridge correspondent of the *Daily Mail*. He wrote up his own account of the Culbertson match entitled *Beasley v. Culbertson*, which listed all the hands played and gave his comments on the match. In later years he became closely associated with the Hamilton Club, just off Park Lane, which had been founded by Baron Repelaer and, until it closed in the early 1960s, was considered the main bridge club in London.

Sir Guy Domville, his usual partner, was a popular society figure in London, debonair and accomplished at many sports. He was a motor-racing enthusiast and a keen and expert card player. George Morris and Percy Tabbush were less well-known, though Morris, an active sportsman, had once made an attempt to swim the English Channel. Tabbush later did something many bridge players threaten to do but few have had the nerve to carry out – he joined a monastery.

Lady Rhodes was well-known both in her own right as a player and as the founder and organizer of the Lady Rhodes Bridge School in Tite Street, Chelsea. Graham Mathieson featured less than the others mainly because he fell through a glass roof on the Wednesday of the match and had to be rescued hanging on to an iron girder by one hand over a forty-foot drop!

The first day went spectacularly well for the English team and they ended the day 1,170 points up, but the Americans were not too despondent. Culbertson had told his team before the match to take it slowly and play themselves in until they got used to the conditions and the opposition. After all, it was a 300-board match and he was confident that his superior teamwork and bidding ability would see them through in the long run. In most of his major tournament matches he was behind on the first sessions. His secret weapon, the 4/5 no trump convention, which this match was to put to the test and which resulted from his conclusion that tournament success frequently hinged on accurate slam bidding, had yet to be properly used.

The convention worked as follows: a four no trump bid was always forcing and promised either three aces, or two aces and the king of a suit previously bid by the partnership. The responses were – holding two aces, or one ace and all the kings of genuinely bid suits, bid five no trumps, inviting a slam. Holding no ace, bid five of the lowest genuinely bid suit. Holding one ace, usually bid the ace suit (but if this was the lowest bid suit, a jump to six was necessary).

This system was a rival to Blackwood or rather they evolved simultaneously. Easley Blackwood devised his convention in or about 1933 but did not submit it for official recognition until 1935 when he wrote to *Bridge World* asking them to publish an article entitled 'Wormwood Convention by Ernest Wormwood' written under this pseudonym as he was then manager of an insurance agency in Indianapolis. Involvement in high-risk activities like bridge would not have looked too good from a business point of view! *Bridge World* did not print his article on the grounds that their subscribers might interpret it as a recommended change in the Culbertson System. Despite this rebuff, his convention continued to gain in popularity. Eventually, in September 1938, *Bridge World* published an article on it which was tantamount to giving it official recognition. A couple of years after this Culbertson, on a trip to Indianapolis, looked up Easley Blackwood to present him with a copy of his recently-published autobiography. The inscription read, 'To my friend, Easley Blackwood, whom I'm trying hard to digest in my system, Ely Culbertson.' Culbertson had made a fortune out of his books describing his conventions, whereas Blackwood never made a penny out of his. As Richard Frey later wrote, 'Of course there is no such thing as patenting a bid and collecting a royalty on it, but if Blackwood had a nickel for every time his bid was properly used he'd be a rich man indeed; if he had a nickel for every time it was misused, he'd be a multimillionaire.'

The second day of the Beasley match saw the English start off by almost doubling their lead, but gradually the Americans began to pull back and they ended the day only 1,440 points behind. It had been another blazing hot day in London and Culbertson claimed to have been more worried by his loss of five pounds in weight than the few hundred odd points at the table. Certainly he seemed to have consumed a record amount of Vichy water, his favourite beverage, during the course of the day.

On the third day, Wednesday, 19 July, the score fluctuated first one way then another, but the tide was steadily turning in the Americans' favour. At the end of the day's play they were only 320 points behind. On the Thursday they really surged ahead and were 5,640 points clear at the end of the day's play. They increased their lead over the next two days, from 9,150 points at the close of play on Friday night to 10,900 points ahead by the time the match ended on Saturday night.

Their victory had been decisive. Hubert Phillips, writing for the *News Chronicle*, was present throughout and put it down to three main factors – superior teamwork, the avoidance of unnecessary risks when vulnerable (and consequently being prepared to risk more when non-vulnerable) and the greater precision in slam-bidding. The record of play seems to confirm this. The American team, especially Culbertson and Lightner, did understand and play better as a partnership than their counterparts. Their years of tournament experience to-

gether and understanding of each other's system bidding stood out.
The English were not always so fortunate. Take this hand played on
the Friday as an example:

North–South vulnerable
Dealer East

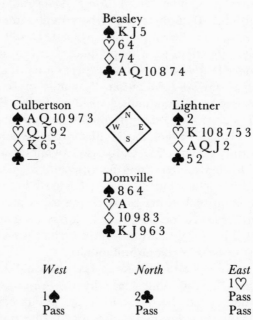

Beasley
♠ K J 5
♡ 6 4
◇ 7 4
♣ A Q 10 8 7 4

Culbertson
♠ A Q 10 9 7 3
♡ Q J 9 2
◇ K 6 5
♣ —

Lightner
♠ 2
♡ K 10 8 7 5 3
◇ A Q J 2
♣ 5 2

Domville
♠ 8 6 4
♡ A
◇ 10 9 8 3
♣ K J 9 6 3

The bidding:

South	West	North	East
			1♡
Pass	1♠	2♣	Pass
2♡	Pass	Pass	Pass

Domville later claimed he was using the relatively new idea of bidding
an opponent's suit to show first-round control of it. But since he had
not made this bid at the first opportunity, Beasley assumed Domville's
bid was genuine and Lightner's earlier heart bid was a bluff. Beasley
later admitted he should have kept the bidding open to find out more,
but he passed and Domville, as South, went down seven, winning
only the ace of hearts for a penalty of 1,750 points.

Culbertson was as busy away from the card-table as he was at it.
He had met an English friend of his, Fraser Mackenzie, who had been
moaning how far the English were behind the Americans in everything as witnessed by the recent American victories in sport. Culbertson protested that this wasn't necessarily the case and to prove his
point bet him a hundred pounds that the 'slow English' could produce
a complete book on the match and have it ready for sale in the
bookshops within forty-eight hours of the match ending. Mackenzie
took the bet.

Culbertson then went to see the editor of the *News Chronicle*, Tom
Clarke, and explained what he hoped to do. The newspaper had

already made a loose arrangement with him for a book about the match, as well as a daily article. They were keen to outdo their arch rival, the *Daily Mail*, who had Beasley under contract. When Clarke heard Culbertson's new proposal he was horrifed. He simply couldn't see how Culbertson expected to produce the book in such a short space of time, and when he was going to get any sleep? The last session's play was not due to end until after midnight.

'Just give me the required men on day-and-night shifts for the duration of the match and I'll do it,' Culbertson told him.

Clarke reluctantly agreed.

So began a remarkable saga of endurance and persistence. The match began on Monday 17 July. After the final session had ended at about one a.m., Culbertson hurried off to a special room set aside for him at Selfridges where a night secretary and two assistants were waiting. He then systematically went through the fifty hands played during that day analysing each of them and dictating his comments on both bidding and play to the secretary. The typescript was then rushed from Oxford Street to the printers in Suffolk Lane, Upper Thames Street about two miles away in the City of London. There the galley proofs were set up and sent back to Oxford Street to be checked by Culbertson. In the meantime he had busied himself writing his two syndicated articles for American newspapers, his article for the *News Chronicle* and, with what minutes were left, preparing his two transatlantic radio broadcasts scheduled for later that week. By now it was nearly five a.m. He read through the proofs, made one or two corrections and then sent them back to the printers. Eventually he got back to his hotel at about eight a.m.

Next day he was up at noon, breakfasted at his hotel, and, carnation in buttonhole, was back on parade again at the bridge-table before three p.m. He kept up this frenetic pace all week, despite occasional twinges of his stomach ulcer. Sometimes he had to forego his dinner to gain extra time. Towards the end of the week, he was so confident of the American victory that he wrote out in advance the introduction to his book explaining why his team had triumphed!

The whole episode was a tribute to his determination, and bore out one of the basic precepts in his life – that when an important opportunity occurred in life, it had to be seized with both hands and with all haste. Machiavelli, his mentor in these matters, would have been proud of him! Almost incredibly the book was completed on schedule. The match finished on Saturday evening, 22 July, and the book was out on the bookstalls by two o'clock on the following Monday afternoon, thirty-six hours later.

It was a stupendous effort. The book itself, *Contract Bridge Champion-*

ship of 1933 (*News Chronicle*), hard-bound in a red cover, contains nearly four hundred pages. It lists every single hand played, the full bidding and, where important, the play of the cards; Culbertson added his own comments on the bidding and play of each hand. Such an outstanding *tour de force* deserves a special place in the annals of publishing.

Hardly had Culbertson drawn breath from the exertions of both the Beasley match and the *News Chronicle* book than he was running a three-day Teachers Convention at the Grosvenor House Hotel in London from Tuesday 25 July until Thursday 27 July. This convention, run along the same lines as the American ones with examinations held at the end and certificates given to teachers who qualified, was an important publicity move on his part and helped put the Culbertson organization on the map in England. Culbertson was on the platform for about eighty per cent of the time – an exhausting timetable but he was the one they had all come to see. Two more bridge matches were played as well. The first was a thirty-two board match on Monday 24 July against a British *Bridge World* team consisting of Beasley, Domville, Hubert Phillips and Bernard Westall and held at the De La Rue offices in Bunhill Row, E.C.1. next door to the Culbertson headquarters in London. The Culbertson side won by 2,690 points. On the Friday afternoon he started on a weekend match at the Savoy Hotel against a team organized by Captain Miller Mundy, who unfortunately had to retire from playing himself through bronchitis. The Culbertson team were beginning to show signs of battle fatigue by now and the standard of play was very erratic. Indeed, it almost became a contest to see which side could throw away the most points. The match was eventually abandoned when the American team was 7,300 points in the lead.

So the gruelling schedule was over. It had been just over three weeks since they first arrived in Paris and they had been playing bridge virtually non-stop. Culbertson had lived on a high throughout – it was one of those periods when his adrenalin was flowing and he had driven himself almost flat out for the whole duration. When he looked back on his trip to England, he had to consider it an outstanding success. He had triumphed in the international match, had introduced his new 4/5 no trump Convention into international competition with very favourable results, had set up a strong nucleus for his organization in England and made, he estimated, over half a million converts in England to the Culbertson System, many of whom would now go out and buy his books appearing in England under the Faber and Faber imprint.

ENTREPRENEUR

Aside from his bridge successes, Culbertson was frequently involved in litigation. In 1933 Culbertson found himself in the courts on no less than three separate occasions. The first was the Hall Downes case. Hall Downes was a Pittsburg Contract bridge teacher who chose to write a book called *The Contract Bridge Self-Teacher* which drew extensively on the Culbertson System. Culbertson was furious. To him it looked like downright plagiarism. Here was an out-of-towner, a nobody, who had the gall to use his system as if it were his own. Culbertson retaliated by publishing, under the *Bridge World* imprint, *Culbertson's Own Self-Teacher*, with a deliberately similar format to Hall Downes's book. He also warned bookshops not to touch the Hall Downes book 'on pain of legal action'.

Hall Downes filed a suit in the Supreme Court on 12 June 1933 to bring an injunction against Culbertson and *Bridge World* their claim to be sole owners of the Culbertson System of Contract bridge bidding. He also alleged unfair competition on their part by producing a book that adopted every feature of Downes's book even down to size and number of pages.

The case came before Supreme Court Justice Sheintag on 10 July. The judge had to admit that he knew nothing about Contract bridge, and appointed a lawyer, H. D. Nims, to act as referee in his place. Nims's findings were not made public until April 1934. He took the view that the name Culbertson had now become public property so far as its use in books and tracts on bridge systems was concerned, and he therefore recommended that the injunction be granted. The case had important repercussions legally. The decision that Culbertson's name was now part of the public domain became a precedent for similar copyright proceedings.

The second case involved Shepard Barclay, who had been general manager of *Auction Bridge* magazine in 1929 shortly before it collapsed. He had remained a bridge journalist on various newspapers including the *New York Herald Tribune*. In March 1933 he wrote an article for the *Saturday Evening Post* entitled 'The First Ten in Contract Bridge for 1932/3'. This list ominously omitted the name of Culbertson. Culbertson, in Hollywood at the time, was sent the article and immediately gave instructions to demolish Barclay's reputation. The June issue of *Bridge World* accordingly carried an article entitled 'Rank Ranking of Rankers' written by G. M. C., a pseudonym regularly used in *Bridge World* that most people assumed stood for 'Great Man Culbertson', but actually, as Bill Huske revealed, stood for 'Give Me Credit'! This article questioned heavily Barclay's motivation for writing the article: 'In these days when it is so hard to keep the wolf from the door, one can hardly blame anyone for compiling anything about anybody that will attract enough attention to yield the compiler a couple of weeks' sustenance...'

Nor did they consider Barclay's bridge reputation sacred: 'Going beneath the verbiage, we discover that Mr Barclay is, as a bridge player, mediocre – so mediocre that, as he would probably admit, he is not even a runner-up for a place on the list containing 5,000 "champions".' What authority, therefore, did he have to compile a list without Culbertson's name on it? Such a list was 'a silly and futile thing' and simply a 'light occupation for the unemployed'.

Any libel lawyer must have whistled through his teeth on reading this and it was not long before Shepard Barclay slapped down a writ suing Culbertson for $100,000 libel damages, which Culbertson naturally contested. The case didn't come up until 6 October when the court found that the offending passages in the article were indeed libellous and ordered Culbertson to file a new answer for them. But, in the ensuing interval, the case seemed to lose impetus. It lingered on for a few months with no conclusive outcome. In the end it was settled with nothing but counsel fees and court costs to pay. Perhaps neither side regretted the extra publicity it brought, as each gained from it.

The third case came up a month later when Culbertson was sued for another $100,000 by one Edgar Hayman of 160 West 77th Street New York, for alleged breach of contract. Hayman claimed that in May 1932 Culbertson had agreed to publish Hayman's own book *Culbertson's Contract Bridge for Husbands and Wives* on a royalty basis, but in fact had never done so. Hence the suit. But this was quickly dismissed as frivolous. The publicity band-wagon had rolled far enough. By now, Culbertson's life was a hectic mixture of bridge, business and social activities. He was centre stage in all three at once. The next enterprise was to test him to the full.

Culbertson later looked back on the Kem card venture as the most exciting, and nerve-wracking business-deal of his entire career. One morning late in 1933 at breakfast-time, Culbertson was in his apartment at the Sherry-Netherland, when the maid let in two foreign-looking gentlemen, both strangers to him. She was a new maid and had not known about his express instructions not to be disturbed early in the morning. The first to introduce himself was Siegfried Klausner who was brandishing a pack of playing-cards in his hands. With him was his assistant Robert Caro.

'At last, Herr Culbertson, we manage to talk to you. We've been trying to see you for two months.'

'Why didn't you go and see my merchandising man?'

'We've seen him already.'

'Did he turn you down?'

'Yes. Only you, Mr Culbertson, have the imagination for this.'

Such an opening gambit was bound to appeal to Culbertson and he listened to Klausner's story intently.

Klausner was a Viennese who, a few years before, had invented a new process for manufacturing playing-cards out of plastic acetate. The pack he was carrying in his hand was an example of this. Normally, acetate cellulose is transparent but Klausner had devised a means of making it opaque, which gave playing-cards better durability. Klausner, himself a chemist and keen bridge player, had limited resources. After patenting his invention in Austria and selling shares in it to various individuals and companies, he decided he had a much better chance of getting his invention taken on in America than in Europe, and so he sold off his Austrian patent to Piatnik, the Austrian firm of card manufacturers.

Hearing this Culbertson first thought he might do a deal along similar lines with the us Playing-Card Company with whom he had good contacts. They held a ninety per cent monopoly of the manufacture of playing-cards in the usa, and might well be prepared to put forward a sizeable sum to buy out this new invention and kill it stone dead, as presumably Piatnik had done in Austria. But as Klausner went on talking something else stirred in Culbertson's mind. He sympathized with him as a European struggling to make his way in America, remembering his own early years and efforts to get established. Now he knew much more about American business methods, and could foresee distinct commercial possibilities. Culbertson studied the samples Klausner showed him. The printing on them was coarse and the backs looked ordinary and poorly-designed, but when he picked them up and shuffled them he noted their fine snap and the smoothly textured sheen on the face-side.

Hitherto, playing-cards had been made of paper stuck together (pasteboards), and usually made oversize so that they could be trimmed down when dirty. But here were cards that offered the possibility of much more. They promised to be long-lasting and good to use. Not only did they need no trimming but they could be washed as well, making them virtually germ-proof, unlike their paper counterparts. Of course they would be more expensive than existing cards. But Culbertson's view was that, in America, you could sell anything for any price so long as it was good. Sold for $3, as opposed to twenty cents for a paper deck, they would need to last twenty times longer. Klausner assured him they would.

The more Culbertson looked at them, the more he could visualize the cards in a streamlined version to suit the American market. Despite the early hour and the unwelcome intrusion, he told Klausner he would do business with him. Their initial agreement was for Klausner and Caro to have a seventy-five per cent holding and Culbertson twenty-five per cent. That afternoon Ely got in touch with a personal friend of his, Jack Dreyfus, President of the Celanese Corporation, to ask him to supply them with acetate cellulose. He explained how Klausner had been to see him, but Dreyfus warned him that it might be difficult to arrange, as his firm had a cartel agreement with a German firm linked to Piatnik. Culbertson kept at him over the next few days and eventually got Dreyfus to agree.

Now that he was taking charge, Culbertson wanted the deal recast. He suggested a corporation be set up with his having the seventy-five per cent holding and Klausner twenty-five per cent. Klausner was in no position to argue and had to agree. Next, Culbertson undertook to locate a printer, not an easy task, as printing on opaque cellulose was in those days an undeveloped technique. Eventually he found the Western Playing-Card Company, who agreed to take on the contract.

He never had any doubts about merchandising. He already had his established chain of distribution and outlets via his bridge organization and bridge teachers, as well as the many department stores throughout the USA where he had lectured at various times during the past two or three years. Later on, Culbertson was able to boast that he had made Kem cards known nationwide, without the aid of a single salesman. But Culbertson also brought to the enterprise his own unique method of financing. Rather than go through the tiresome business of regular accounts and balance-sheets, he hoped to finance the whole operation out of income (which at that time was running at well over $250,000 per annum). This, as could be expected, led to all sorts of complications, not least his rupture with Mrs Farrelly at Crockford's Club.

In business matters, Culbertson was an unashamed optimist. Economic forecasting was based on the unshakeable principle that everything would come right in the end. Fortunately his income stood up to it initially. Albert Morehead, his right-hand man, later calculated that for the year 1933 to 1934, the joint income of Ely and Josephine amounted to over $350,000 per annum, made up of (the figures are approximate) $140,000 from royalties on his books (mainly the best-selling Culbertson summary), $135,000 for his movie shorts, $40,000 in other royalties, $22,000 for newspaper and magazine articles, $10,000 for lectures and $10,000 for miscellaneous endorsements.

A major boost to the Kem cards campaign was the arrival in early 1935 of Richard Frey to the *Bridge World* organization. Previously advertising manager for a clothing manufacturer, he had been approached by Albert Morehead and offered the post as Sales Manager for Kem cards. He could hardly refuse from a financial point of view, as the pay was $300 per month – though it meant he had to give up being a member of the Four Aces team, of which he was a founder-member. He duly resigned, not without a little acrimony as he soon found his name taken off the cover of their about-to-be published book, *The Four Aces System*, to which he had made a sizeable contribution, and he was given only a short acknowledgement in the preface. Frey became a long-time contributor to *Bridge World*, writing the Tops and Bottoms column, but his immediate task was to look after the sales of Kem cards. Culbertson agreed to give him a one per cent share in the company (Albert Morehead was already on ten per cent of all the Culbertson enterprises).

But hard as they tried to promote Kem cards, the expected breakthrough never came. The American public resisted the idea of paying that much for a single pack of cards. Culbertson was worried as he had staked heavily in Kem cards. His financial position took a turn for the worse and he was forced to cut down dramatically on his business and living expenses.

Then, like a *deus ex machina*, Theodore W. Herbst suddenly appeared. Herbst was a German by birth who had lived in the USA for some years and in 1931 married Cynthia Kuser, the daughter of a prominent and wealthy senator from New Jersey. They lived in Barnardsville, New Jersey, and mixed with a rich and affluent social set. It was this as much as any strong business sense that was a direct cause of Herbst's interest in Kem cards. Herbst did not have a job so that when, as often happened, they were invited on friends' yachts and to country-houses, and businessmen there began to discuss their latest acquisitions and dealings, Herbst felt very left out. He resolved to find himself a business. Through Robert Caro whom he knew personally, he heard that Kem cards was going through a difficult stage and sought out an introduction to Culbertson.

Culbertson initially remained cool and impassive. He enquired about Herbst's background and his reasons for wanting to buy Kem cards. Then he decided on a campaign of subtle psychological warfare, or rather a campaign of nerves directed against Herbst and his advisers. For the best part of 1935 there were manoeuvres and counter-manoeuvres, approaches made, a tentative price suggested, and then the matter was dropped for weeks, even months. Culbertson based all this on his view that the longer he waited and delayed, the more Herbst would want to buy the company. When, eventually, in January 1936 an offer of $300,000 was made, Culbertson unhesitatingly turned it down. Jo and his business associates were surprised and dismayed. To them it seemed a fair price. Kem cards might eventually be worth more but its present financial state was in such a parlous condition, with a floating debt of $200,000, that a sale for $300,000 seemed like a godsend. But Culbertson would not hear of it. He wanted more, much more. Moreover, he sensed that the other side had heard of his financial difficulties and were trying to buy him out cheap – nothing was more likely to offend his pride and compel him to hold out even longer.

The atmosphere changed from parlour bridge to a game of barroom poker. If he lost, Culbertson would be several hundred thousand dollars worse off, but if he won, he would make a fortune. He decided to up the ante and told Herbst that the company was worth at least one million dollars, take it or leave it. Weeks and many anxious hours passed in the Culbertson camp before he got a reply. Their best offer, they stated, was $400,000. Culbertson reckoned this was a tactical mistake on their part. The sudden jump of $100,000 revealed their unmistakable intention to buy. Jo, however, by now was getting desperate. She berated him for putting their and the children's welfare at risk. As she saw it, this sum would not only pay their debts but leave them $200,000 besides. But Culbertson turned a deaf ear to her entreaties.

Two months elapsed and even he became nervy. His creditors were pressing. Then came a final offer of $500,000, cash, for all the rights.

'Gentlemen,' Culbertson told Herbst and his associates, 'you're getting warmer, but you're not hot enough.'

The other side were furious. As they rose to go, one of them said, 'Well, Mr Culbertson, I guess that ends the matter,' and threw the proposed agreement on the floor. Culbertson took this as a good sign. 'Did you see the way they threw that agreement on the floor and not at me? It shows they're still interested,' he commented.

Another three months passed. By now it was January 1937. All around him everyone feared the opportunity had been lost for good. But Culbertson still held on. His intuition told him they were still interested. His view all along had been that Herbst was emotionally committed to buying Kem for reasons of social prestige, and would not want to back down now. Money, so far as Herbst was concerned, was not the main issue. In the meantime Culbertson upped the stakes by putting in a couple of home-made 'forcing bids'. First he let it be known that another company, a phantom buyer, was interested in Kem. Then he made sure the newspapers announced that he and Josephine were due to leave for Europe in the spring of 1937 to play in the World Championships in Budapest.

His strategy had the desired effect. Ten days later an offer of $600,000 came through – again in cash. 'Gentlemen,' he told them, 'you're getting hot, but not hot enough.'

Finally, in frustration, they asked him to name his price – something he had been careful to avoid doing all these months.

'My price is $600,000 cash, and . . .'

They waited.

'. . . you'll want to use my name and experience, won't you?'

'Of course. But we won't pay a cent more.'

'That's up to you. But I wouldn't be doing justice to my name and business sense if I took less than five per cent gross on all the money received by you.'

'For one year?'

'No,' Culbertson said blandly. 'For fifteen years.'

They snorted, muttered 'ridiculous' and walked out.

This time Culbertson's nerves really were on edge. Jo pleaded ceaselessly, and even Al Morehead was frantic. Culbertson waited tensely at home. The next evening they returned and said they would do business.

In the end, the price was lowered by ten per cent in return for a fifteen-year personal royalty on Kem cards. Lawyers on both sides were closeted for twenty-four hours before the final contract was drawn up. Culbertson was taking no chances on a last-minute change of mind! The revenue from Kem cards was to become his main source of income almost up to the time of his death.

By the mid-1930s, Culbertson had assembled a formidable staff at *Bridge World*. The key figures were Albert Morehead as editor, and Alphonse Moyse, Alfred Sheinwold and Sam Fry as technical editors. When Al Sobel joined the staff in 1937, a cry of 'Al' from the editor-in-chief was likely to bring any one of four Als running! Albert

Morehead joined the *Bridge World* staff in 1932, and after becoming its technical director in 1933, was made editor the following year and general manager of all Culbertson enterprises. From then on he became Culbertson's right-hand man and most trusted adviser. As these expanded, so did Morehead's involvement. He was a director of Crockford's Club, of Kem cards, of the USBA and had a hand in writing most of the Culbertson books from 1933. For *Bridge World* he wrote both under his own name or used pseudonyms like Turner Hodges (two of his family names). His column 'Paragraphs' loosely resembled the *New Yorker's* 'Talk of the Town' feature and was always entertaining. He was a tall, saturnine figure, always seemingly relaxed and assured, a cigarette permanently in his hand (a likely cause of his early death in 1966, aged fifty-seven). He was widely liked and respected, and had a rare gift for friendship. Many leading bridge players of the time considered him their closest friend. He was accomplished in many fields, was an expert lexicographer and from 1935 until the end of 1963, was bridge correspondent for the *New York Times*, a post he originally acquired through his friendship with the Ochs family, fellow Southerners like him.

The standard of writing in the magazine was high, though who did it depended mainly on who was in the office at the time. Certainly most of Culbertson's and Jo's articles were ghosted by one or other of the staff. The technical editors were often called upon to write Culbertson's syndicated articles that appeared in the *Chicago Tribune* and the *New York Daily News* under the title 'The Daily World of Bridge'. Sam Fry recalls having to write fourteen syndicated articles a week, seven for Culbertson and seven for Jo. If Fry was not there, Alfred Sheinwold would write them. Once, Sheinwold was in the office, having completed his stint in what seemed record-breaking time, and was bragging to the office staff about beating Sam Fry's record by dictating the week's articles in one hour and ten minutes when he heard a cough behind him. It was the editor-in-chief: 'Sheinwold, you're fired.'

It was not the first or last of Sheinwold's hirings and firings. He joined *Bridge World* in December 1934 as technical editor soon after it moved to its new offices in the old RCA building in the Rockefeller Centre. Initially, he was paid the not-so-princely wage of $25 per week, but for a young (he was then only twenty-two years old) and aspiring bridge writer, this was quite a coup. For anyone in his position and for many others besides, *Bridge World* was the 'only show in town'. He had learnt his bridge in college and it was while playing in New York bridge clubs that he had met Al Morehead who recruited him. Sheinwold's first article, entitled 'O Tempora', appeared in the

December 1934 issue. Lilian Brunesen, the circulation manager, came into his office shortly afterwards with a sheaf of mail for him and Sheinwold's eyes lit up at the sight of so much immediate fan-mail. He picked up the first letter on the pile and read, 'I have read Mr Sheinwold's article. This is not how I play bridge, nor do I want to play this way. Please cancel my subscription.' So much for a flying start!

Sheinwold's relationship with his boss Culbertson was never easy. The first of his firings set the tone for the others. One of his first duties was to proofread copy from other contributing bridge writers and this meant dealing with the writers in person. One or two of these let it be known that they had not yet been paid for previous articles. Sheinwold rashly mentioned this to Culbertson, whose immediate response was, 'I don't like your tone. You're fired!' Culbertson took the view that money should only be paid out under dire emergency and then only to key suppliers. Sam Fry remembered trying to get some money he was owed by Culbertson when he was about to go into the army and he had to leave his wife and young son behind. Culbertson owed him $300 and Fry needed the money for his wife while he was in service. He approached Culbertson about it. Culbertson listened sympathetically and called his secretary over, 'Miss Hazen, see that two bottles of milk are delivered every day to Mr Fry's household.' Only much later did he agree to pay the $300, at the rate of $50 per month.

Sheinwold was soon reinstated. However, $25 a week was not very much to get along with, particularly when, for instance, the cost of a dinner-jacket (obligatory for him at Crockford's in the evening) also amounted to $25. One morning in 1935, Culbertson had gone out on his famous shopping expedition to Sulka's on Fifth Avenue, and managed to spend $5,000 on shirts, pyjamas, neckties and other accessories. After lunch, he was telling everyone in the office about his escapade. Sheinwold, encouraged by such signs of largesse, felt emboldened to ask for a rise from $25 to $35. Wrath descended on him and he was summarily fired a second time.

Had he wanted, Sheinwold could have taken his revenge on Culbertson. When the draft of the *Red Book* was finally completed Culbertson asked him to proofread it from a literary and bridge point of view. As he read through the proofs, he exploded into laughter at one point. Culbertson was writing about the principle of preparedness and how essential it was to get the timing right in bridge. Culbertson's prose rolled by, drawing high-flown comparisons: 'The bullet winging its way to its target, the graceful feet of the classical dancer in their exquisite struggle with the blunt law of gravitation, the juggler with his balls in the air...' Sheinwold was sorely tempted to leave

this last phrase in, but, considerately, changed it to the more inno-
cuous 'Indian Clubs in the air' – as it now appears in the finished
version.

Another member of staff at *Bridge World* to cross swords with Culbertson was George Beynon, recruited by Culbertson in 1935 as his
press agent. Beynon started life as a professional hockey-player in
Hamilton, Ontario. After studying music at La Scala, Milan and
directing orchestras in Europe and America, he was quick to spot the
possibilities of the movie industry, then in its infancy, and devised a
method of synchronizing music with silent films, becoming musical
director for Griffith's *Birth of a Nation* (1915). Indeed, he did so well
out of the movie business that he was able to retire to East Orange,
New Jersey in 1917. Forced out of retirement in 1929 after the Wall
Street crash he made a new career in bridge directing games in New
Jersey and writing a Newark bridge column. In 1935, he joined the
Culbertson organization. Initially, all went well. Then, after a few
months, Culbertson told Beynon he had no further use for his services.

'What about our year's contract?' Beynon asked.

'Don't talk to me about contracts,' Culbertson replied. 'Sue me, if
you like. Maybe you'll win and maybe not. But if you're ever broke,
call me.'

Beynon could not afford to sue so he had to accept his dismissal.
Months later, stranded somewhere in the hinterlands of the USA Beynon remembered Culbertson's offer and rang him asking for $75.
Much to Beynon's astonishment, the money arrived in two hours. A
few years later, Beynon tried to return the loan.

'You don't owe me a cent,' protested Culbertson. 'Don't talk to me
about money. But tell me, how are your tournaments going ...?'
Beynon was at that time ACBL Field Tournament Director.

The story is revealing in that it shows how varied and unpredictable
Culbertson's generosity was. Beynon later moved to St Petersburg,
Florida, in 1955 where he wrote a weekly bridge column for the *St
Petersburg Times*. He was still writing it on his hundredth birthday and
could justifiably claim at that moment to be the oldest working news-
paperman in America. He died in 1965 at the age of 101.

For Culbertson the characteristically 1930s notion of conspicuous
consumption became almost second nature. He owned a Rolls-Royce
but allegedly gave it away when in 1934 it was replaced by a Due-
senberg. He travelled *super de luxe*, wore the most expensive clothes
and could never resist buying expensive watches and gold cigarette
cases. Jo too enjoyed the fruits of their success. She sported an impressive solitaire diamond on one finger. Every summer in Europe she
filled her wardrobe by visits to the couturiers in Paris. Once, in

1937, they were held up at the frontier into Turkey as the customs officers were unable to believe that a couple of bridge players needed to travel with twenty-two pieces of luggage! Culbertson spent $7 a day on his own specially-made Melachrinos cigarettes, and was just as lavish in his choice of food and drink. But possibly his greatest extravagance, and in keeping with the Gatsbyesque era in which he lived, was the country estate at Ridgefield he bought for himself at the end of 1934.

Ridgefield is an attractive tree-lined Connecticut town about forty-five miles north-east of New York, dominated by a broad, main boulevard over ninety feet wide. It still retains an eighteenth-century feel about it. In earlier days, the town was the scene of the Battle of Ridgefield when in 1709 Benedict Arnold set up barricades against General Tryon's troops. Whether Culbertson conceived this as a good omen is less clear, for the only battles he fought there were in the law courts.

He came across Ridgefield in 1934 in his search for a country estate. Surrounding the town were many fine properties such as Sugar Hill, belonging to his later friends Henry and Clare Booth Luce, but the one that caught his eye was the F. E. Lewis estate on West Lane, about a mile from the centre of the town. Named implausibly by its millionaire owner, Upagainstit, it was set in sixty acres with a home farm attached. Lewis, a railway magnate, had reputedly spent $3,000,000 improving it, as was evident from the huge, glass-domed swimming-pool, with its sliding roof, the palatial greenhouses and the extensive gardens with exquisitely tended lawns running down to a lake full of swans and snapping turtles. Six cottages were included with the estate. The main house had forty-five rooms and enough accommodation, if needed, for twelve indoor servants.

Culbertson completed his purchase in December 1934 and paid $125,000 for the whole estate. The possession of a magnificent country estate was an essential requirement for a newly-arrived millionaire, which, on paper, Culbertson certainly now was. But he had other reasons as well for buying it – in the bridge field he wanted to emulate Vanderbilt with his mansion at Lantana, Sims with his Deal Estate and von Zedtwitz with large houses both in Deal and Florida. Then, harking back to his own childhood, when his first pretensions to grandeur were stirred by his mother's ambitions for him, he felt drawn to living, as his Russian forbears had done, in a seigneurial way, as lord of the manor.

In practice he used the estate much less than he might have done – it became more of a showpiece. Guests were invited for occasional week end house parties and it was used for the children as a summer residence. But it soon proved a costly place to run, demanding the sort of cash Culbertson was always short of. The swimming-pool, for all its glamour, cost $40 each time to fill and heat, and was therefore little used. The heating bill for the hot-houses alone ran to $500 per month in the winter months. Even the dairy farm was an expensive item. When a guest at breakfast once asked Culbertson for a glass of milk, he was offered champagne instead, as this was reckoned to be cheaper than home-produced milk. Matters were to get worse.

CULBERTSON v SIMS

At bridge, 1934 was noted principally for Culbertson's tussles, or rather non-tussles, with the Four Aces team. January 1934 saw the first USBA-sponsored Grand National Tournament played at the Hotel Pierre in New York. The winners were the Four Aces (Michael Gottlieb, Oswald Jacoby, David Burnstine, Howard Schenken and Richard Frey). Culbertson had strong hopes that his team would win the inaugural tournament but they were defeated in the semi-final. Indeed so confident was Culbertson of victory that he had pre-arranged a radio broadcast on NBC to follow on to the end of the tournament. When the Four Aces won, the broadcast had to go ahead just the same. He told Gottlieb and his team that he would simply introduce the programme and then they could say their piece. It was a fifteen-minute programme. They could each talk for two minutes and he would sum up at the end. They all gathered round the microphone and Culbertson started off but he simply would not or could not stop. He talked right through, extolling the merits of the Culbertson System so that listeners had to assume that a Culbertson team had won. After thirteen minutes, an exasperated David Burnstine leapt up and grabbed the microphone and blurted out: 'Mr Culbertson hasn't left us much time, just enough to say we are the Four Aces and *we* won the tournament and we *don't* play the Culbertson System.'

The Four Aces dominated tournament competition in the mid 1930s. Their first public appearance was at the Summer Nationals at Asbury Park in 1933 when they won the City of Asbury Park Trophy, later to become the Spingold. In 1934 they swept the board winning the Grand National Tournament in January, the Reisinger Team-of-Four at the Eastern Bridge Championships in March, the Spingold in September and the Vanderbilt in November. They felt entitled to consider themselves the champion team and hoped to knock Culbertson off his pedestal.

Culbertson had deliberately avoided meeting them. Like a champion boxer, he was careful these days to choose his opponents. The Four Aces offered him repeated challenges but he declined them all. They published a book on their system, *The Four Aces System of Contract Bridge*. Here Culbertson felt on surer ground and he immediately offered Mike Gottlieb a bet of $1,500 that their book would not sell more than 10,000 copies within a year. Gottlieb, not unreasonably in view of his team's tournament success, took the bet and set about promoting the book with all his professional experience as a real estate broker, personally visiting book-shops and chasing up sales wherever he could. But the sales never reached their target figure and Culbertson won his bet. The fact was that the public had become accustomed to Culbertson, they knew where they were with him and, however glamorous the Four Aces' success, they were in no mood to change horses. Irked by this setback, in August 1935 the Four Aces served Culbertson with a summons claiming that he had 'injured their chances of success as authors' by writing about them in *Bridge World* in a derogatory way. This slightly unworthy attempt on their part was deemed by Culbertson as a 'psychic bid for publicity' and he suggested instead that if they sued him for 'alienation of affection', they might stand a better chance of winning!

In October 1934 the Culbertson team defended their title in the second international Schwab trophy. This time the English team consisted of two experienced partnerships in Lederer and Rose, Ingram and Hughes against the American team of the Culbertsons, Lightner and Albert Morehead. The match was played over five days at the Dorchester Hotel in London. It was a 300-board match and Culbertson later called it 'the most gruelling and nerve-racking five days of play that I have ever experienced'. He rated the English team the most skilful of the four he had played against in international competitions over the past four years.

It was a close run thing. After the English had taken an early lead and looked set for a historic victory, their stamina began to give out over the last two days and the Americans snatched a win. Terence Reese in his *Bridge at the Top* (Faber, 1977) gives an entertaining and informative account of this match.

By the end of 1934 Culbertson felt it was time to stimulate public interest again in the Culbertsons as a bridge-playing married couple. His message came out in a radio broadcast for NBC on 14 December on a coast-to-coast hook-up. The Culbertsons, he told his listeners, were willing to take on a challenge from 'any pair in the world ... be it a team of Simses or a team of Aces with a few jokers, or half a dozen horsemen, not to count the few donkeys. All we ask is that a sufficient number of rubbers be played to ensure a real test of skill, that the match offer sufficient public interest, and that the challengers be of sufficiently high calibre. So long as my wife is in good health and not too busy with children, I don't believe I will lose a big match. Far from avoiding challenges, we are seeking them, and let this be a notice for any *bona fide* challenge from any logical candidate.'

A flood of offers came in, mostly from publicity-seekers, but on Christmas Eve the postman brought the letter he had been waiting for. It was from Hal Sims and stated:

> For years, you have been subtly instilling into the minds of a more or less unsuspecting public the idea that you and Mrs Culbertson are the leading pair in the world. After listening to your most recent boastful claims in the press and over the radio it occurred to me that you might be in a frame of mind to accept a challenge from Mrs Sims and myself. Contract is really a fascinating game, and I am sure that if you found the time to take it up, you would derive tremendous enjoyment from it.

Culbertson could not wait to reply:

> Your challenge is accepted with pleasure. All these years I have been itching to lay my bridge hands on you. At last you have emerged from your hiding-place to meet your master. Though I consider you one of the world's finest card players even your brilliancy cannot overcome the handicaps of your atrocious system. Let it be a real tough but clean fight to the finish.

The publicity machine was at full stretch and Culbertson entertained hopes of a repeat of the Lenz match.

Hal Sims had been one of Culbertson's earliest friends in the Auction bridge days at the Knickerbocker Whist Club in the early 1920s. They had taken to each other immediately, in spite of their many physical dissimilarities (Sims was big-boned and muscular, six foot four inches tall and weighed over 300 pounds), but they had much in common in other respects. They both liked to 'outsmart the other guy' and used whatever form of subterfuge or psychological advantage they could to achieve this. Culbertson remembered that when he first met Sims he could usually tell when the latter had a bad hand. If he had been dealt poor cards, Sims, like a true Southerner, would play possum and lapse into a dreamy silence. Someone would then have to nudge him and say, 'Come on, Hal, your bid. Wake up.' Then his big grey eyes would open sleepily, and he would mumble 'What's that? What? My bid?' and it wouldn't be hard to guess the state of his hand. Many a new partner trembled at the prospect of playing with him enough. On hot days he had a disconcerting habit of chewing ice throughout the afternoon. His technique, as his wife Dorothy related, would be to fix his new partner 'with a hungry glare, then let out a couple of roars, like a wounded lion in anticipation of the wrong that will shortly be done him and, in a tense silence, await results to prove his judgement correct'.

Tournament directors liked having both of them play in the same tournament. The sight of the two of them arguing ferociously across a table or, while spectating, trying to goad each other into a near rage was always good news value. But behind the apparent rivalry they were still friends, at least up till 1934. After a tournament, they were just as likely to go off together arm in arm to see a movie or eat in a restaurant, at Child's or at another one they liked, a chop suey joint near Columbus Circle.

Their wives had always remained friends. Dorothy Sims was a spectacular and unusual woman. Born in 1889, she was one of three talented and original sisters, daughters of Isaac L. Rice, a well-known lawyer, chess player and inventor, involved in the first manufacture of the submarine. Dorothy grew up at Asbury Park, New Jersey. Even at an early age, she was something of a rebel:

> At twelve, after a rather uneventful childhood, [she later wrote] I retired from school. The school took this in its stride. I was not a bad student – I was not a student at all. I saw no point to clogging my mind with things that everyone knew. Father and Mother were pleased at first to have me home. Father knew so much that ignorance fascinated him. He saw charm in it that stupid people overlooked. He called my spelling 'original' and 'phonetic'. I was delighted to have it appreciated. Only father could have made it sound so classical.

Her spelling never improved. Indeed her good friend George S. Kaufman, the playwright, joked about her spelling by telling her that there was only one 'z' in 'is', Dorothy's comment being: 'I thought this funny – till I thought it over.'

As a teenager she was known locally as the 'Red Devil' because of her prowess on the motorbike. By 1911 she was the US Women's Motorcycle Speed Champion. Once, had up for speeding and appearing before the local judge, she told him that, in modern traffic, it was safer to be reckless than careful; she followed much the same creed at the bridge-table. She was the first woman in the USA to hold a pilot's licence and it was through this that she met Hal Sims. At the outbreak of the First World War she joined Air Transport and came across Hal who was serving in the US Army Air Corps. They got married soon afterwards and eventually set up home at Deal, New Jersey, not far from where she had been brought up. In later years her devotion to speed mellowed and she founded the Anti-Noise Society.

It was to Deal that the Culbertsons had come for the summer of 1928. They had rented a cottage on the Sims estate there. This estate, on Roosevelt Avenue, overlooking the ocean, was something of a showplace with its ten bedrooms and hundred-foot combination living and dining-room. In the early 1930s, the Simses held celebrated bridge weekends there, managing at times to sleep as many as forty people in a state of modified chaos. This created, as Dorothy noted,

> slight trouble with servants. They came down in gangs from New York (we exhausted the Jersey supply early). We had Chinese, Filipinos, Swedes, and combinations; but when we found one that suited us, we didn't suit him. I suppose they felt like the butler Mother had on East 87th Street. He wanted to leave. Mother said, 'Why?' He said, 'This place is peculiar.' Mother said, 'But all places are peculiar.' He said he knew but ours was *very* peculiar.

Invitations to these weekends or bridge weeks were much sought after. Regulars there included Oswald Jacoby, Willard Karn, Walter Malowan, David Burnstine, Michael Gottlieb, Howard Schencken, Waldemar von Zedtwitz, Theodore Lightner, Sam Fry, Derrick Wernher, Dick Simon and many others. To quote their hostess again:

> All day and all night the games went on. Occasionally someone caught a train or went to bed, but there were always others getting up out of bed to replace them. The conversation was entirely devoted to 'hands' – the narrator's good ones and his partner's horrible plays, who chucked who, when and how. There was generally a courteous understanding that if you listened to someone, he must listen to you. There was talk for a while of hiring the unemployed for an audience.

The games varied in stakes from two-cents tables to ten- and twenty-cent games, and there were tournaments every so often.

So popular were these events that the Simses, to cater for the overflow and because they were 'sick of running a hotel', started up the Deal Club nearby. This was in a majestic frame building on the ocean front, designed by Stanford White, with a private pier and about thirty rooms, each elaborately furnished. Guests had to pay for their own accommodation and meals and Sims hired a chef and staff to look after them, but many found it too expensive and sought cheaper lodgings.

In 1928 the Culbertsons were very hard up and were grateful for Hal's generosity in renting them a cottage at minimal rent. Indeed it is probable that Sims lent Culbertson money once or twice at crucial times in the 1920s. People said afterwards that, as a result, Sims had a sort of Indian sign on Culbertson. Certainly when they fell out with each other in the early 1930s, there was an acrimony to their dispute that hardly seemed merited by the circumstances. For most of the year preceding the 1935 Sims–Culbertson match, they were hardly on speaking terms. Sims accused Culbertson of pinching bits of his and other people's systems and then including them in his new version of the Culbertson System. This hardly seems a justified allegation. Of course there was bound to be a certain amount of duplication among systems and Culbertson was always a great 'borrower' of ideas. Richard Frey remembers him coming into his office when he was working for him at *Bridge World* one morning and saying, 'Dick, Deeck, I have the most wonderful idea ...' and then proceeding to tell him something that Frey had suggested three weeks before.

That Sims was jealous of Culbertson's tournament success and the way his books and system had caught on was undeniable. In the early 1930s, the Sims-sponsored team, the Four Horsemen, had met with a certain amount of tournament success, easily winning the 1932 Vanderbilt and Asbury Park trophies and the 1933 Reisinger Trophy by a convincing margin. But they were then disbanded as two of the key members, Oswald Jacoby and David Burnstine – the other member being Willard Karn – were unwilling to be tied so closely to Sims's efforts to promote his own system in opposition to Culbertson's. Jacoby and Burnstine went on to form the Four Aces.

Sims made up a new team, mainly with his wife or Willard Karn, but his system never caught on in a big way. Sims described it in his books *Money Contract* (1932) and *Master Contract* (1934). It was really a system geared to Sims's own individual approach to bridge and his desire (of necessity in Dorothy's case) to dominate the partnership and permit him to play the hand. Its lack of success left him disgruntled and as a form of retaliation he refused to let *Bridge World* publish any articles on the Sims System.

Despite his too individualistic system, Sims was a naturally gifted bridge player. He had a remarkable memory and an incredibly sharp eye. He could summon up the laws of percentages at will. Once, playing in a tournament, he called off every card in both opponents' hands. Then he explained to the director of the tournament that the same board had been played several days before and not been reshuffled. At gin rummy this ability to memorize long sequences of cards made him warn challengers: 'It wouldn't be an equal contest. Unless you get a perfect shuffle some cards will stay in the same order they came up on the last hand. And I'm the kind of fellow who can't help remembering the exact order in which the cards turned up for the previous three deals.' At bridge, Sims was a masterful handler of dummy and a shrewd analyst of defence. Like his wife, Dorothy, he used psychics daringly and was always keen to outmanoeuvre an opponent in the bidding. Dorothy was less effective as a player, only

Crockford's Club and the Culbertsons' own apartment on upper floors at 14 and 16 East 62nd Street, New York.

Thirties-style bar at Crockford's, with Raymond Modolo in attendance and Culbertson keeping a watchful eye on the Schwab Trophy.

Main house on Ridgefield estate.

Webster cartoon

Hal and Dorothy Sims.

ELY CULBERTSON
*who accepts with pleasure the challenge
of P. Hal Sims to a Bridge battle that
will rival the Culbertson-Lenz match*

THE CHALLENGE

PHILIP HAL SIMS
DEAL, NEW JERSEY

December 20, 1934.

Mr. Ely Culbertson,
Editor In Chief of 'The Bridge World',
Radio City, New York, N. Y.

My Dear Culbertson:-

For years you have been subtly in-
stilling into the minds of a more or less unsuspecting
public the idea that you and Mrs. Culbertson are the
leading pair of the world. After listening to your most
recent boastful claims in the press and over the radio
it occurred to me that you might be in a frame of mind
to accept a challenge from Mrs. Sims and myself.

Conditions: CONTRACT BRIDGE.

Contract is really a fascinating game, and I am
sure that if you found the time to take it up, you
would eventually derive tremendous enjoyment from it.

Yours sincerely,

P. Hal Sims.

From the Bridge World, New York.

RELEASE TO ALL MORNING AND AFTERNOON NEWSPAPERS.

NEW YORK, December 28. Ely Culbertson, today, definitely
accepted a challenge for a Contract Bridge fight to a finish,
from P. Hal Sims of Deal, New Jersey, his bitter Bridge rival.
Mr. Culbertson's statement read:

"Dear Sims:
"Your challenge is accepted with
pleasure. All these years I have been itching
to lay my Bridge hands on you. At last you have
emerged from your hiding place to meet your master.

"Though I consider you one of the world's
finest card players, even your brilliancy cannot
overcome the handicap of your atrocious system.

"Let it be a real tough but clean fight
to the finish."

(signed) Ely Culbertson.

The detailed conditions of the match which include provisions for
possible fistic encounters are being worked out in a formal contract.

P. HAL SIMS
*who challenged Ely Culbertson to
prove his right to the title of leading
Contract Bridge player of the world*

IS ANSWERED

The Sims Challenge letters.

Oswald Jacoby and Al Morehead at a tournament.

Webster Cartoon

Ladies' Man!

Culbertson in London in 1938
shortly after his divorce.

Dorothy, his second wife, as 'Galatea'.

Family group in 1952. Culbertson with Dorothy, Bruce with his wife Carolyn, and Nadya's son Stephen.

passable as a declarer and fairish on defence, but she had flair and occasionally pulled off some stupendous contracts. If luck was running against her during a tournament or a match at Deal, she liked to put all the opposing women's hats on a bed to bring them bad luck!

From a publicity point of view, Culbertson had timed the match to coincide with the introduction of the latest version of his system in the *Red Book*. But even greater gain would come from demonstrating that two sets of married couples could play a long-drawn-out match harmoniously and with little cause for argument. Such a triumph of domestic bridge would reinforce the appeal of bridge to the ordinary player who, presumably, if the Culbertsons won, would go out and buy their books.

Culbertson drew up a contract for the match but had some trouble getting Sims to sign it. He did not despair. Dorothy noted, 'Ely never despairs. While you have life, he has hope.' Eventually Culbertson ran into Sims in a restaurant off Fifth Avenue and asked him to sign the agreement there and then. Sims was not keen to sign a contract away from a lawyer's office. Important documents, he reminded Culbertson, needed witnesses. Culbertson was not to be put off. He jumped up, surveyed the restaurant and spotted a man and a woman he knew in evening clothes. Before Sims could stop him he was across the room and returned with the two in tow. He had got his witnesses and Sims, admiring his nerve, had to sign.

The conditions of the match were arranged as follows: 150 rubbers to be played over twenty-one days, starting on 25 March 1935 with play in the afternoon from two-thirty to five and evening from nine to eleven-thirty, one rest day per week. The referee was to be the familiar figure of Lieutenant Alfred Gruenther. A large side bet, reputed to be nearly $10,000, was involved.

The Simses, with typical flamboyance, set up a training camp at the Molly Pitcher Hotel at Red Bank, New Jersey – following in the footsteps of the recent heavyweight champion boxer, Max Baer, who had trained at their oceanside home the previous spring in preparation for his Carnera fight. Someone said at the time that if he could handle the Sims group, he could handle Carnera! Their schedule involved getting up at nine a.m. (anathema to Sims) to go road jogging, followed by setting-up exercises. The whole Sims entourage, including the Great Dane, Duke, wore white turtle-necked sweaters with a large scarlet s on the front. They kept to a strictly controlled diet, had dry toast for dinner and then steeled themselves for some 'shadow bidding' with their sparring partners, Derrick Wernher, George Unger and others. Curfew was strictly enforced at eleven p.m.

Sims for all his bulk was a remarkably fit man; he had always been an all-round sportsman, a near-scratch golfer and skilled tennis player.

Culbertson, for his part, was forced to confine his training and roadwork to one-night stands on his pre-arranged lecture tour of the Middle West and Texas. For nearly a month he lectured twice a day, except when travelling from one town to the next. But before he left he made sure that the newspapers were already priming their readers for the match. Robert Neville of the New York *Herald Tribune*, who so assiduously reported the Lenz match, wrote setting the mood for the encounter: it was going to be 'a goat-getting, coffee-housing rodeo of the first water'.

The whole of the second floor at Crockford's Club was given over to the match. Special bridge furniture of modernistic tubular stainless aluminium was commissioned from the Warren McArthur Corporation of Park Avenue, for players and score-keepers alike. The latter were also given a block-rubber grip on each arm-rest either for writing the score on, or, it was suggested, for holding on to in moments of convulsive excitement. The bridge-table was extra-large in deference to Sims's giant frame. Size became an issue at a later stage of the contest when Culbertson, as part of his endless jockeying for position, insisted on drawing a chalk demarcation line under the table to mark where the legs of each of the contestants were allowed to be. Sims, squeezed for room, was not at all amused.

Play got under way rather belatedly on the evening of Monday, 25 March following a dinner at Crockford's for about thirty friends and associates. By the time they had finished their eight-course meal, with its *pièce de resistance* of *Poussin aux Olives* prepared by Raymond Modolo, it was nine forty-five p.m. Champagne had flowed liberally throughout the meal and compliments had flown almost as fast across the table between Ely and Hal. Culbertson managed to 'lose' a card on the first hand. A hurried search revealed that it had fallen under his chair! As the evening progressed the good-natured murmur from the spectators increased to such an extent that Culbertson complained that he could not hear the bidding and insisted that the kibitzers keep quiet and 'just look significant'. By the end of the first session the Simses had taken a lead of 2,200 points partly thanks to a small slam which Dorothy freely admitted she had bid up to make sure that Hal played the hand.

The second day started badly for the Culbertsons. Jo at one point managed to pass her partner's forcing bid. This was *lèse majesté* of the highest order, since forcing bids were the cornerstone of the Culbertson system. After Jo's mistake Culbertson seemed to go into a sort of trance and played in listless fashion for a while.

As the second day had seen no improvement in the Culbertson fortunes, in mid-afternoon Culbertson ordered his Crockford's house flag, bearing the apposite Latin motto 'Fair Play and Good Fortune' to be lowered to half-mast. There, it fluttered mournfully awaiting better times. And sure enough, in the evening session, Culbertson rose from his table and signalled to an attendant to hoist the flag to the end of its staff. A few moments later the night breeze caught it in a proud wave. The Culbertsons were now in the lead for the first time in the match by 130 points; a short while later they captured the rubber, eventually ending the day with a plus score of 1,750 points and never losing the lead again.

This match was conducted throughout with good humour. Communications between partners were always a rich source of entertainment to the spectators. Once, when the Simses went off three tricks in a three no trump contract, Hal reminded Dorothy, 'Darling, must I tell you every time you have a king and one in a suit that I have bid, you must raise?' 'But Hal I thought...' 'Thought,' thundered her husband. 'How many times have I told you not to think. Just do what I tell you!'

There was constant badinage and repartee between players. Each had his or her way of addressing the other. Sims called Culbertson 'Professor' and was himself called 'Maestro' or 'Petronius' by Culbertson. Dorothy's husband called her 'my sweet' or 'my angel', while Culbertson addressed Jo as 'darling' or 'sweetka' (Russian for the same thing, as he quickly explained). Culbertson was rather proud of his appellation for Sir Derrick Wernher, one of the main referees, or umpires – he kept calling him 'the British Empire'.

Name-calling reached its peak and bordered on adulation after this hand:

Neither side vulnerable
Dealer East

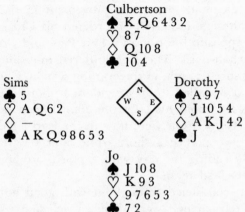

Culbertson
♠ K Q 6 4 3 2
♡ 8 7
♢ Q 10 8
♣ 10 4

Sims
♣ 5
♡ A Q 6 2
♢ —
♣ A K Q 9 8 6 5 3

Dorothy
♠ A 9 7
♡ J 10 5 4
♢ A K J 4 2
♣ J

Jo
♠ J 10 8
♡ K 9 3
♢ 9 7 6 5 3
♣ 7 2

Dorothy dealt and made a characteristic opening bid of one club on
the East hand. Sims bid seven clubs straight off and the contract was
made. As the last trick was played, Sims, in a husky voice charged
with emotion, declared 'My angel!' Then, after a moment's thought,
he added (fearing his first declaration had been inadequate), 'My
sweet!'

Some of the most interesting play of the match occurred in a running duel of wits that Jo and Sims engaged in midway though the
match. The final score was one victory each. Jo started matters off.

North–South vulnerable
Dealer North

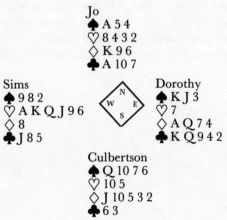

Jo
♠ A 5 4
♡ 8 4 3 2
♢ K 9 6
♣ A 10 7

Sims
♠ 9 8 2
♡ A K Q J 9 6
♢ 8
♣ J 8 5

Dorothy
♠ K J 3
♡ 7
♢ A Q 7 4
♣ K Q 9 4 2

Culbertson
♠ Q 10 7 6
♡ 10 5
♢ J 10 5 3 2
♣ 6 3

The bidding:

North	East	South	West
Pass	1♣	Pass	1♡
Pass	2◇	Pass	3♡
Pass	3NT	Pass	4♡
Pass	Pass	Pass	

Jo opened with the five of spades, Sims played dummy's three, and Culbertson's ten won the trick. A heart return put Sims in. He drew trumps and then led a club, which Jo won with the ace. She promptly led the four of spades. Sims gave the matter some thought, but finally decided that Jo would not underlead the same ace twice. So he played the jack, and the queen won. Culbertson returned with a spade, and Jo's ace was the setting trick. The microphone for the radio broadcast had been on throughout this hand and when it was over, Culbertson leaned over and said into it: 'It is a very rare but a very great pleasure to fool Papa Sims. In this instance Mrs Culbertson fooled him twice on the same hand. It has never been done before.' But Papa Sims got even three days later with a superb piece of deceptive play along similar lines (underleading an ace-queen and causing Jo to guess wrong) and that made the honours even.

By now Culbertson was back to his old habits of arriving late. Notwithstanding having to pay the forfeit of $25, he insisted on 'breakfasting' at the table on spaghetti, or sometimes spinach, followed by ice-cream. In a manner reminiscent of the Lenz match, he would delay for endless minutes before the play of a card. His timewasting earned the first formal protest of the match in the 113th rubber on 9 April. This was dubbed the 'huddle hand':

Both sides vulnerable
Dealer West

Jo
♠ Q J 7
♡ J 5 4 3
◇ 9
♣ A K 10 5 2

Sims
♠ A
♡ 10 8 6 2
◇ K Q J 8 6
♣ J 9 7

Dorothy
♠ 10 9 6 4 3
♡ 7
◇ 7 5 3 2
♣ Q 6 3

Culbertson
♠ K 8 5 2
♡ A K Q 9
◇ A 10 4
♣ 8 4

The bidding:

West	North	East	South
Pass	Pass	Pass	1♡
Pass	2♣	Pass	2♠
Pass	5♡	Pass	Pass
Pass			

Culbertson, after three passes, bid one heart, Jo replied with two clubs and Culbertson's next bid of two spades, being a reversal of suits, was semi-forcing. While Jo was pondering what to respond, Dorothy turned to her enquiringly. 'I'm thinking, Dorrie,' Jo said quietly. Minutes passed and Culbertson, never slow to let an opportunity slip by, remarked, '*Cogito, ergo sum.*' Hal Sims was not impressed by this invocation of Cartesian logic and insisted, 'Speak English, Professor.' 'The referee understands me,' replied Culbertson, and true enough Sir Derrick Wernher, the referee, had to smile in acknowledgement. 'That makes no difference,' protested Sims. 'I'm the one concerned; I am playing the cards, not the referee.' Jo finally decided to bid five hearts and everyone passed.

Sims led the diamond king to declarer's ace. Culbertson then drew two rounds of trumps, revealing the unfortunate division of the suit and then led the two of spades. Sims won with the ace and returned the diamond queen, which dummy ruffed. Culbertson then went into his great huddle. During the following eighteen minutes Culbertson sat thinking about his next play. Dorothy began to fret after five minutes and Culbertson protested that his train of thought had been interrupted and he would have to start all over again. Another five minutes elapsed and Dorothy again asked him to resume play but he was still not ready. So she took a walk around Crockford's Club and, after eight minutes more, was summoned back 'Ready to go, Professor?' she enquired as she sat down. 'What was the big problem?' 'I was thinking whether I was going to go one or two tricks down,' he replied. Then he led the jack of spades from dummy which Sims trumped and played a further diamond to be trumped in dummy. The ace and king of clubs were now played and the third round of clubs ruffed in hand. Drawing out the remaining adverse trump and returning to dummy with a spade, Culbertson claimed the rest, as the clubs in dummy were now good. Five hearts had been made.

The moment the hand was over, Sims woke up to the fact that if, instead of ruffing dummy's jack of spades, he had discarded a club, he could have defeated the contract by ruffing the last spade and forcing dummy with another diamond, leaving Culbertson with no means of getting off the table to draw the last trump. Sims protested, saying that he had been misled by Culbertson's remark and he asked for a fresh deal but the referee saw no reason to allow this.

By Wednesday, 10 April they had played a total of 133 rubbers and the Culbertson lead had reached 14,720 points. The Culbertson children visited the tournament just in time for the radio broadcast and were introduced on the programme. Joyce showed no sign of 'mike fright' and Sims observed, 'It's easy to tell whose daughter Joyce is. Just look at the way she grabbed that microphone.'

The following day, Thursday, the two ladies took a rest and had the day off as it was Bruce's birthday. The two substitutes stood in for them, Al Morehead for Jo and B. Jay Becker for Dorothy. Being a men's foursome, hefty side bets were struck at twenty-five cents a point – Culbertson ended up losing $750.

By Friday there remained only three rubbers of the 150 to be played. Before a bejewelled and somewhat chatty gallery, the two partnerships hurried through the remaining hands. On the very last rubber, Dorothy had a chance to cut the final total by an appreciable amount but she missed playing the right card:

East–West vulnerable
Dealer South

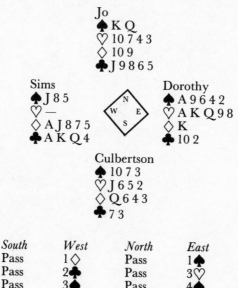

Jo
♠ K Q
♡ 10 7 4 3
♢ 10 9
♣ J 9 8 6 5

Sims
♠ J 8 5
♡ —
♢ A J 8 7 5
♣ A K Q 4

Dorothy
♠ A 9 6 4 2
♡ A K Q 9 8
♢ K
♣ 10 2

Culbertson
♠ 10 7 3
♡ J 6 5 2
♢ Q 6 4 3
♣ 7 3

The bidding:

South	West	North	East
Pass	1♢	Pass	1♠
Pass	2♣	Pass	3♡
Pass	3♠	Pass	4♠
Pass	6♠	Pass	Pass
Pass			

Culbertson led a club, won on the table. Dorothy studied the cards: 'This will take more than a miracle, Hal. We have duplication of values.' Then she led a small spade and the miracle happened. Jo dropped the king and Dorothy's ace took the trick. She then returned a small spade to the jack-eight in dummy, and when Culbertson played low, put up the jack. Jo won with her queen and now Dorothy had to concede another spade trick. Her husband glowered. 'It was a guess, Hal,' she pleaded. 'Dorothy,' he replied, 'there was no guess at all. If Jo had the ten, she would have played it instead of the king. If Ely has the rest of the spades you're set anyway.'

In the end the Culbertsons won by a margin of 16,130 points. Of the 150 rubbers played, the Culbertsons won eighty-two and the Simses sixty-eight but the Simses held twenty-two more aces, fifty more kings and eighty-six more queens. Yet the margin to the Culbertsons was decisive. The partnership factor had once again proved too strong; both of the Simses were individualists with Dorothy very much the weakest player among the four. But the match achieved what it set out to do. It proved that two sets of married couples could play a long match together, and it proved to the public at large that the Culbertsons still seemed to be as good as ever at bridge. In reality it was his way of avoiding the real challenge from the Four Aces.

CHAPTER 13

DIVORCE

Meanwhile Culbertson's children were growing up, and their education was crucial: 'This boy Bruce and this girl Joyce were our most hazardous enterprise; our laboratory, our theatre, our circus, our temple.' His choice of words is highly revealing. His children had the highest expectations placed on them from an early age. Not surprisingly from a man imbued with such a strong ego, they were expected to become some sort of embellishment to him. Success and the pursuit of excellence were paramount and so an immense amount of effort was put into their upbringing.

Predictably after the success of his bridge system, a system was evolved for their education. The same principles were followed. It had to be scientifically based with little left to chance. Their lives were to be mapped out as fully as possible. The key text for their early up-bringing was the Yale Professor of Child Hygiene, Arnold Gesell's *An Atlas of Child Behaviour*. This, as its title implies, gave a thorough, step by step, analysis of child-rearing but Culbertson chose to add a few of his own 'scientific' theories. He wanted his children to be inured against sudden frights and childish fantasies. Thus they were subjected to just those things they might be frightened of. He fed them during storms to condition them; at times they slept in darkness and at other times with the lights on; they were taught to handle all sorts of crawling things, including frogs, lizards and snakes.

Culbertson was scornful of ordinary education. Too much time at school, he argued, was wasted on 'antiquated curricula, large classes and fruitless vacations'. Private schools were little better and seemed to breed only a narrow class-consciousness. He wanted to create strong individuals, rather than 'moulding children to the crowd'. The American education system had, he felt, gone overboard on the issue of social adjustment. It had become a fetish, 'sacrificing the individual for the standard'. He did not want anything to do with the 'levelling influence of the herd', and was prepared to let his children join the hurly-burly of ordinary school life only once the essential character formation had taken place. Their education for the first few years was to be at home, in a controlled environment, with selected private tutors.

Bruce remembers his early education with horror. Culbertson appointed Professor Leta Hollingsworth from Columbia University to oversee the children's education. She was the author of several books on education, her best-known being, appropriately enough, *Gifted Children* (1927) where she advocated the discovery and development of the gifted child as the surest means of social progress. For the day-to-day organization of the children's education, the person in charge was Miss Bilz, a German lady with the disposition of a martinet.

From the age of five onwards, the two children underwent a planned and rigorous regime. A special classroom was constructed inside the apartment at East 62nd Street. Vacations were regarded as time-wasting and the elaborately worked-out programme continued all year round. Miss Bilz accompanied them to their summer estate at Ridgefield, where their studies proceeded as before. Foreign languages were another key part of the programme. Miss Bilz, fluent in German and French, instructed the children in those two languages, training their voice-boxes to foreign sounds 'before they became petrified in the Anglo-Saxon mould'. An art tutor, Mr Raymond Mack, was brought in and in a corner of the classroom was set up a mini-laboratory for Mr Nethery, the physics and chemistry teacher to teach Bruce. Later on in 1941, as an unusual 'treat', Bruce was given an individual physics lesson by Bertrand Russell, by then a family friend!

Culbertson, consciously or unconsciously, was repeating many of the patterns of his own upbringing and education. He too had spent much of his childhood being tutored privately at home and his father held equally high expectations for him, hoping that he would become a scientist. Now Culbertson was doing the same thing with his own son, Bruce. Education, as ever, was proving to be as much to do with parental aspirations as with the actual abilities of the child. It tied in too with Culbertson's current political thinking. He believed strongly in the power of leadership. In his view, the education system sought either to imitate the 'moribund pattern of European aristocracy', or to produce a level of standardization that he found unacceptable. It had sacrificed the concept of leadership for that of standardization. In the 1930s such ideas held considerable persuasive force, as was only too evident from contemporary events in Germany and Italy. In Culbertson's own field of bridge, he had built his organization of Culbertson teachers round their group-leaders. He believed in hierarchy. The borderline between acceptable modern organizational methods and structures that became nefarious political machines was often thinly drawn.

Eventually Joyce and Bruce did enter the mainstream of the education system, attending Browning High School, but Joyce (or Nadya, as she was always known) flunked out early on. Bruce persevered and was due to go to Harvard in 1947 when he got involved in a teenage prank which scuppered his chances. But the scars of those early years of 'force-feeding' remained with both of them for life. Neither emerged unscathed, and in Joyce's case it had tragic consequences.

The children's education caused a serious rift between Jo and Ely; Jo was horrified when Ely spelt out the regime he was planning for them. For her the upbringing of children ought to be a slow and gradual process. They needed nurturing, while their separate individualities became apparent. Later, perhaps, they could be committed to a programme. She wanted to wait and see how they developed first. It was to no avail. Culbertson was quite inflexible, his mind was made up and nothing was going to put him off.

By the mid-1930s their relationship was beginning to show signs of strain in other directions as well. Success had had different effects on them. Jo felt she had been thrust into the limelight too often. For her, it was like being permanently on display, having to live up to the image that had been created for her as a model of decorum, restraint and good behaviour. It became a glass menagerie kind of existence, and it did not suit her. Essentially she was a private, quiet, home-loving, rather withdrawn personality. Culbertson, on the other hand, seemed to thrive in the limelight. He had the gambler's addiction for being centre stage, with the spotlight focussed on him. He expected Jo to join him there, in the full glare of publicity; as he saw it, their success depended on it. But even he, in the second half of 1936, was beginning to feel the effects of over-exposure. Behind the closed doors of their apartment, he was often moody and irritable and Jo would receive the brunt of any frustrations. Once, during a bridge game at Crockford's, Jo reprimanded him for behaving like a prima donna. 'But I am a prima donna,' Culbertson at least had the humour to reply.

Jo had known from the start that it was going to be a difficult marriage. She recognized that Culbertson was a restless, nomadic type and she had hesitated before marrying him. This side of his nature had not changed over the years; in fact his restlessness had increased. The gap between his public persona and the private individual widened. It made him harder to live with, and his demands on his wife and children became greater. The first to crack was Jo. She took to drink, or rather she stepped up her drinking. She had always been a moderate drinker but now, with few close friends to unburden herself to, she found drink a consolation and became more dependent on it.

Indeed, she soon needed it to see her through public events. Once she had gone to an exhibition match that Culbertson was sponsoring to promote a new kind of display-board for showing the cards. Alfred Sheinwold was taking turns with Al Moyse in doing the commentary and explaining how the display-board worked. Sheinwold came back into the audience at one point when Moyse relieved him and saw Jo there with Morehead sitting next to her. She was in tears and Sheinwold, who had only just joined the Culbertson organization, was puzzled at this and started to ask, 'Is she all right?' But one look from Morehead told him all he needed to know. Such occurrences became more frequent. Once Sims and Jacoby had to get her out of a tournament at the Ritz in New York before the press got wind of it. Culbertson's instructions to his associates were to hush it up at all costs. The last thing he wanted was this kind of adverse publicity.

Whether Jo ever really enjoyed being such a well-known professional bridge player and one half of a famous team remains open to doubt. Certainly some of her photographs capture a pained expression on her face. She was having to mix with rich and glamorous people, such as those who frequented Crockford's, and she may have felt ill-equipped for this. Her own make-up and early background in Queens had not necessarily prepared her for it. Once her mainstay became drink, her famed sense of decorum lapsed at times and occasionally a few unladylike phrases passed her lips!

Culbertson usually had a way of talking to her that seemed affectionate but a bit overblown. By the mid-1930s, their relationship had noticeably altered. The strong bond that held them together in their early years and his reliance on her strong support, her belief that he could 'do it', had been replaced on Culbertson's side by indifference as Jo receded more into the background. Now that his fame was assured, he was sometimes less considerate. Once, leaving a tournament, he met Richard Frey who asked him how they had got on. 'We played perfectly – except Jo,' was all he would say.

How much Culbertson's womanizing contributed to the instability of their relationship is hard to verify. In his later autobiographical writings, he claims not to have indulged in extra-marital affairs until his marriage was already on the rocks. This seems unlikely. His temperament was always that of a womanizer. He liked the company and affection of women and valued his success with them. There was a magnetic, charismatic quality to him that undoubtedly contributed to this success, a mixture of comforting worldliness and child-like obstinacy that was both appealing and offered a challenge. The Slav in him considered the pursuit of women as an everyday activity, with little of the attendant guilt felt by many of his fellow Americans. Bridge tournaments in particular lent themselves to casual, shortlived encounters. Sam Fry, his confidant in such matters, remembers a long train journey with him to Chicago for a Teachers Convention in 1935 where he talked of little else but sex. Sex, he assured Fry, was the world's best indoor sport – and should not be wasted! As a young man, though, he told Fry, he had not always felt so confident. In Paris, as a callow adolescent, he had looked at himself in the mirror. 'Culbertson, you are ugly,' he announced brusquely to himself and then proceeded to make up for it by getting hold of all the erotic literature he could lay his hands on. His technique improved, and he never looked back!

But success with women and success in marriage are clearly not the same thing. Both his marriages ended in divorce – the second on grounds of 'intolerable severity'. The women closest to him throughout his life were expected to fulfil some impossible ideal, compounded of his earlier relationship with his mother ('I am one of those in whom mother-worship is writ large,' he once wrote) and the left-over feelings of his romantic attachment to the youthful Nadya, in Russia. She became the ideal against which all others were measured. Neither Jo nor his daughter Joyce, on whom he placed such high hopes, could stand up to the pressure and they both retreated into the private world of alcohol. As Culbertson grew older, still searching for his ideal – the Galatea he could mould to his liking – he grew more attracted to younger and younger women. At *Bridge World* in the late 1930s the story went round that he would only employ secretaries who looked good in a sweater! Once he even tried to take a young secretary with him on holiday to Cuba. But she was only sixteen years old. His office colleagues told him, as he was about to embark on the ship, 'Mr Culbertson, you can't do it.'

'Why not?'

'Mr Culbertson, you may be used to doing it, but you're not permitted to do it.'

So reluctantly he had to get off the ship and cancel his trip to Cuba.

Later he was extraordinarily fortunate to meet such an attractive and vital woman as his second wife, Dorothy, in 1946, then aged twenty. But to some extent he made his luck. In bridge as in life, he had what card players term *'présence de table'*, that mixture of skill and luck that enables the born gambler to pick winners.

As the relationship between Jo and himself deteriorated at the beginning of 1937, Jo felt impelled to do something about it. By now, Culbertson had withdrawn more and more, sitting for hours in his room brooding about his business worries, his Crockford's dispute with Mrs Farrelly and the uncertainty hanging over Kem cards. His only reading seemed to be 'confession-type' magazines and Sears Roebuck catalogues. One day Jo went in to see him.

'You know, Ely, we've never been separated for more than a month?'

'Yes, I know it's true.'

'Well, I want a rest from you. Why don't you go on ahead to Europe by yourself and I'll join you in time for the international championship in Budapest in June. We can meet in Paris and travel to Hungary together. It will do you a lot of good.'

He agreed – it seemed the right solution.

Culbertson sailed for Europe on the *Normandie* in April 1937. Once aboard he let himself relax. Freed from the pressures of his business and personal life he set out to enjoy shipboard life to the full. Transatlantic crossings still held a magic of their own and the *Normandie*, with its Art Deco furnishings, had a distinct, cosmopolitan elegance. In London he stayed at the Savoy Hotel. His visit coincided with the preparations for the coronation of George VI but he was in no mood to join in the festive spirit. The Savoy was full of other foreign visitors for the coronation, and a number of his friends were in London as well. But he found many of these social occasions tedious. Nor could he easily escape his bridge celebrity status. There would always be someone who assailed him with the familiar remark, 'You know, Mr Culbertson, I ought to be a museum-piece. I don't play bridge.' He found it harder and harder to respond to the jest.

London life soon palled. He was tired of café society, the same faces in London at the Ritz, the Dorchester and the Savoy, and at the Four Hundred night-club with its reputation for being 'too dark to see anyone, but not dark enough to do anything'! He went to Paris instead and stayed for a week at the George V. Then, one day, he suddenly packed his bags, left them with the hall porter, gave no forwarding address and took a taxi to the rue Tournefort where he had lived all those years ago as a student in Paris. The same *concierge* greeted him. She had grown stouter over the years and her moustache was even more pronounced but she recognized her former *locataire*, Monsieur Culbertson, taking care, as always, not to put undue emphasis on the first syllable with its derogatory meaning in French! His old room was even free. He planned to spend the next month there, before Jo arrived, in an attempt to recapture some of the feeling and exuberance of his youth and some of his lost idealism. He wanted to become a student of political science again. He was fascinated by the political developments in Europe; they revived his interest in his theory of the mass mind and how large-scale movements were created through the efforts of group-leaders. In his own bridge organization he had adopted much the same method. His basic thesis, which he explained in a talk to the American Club during the first week of his stay in Paris, was that the crowd by itself was a dead, inert body but within it were potential group-leaders, perhaps one in every ten, who had the ability to transform the crowd into something positive and vital. The Bolsheviks had done it with their revolution which had started, he said, with a mere two hundred adherents, who had then gone out and recruited further group-leaders to spread their gospel. He had done the same thing with Culbertson National Studios and now he saw much the same process happening in Germany.

The Café Soufflot, close to the Pantheon, became Culbertson's head-quarters. It was a rendezvous for students and journalists interested in politics. They were a mixed bag, of every nationality and political creed and Culbertson soon became part of their group. They talked for hours debating the issues of the day, paying him a deference due both to his sense of authority and his readiness to pick up the tab. He marvelled once again at the heady optimism of the students – out of such stubborn hopes revolutions are born, he mused. He frequented the Bibliothèque Sainte Geneviève again and bought himself dozens of books on political subjects.

Only once during that month did he go back to the George v to collect his mail. Frantic cables and telephone messages awaited him from New York and from European business associates. He heard too that Jo had already left New York for France. He returned for his last night to the rue Tournefort. As he lay in bed, he reflected on his life and the words that kept coming back to him after all these years were Nadya's: 'You can do anything you like – as a vacation.' It was a timely reminder that he had foresaken his earlier ideals.

Jo arrived in Paris and they spent a week there together. It was a tense reunion. They were both unsettled and ill-at-ease with one an-other. They travelled down to Budapest a few days before the World Championship was due to start on 13 June. On the train, his nervous attacks came back and his stomach ulcer started playing up again. He became irritable and sarcastic, but he had to put a brave face on it in front of the other two members of his team, Helen Sobel and Charles Vogelhofer, who were already waiting in Budapest. They had arrived with the second usa team, from Minneapolis. This latter team's presence in Budapest had come about in dramatic circum-stances. Earlier in the year, Culbertson had held the fourth annual Grand National Tournament. He had stated in advance that the winners of this nationwide tournament would get, as their prize, a free trip to Europe to play for the USA in the forthcoming World Championship in Budapest, all expenses paid by Culbertson. Clearly he was hoping that a Culbertson or Culbertson-System team would win, but the victors were once again the Four Aces. They claimed their right to go. Shortly afterwards they learnt, to their surprise, since no mention had been made of it previously, that they would have to play the Culbertson System once they were there. They were furious, felt cheated and had no intention of doing so. But Culbertson was adamant and so they refused to go. They thought of suing him but knew it would be a costly and drawn-out affair. In their place Culbertson substituted the runners-up in the tournament, a lesser-known team from Minneapolis. His own team qualified as the winners of the previous International Schwab Trophy competitions.

New to his team was Helen Sobel. She was to become the outstanding woman player of her era, some say of all time, particularly in her partnership with Charles Goren. Just a short time before the Budapest match she had become hostess at Crockford's and Al Sobel, whom she had recently married, editor of *Bridge World*.

The Hungarians were determined to make these championships a memorable affair. As hosts they certainly did things in style. Pre-war Budapest had a deserved reputation for being one of the most exciting and convivial of cities and it lived up to its name. The contestants were taken on a conducted tour of Budapest visiting its immediate surroundings, Mounts Janoshegy and Svabhegy, as well as being taken on trips on the Danube, with tea on St Margaret Island and a splendid pre-match banquet at the Hotel St Gellert.

The American participation in what had previously been only a European championship justified this being called the First World Championship. European championships had been played annually since 1932, following the founding of the International Bridge League in the same year. The first had been held at Scheveningen in June 1932, arranged by the Dutch Bridge Union. At Budapest, fifteen European countries (the current European champions Austria, the runners-up Hungary and Holland, together with Belgium, Czechoslovakia, Denmark, England, Estonia, France, Germany, Italy, Norway, Sweden, Switzerland and Yugoslavia) were represented, plus one African one, Egypt.

The four seeded favourites, USA 1 and 2, Austria and Hungary reached the semi-finals, played over seventy-two hands. Austria and USA 1 emerged for the final over ninety-six boards. The Austrians were a powerful team, captained by Dr Stern and comprising Jellinek and Schneider, Herbert and Frischauer. They had trained hard for the match at their headquarters at the Bridge Club in Vienna's Grand

Hotel. They were strong on partnership understanding, the original Culbertson tactic. It was a close-fought match for the first eighty boards, the difference standing at no more than 800 points in the Austrians' favour at that point. Then, with neither of the Culbertsons concentrating fully, the Americans made one or two bad mistakes, tried to recoup, got into deeper water, and the Austrians, with some enterprising slam bidding, eventually ran out winners by 4,740 points. The Austrians, including the young Rixi Markus, won the ladies' competition as well, in which Jo captained the American team. So the Culbertsons had to come away from Budapest empty-handed.

After the match a banquet was held, attended by the players and dignitaries such as the Archduke Frederick, honorary President of the Hungarian Bridge League. Jo was seated on his right. Speeches and toasts to the various participants followed the dinner. One of the last was to 'Mr and Mrs Ely Culbertson, the King and Queen of bridge, to whom millions of players owe a debt of gratitude'. Prolonged applause followed and Culbertson stood up to reply. He described this graphically in his autobiography.

'Your Highness, ladies and gentlemen, I am most deeply touched ...'

'Apple sauce!' a voice to his right interjected.

'... by this undeserved welcome to me and ...'

'Quite undeserved,' the voice repeated.

'... and my wife.'

Culbertson turned and smiled towards Jo, whence came these interruptions. Fortunately another round of applause drowned any further comment.

'We came across from America, expecting to find rivals in the Championship fight. Instead we found friends. And in a few short days, they have become very dear friends ...'

'Don't believe a word of it.'

As he continued his speech the bibulous interruptions from Jo went on. Her current unhappiness and the champagne she had drunk were behind it. Culbertson tried speaking in French, but she was not to be put off. Her interruptions continued. She sat there muttering and shaking her head. As a last resort Culbertson fell back on an attempt at old-world gallantry. He proposed a special toast to Jo, addressing her as the person to whom he was most indebted, 'the greatest woman player and his favourite partner'. As the assembled company stood up to salute her, Culbertson was relieved she could remain seated.

Back in their hotel, Culbertson was taken aback by her distress. They agreed to give their relationship another try and extended their stay in Europe a further two months, visiting Yugoslavia, staying at the small summer resort of Abbazia on the Dalmatian coast, then went on to Greece and Constantinople. Given time to reflect, Culbertson made up his mind now that his tournament bridge days were over. The Budapest match had taught him that. He would have liked to have gone out in a blaze of glory, like a champion boxer, but it was not to be. Deep down he had lost that real hunger for success, without which tournament success at the highest level was not available. His stay in Europe had reawakened his interest in political matters. He would turn his attention to that now. As he set sail for New York in September such thoughts were very much on his mind.

On the Atlantic crossing Culbertson's moods returned and he stayed in his cabin most of the time. Back in his New York office after a six-month absence, he was swamped with business affairs and for a week he worked at full speed to help straighten them out. But he found it an effort to talk, to plan, to decide. A strong inner resistance kept tugging at him, pulling him away. One morning he simply stayed in bed and pretended to be ill. He had a sudden craving for solitude. The two-month interlude in Europe had made little difference to his relationship with Jo. Eventually they had a major row – all the accumulated frustrations of the past few months spilling out. Culbertson packed his bags and went to stay the night in the Hotel Ambassador. Next morning, full of regret, he rang Al Morehead and asked him to call Jo and intercede on his behalf. He went back home but it was apparent that the core of their relationship had snapped. Their European trip together had not healed the wounds. Jo had wanted to tell him in Budapest how much he had changed over the past two years, but had not been able to. Now back in New York, they had reached an impasse.

Jo took the initiative and suggested they get divorced. Culbertson agreed but with the stipulation that their lives should go on much as before. He was worried about the effect on the children. He was aware that they would have to live through the drama of divorced parents, not to mention the burden of the crippling handicap of wealth, and the 'curse of parents whose fame shone malevolently as an unjust and invidious reproach to them'. He still wanted them to have a joint home, so East 62nd Street was remodelled. Jo and the two children were to live in the two adjoining apartments on the fifth floor while Culbertson moved down to the fourth floor directly below the children's rooms. In this way, the children's area could become a sort of neutral territory where both parents could meet and at times all dine together. Jo and Culbertson agreed that their corporation, Culbridge Inc., should share all assets and future incomes. Thus, to all intents and purposes, Jo remained both a business and bridge partner.

In his own apartment, Culbertson created a hideaway, 'an oasis of solitude' accessible through a secret panel built into one wall. It was a huge room, sound-proofed and air-conditioned, containing a studio, a dining-room, a bedroom, a bridge corner, a bar and a reception room all rolled in one. No incoming telephone calls were allowed, and no servant could enter unless summoned. This was to be his place to work on the great project he had in store for himself – his plan for a World Federation that would bring lasting peace to the world, no less. But he had other, more immediate worries to attend to. Foremost were the problems arising from his Ridgefield estate.

When he bought the estate off the Lewis Trustees in 1934, he had paid only $27,000 cash, and taken out a mortgage for the remaining $98,000 with the trustees, the City Farmers Trust Company of New York. In August 1936, a fire broke out in outbuildings by the stables and a large barn was destroyed. Culbertson was away at the time, the cause was probably summer lightning. His insurance company paid up but told him he would have to look elsewhere for future insurance. Rather than reconstruct the damaged buildings, he used the insurance money to reduce the mortgage debt. He took out a fresh insurance policy for only $80,000 on the property, much less than the real value of the estate but enough to cover his outstanding mortgage debt. The trustees were not at all pleased to hear this and sent him the extra annual premium of $310 for the full insurance of the estate. He refused to pay it and, in May 1937, transferred the title of the estate from his name to his holding company, Culbridge Inc. Such high-handed tactics aggrieved the trustees and they decided to bring a foreclosure action on the estate. The case came before the Superior Court at Bridgeport, Connecticut in November 1937. Culbertson appeared in person and put on his usual, lawyer-wincing performance on the witness stand. Asked at one point by opposing counsel whether he intended to pay Federal income tax on any income in excess of the $24,480, plus expenses, he received from Culbridge Inc., he blandly replied, 'That depends on what the stock market does in the next few weeks and months.' He chose to tell the court that he was spending $250,000 on a fund for 'the advancement of physical–chemical research'. Why then, many a court spectator must have wondered, was he making such a fuss about paying up $310!

He won the case, to his surprise, and much to his lawyer's relief (as he was granted costs). The trustees appealed and a retrial was ordered. Culbertson lost this one, and was told either to repay the balance of the mortgage ($78,000) or forfeit the estate. Short, as ever, of ready cash, Culbertson hunted around for an alternative. He came across W. Roscoe Slack from Stamford, Connecticut, who was looking for somewhere to open up a girls' boarding school. Slack paid him what he needed, letting him retain an outlying part of the estate, the Hague property, for himself. After three years in existence, the girls' school, Gray Court School, closed down – their heating bills too were prohibitive.

By November 1937 the legal preparations for the divorce were under way but were kept a closely guarded secret. Ironically Culbertson, who had spent so much of his life seeking publicity, now did everything in his power to avoid it. He timed the newspaper release for 1 December, the day on which Jo would be on the high seas *en route* to Reno via Panama and he himself would be leaving on the *Queen Mary* for England.

The announcement duly appeared on the scheduled day. To millions of bridge players, it came as a great shock. The Culbertsons had always been held up as the epitome of the happily married bridge couple. Now they were separating. Culbertson, on the quay before his ship sailed, moaned, 'I have lost a grand slam doubled and redoubled.' Then, in case any lingering doubts remained, he added, 'I am a married man with bachelor instincts. If disturbed, I become unbearable.'

The divorce decree – on grounds of mental cruelty – came through on 26 January. Jo, who had earlier been quoted as saying 'We are still very friendly. Ely is my best friend and favourite partner in bridge and business, but I do not want to be married to him,' appeared nervous as she left the courtroom. Faced by reporters she spoke of her husband's 'ultra-temperamental moods' and his insistence upon publishing 'a brutally frank story of his life to teach the children how to do things' – a reference to his forthcoming autobiography.

On the *Queen Mary*, Culbertson dined alone the first night in his cabin. Feeling restless at about midnight he went up to the bar and ran into Noël Coward who was sitting there by himself. Coward invited him to join him for a nightcap. They talked of Coward's recent autobiography which chronicled his brilliant theatrical successes of the 1930s. Culbertson too had reached the pinnacle of his fame during that time, but for him it was an era that was coming to an end. He felt he needed 'to draw some sort of line at the end of this cycle of life'. In the introspective mood that had dominated him of late, he thought about his past life, of the life he had not led as much as the one he had. It was his mid-life crisis – he was soon to write in his autobiography that he could only see his life up till now as a 'series of failures'. He felt he had failed as a revolutionist, as a scholar, as a sophisticate and now as a husband. Only in material things had he achieved any success. In keeping with this phase of his life had been

his attempt to recapture lost youth during his trip to Paris the previous year. Yet not all the picture was bleak. Rather than rely on the
inspirational success of his bridge years he now sought a more solid,
sculpted achievement – he was going to pin his hopes for the second
act of his life on his role as an internationalist and the creation of his
wide-ranging plan for world peace.

In London, Culbertson felt liberated and at the same time slightly
insecure like many a recently divorced man. He stayed at the Dorchester Hotel. He thought he would embark on a last fling before settling
down to the serious business of saving the world! With any luck he
might even find a soulmate to help him with his task, a *femme extraordinaire*. Footloose and fancy free, he kept an eye out for unattached
women. Four Hungarians also staying at the hotel seemed to fit the
bill. But before he could make any headway with them, he was distracted elsewhere.

Shortly after his arrival, a press conference was arranged by his
London publicity agent. Reporters were questioning him about his
divorce and his future plans when through the door walked a young
woman, who came straight up to him, held out her hand and said,
smiling, 'Hello, Elie.' He had never seen her in his life before. But his
gallantry came to the fore and he leapt up to offer her a seat next to
him. From her accent he could tell she was French – blond, petite,
tough beneath a soft exterior. His own publicity agent hissed in his
ear, 'It's Margot Deville, the French film-star.' Not of the first rank,
she had starred in one or two Parisian gangster movies. Hers was one
of the oldest publicity tricks in the book and she had been put up to
it by her agent who accompanied her. Glancing at the assembled
crowd and hardly pausing, she went on 'You have many bridge dis-
ciples, Elie.' Flattered by her attention, admiring her boldness and
already entertaining hopes of a suitable reward, he went along with
her outrageous prank. 'Yes,' he told the reporters in answer to the
obvious question, he had known Miss Deville for some time. They
were good friends. Suddenly the whole gathering perked up. The
newspaper reporters tried to insinuate a connection with his divorce
and even printed as much in the next morning's newspapers. In the
general mêlée that ensued, only his publicity agent slinked away in
disgust, incensed at his gullibility. But Culbertson had his date for the
evening.

They went for dinner at a restaurant in Soho and spent the night
together. But it was a short-lived affair. Neither was exactly what the
other was looking for, they were more like a couple of seasoned trou-
pers whose paths were crossing, each at a turning point in their lives.

Culbertson suspected she was after his money and on the train to Paris where they were both bound, they had a row that terminated their relationship. In Paris he stayed as always at the Hotel George v. Max Blouet, the manager and his long time friend, tried to commiserate with him about his divorce. He kept up his social round. Through a friend of his, Etienne Azarian, he met a woman who came closest to matching the *femme extraordinaire* he was seeking.

They had gone together to a dinner party at the home of a friend of Azarian's. It was a black tie affair and a rubber of bridge was played before dinner, Culbertson cutting his hostess as partner. He studied her closely, she was in her early thirties, ash-blond, with large grey-green eyes and well-built. Culbertson felt immediately drawn to her. Their rapport was self-evident as they discussed the cards and play of the hand. After dinner they went to the Schéhérézade, a fashionable night-club, where they talked against its backcloth of silk walls and oriental tapestries. Culbertson told her about his plans for a blueprint for world peace. She seemed to understand and support what he was saying. As another displaced person, an exile too from Russia where she had been brought up, she sympathized with his endeavours. They agreed to meet the next day and soon became inseparable. Her husband was away investigating archaeological ruins in North Africa. Culbertson entertained visions of her coming back to America with him. He pressed her to do it, she hesitated but could not agree to leave her husband. For Culbertson it was now all or nothing. His ideal woman had to be prepared to drop everything for his sake.

From Paris he went on to Rome where he spent another six weeks, and played bridge with Alfonso XIII of Spain, as was mentioned earlier, before travelling back to New York on the ss *Bremen* where he arrived in mid February.

In New York, Culbertson had to deal with another spectre from his past, the Willard Karn case. He had known this was coming up, and on 18 March the story hit the newspaper headlines. He had paved the way for it a few months previously by running a series of articles in *Bridge World* about hustlers and card-cheats in well-known bridge clubs. The October 1937 issue editorial was headed 'Hustlers – the Bane of Bridge Clubs' and referred to 'those professional gamblers who prey on weaker players'. Culbertson made it clear that Crockford's had barred them from playing there. The origins of this case went back to 1933. At that time, Willard Karn was among the select band of top Contract bridge players. Indeed, Shepard Barclay in his infamous ranking of the top players of 1932-3 had put him at the head of his list. He had been Sims's regular partner, he was one of the original members of the very successful Four Horsemen team, he had twice in 1931 and 1932 been part of the team which captured the Vanderbilt Cup, and he had even presented his own cup for pairs competition in 1932, and won it first time round with Waldemar von Zedtwitz. In 1931 he had just published his own book on bridge, a loose-leaf publication entitled *Karn's Bridge Service* – in fact his record was quite outstanding and he looked all set for a long and distinguished career in bridge.

Then, quite suddenly, Karn had disappeared from the bridge scene. In the middle of 1933, Culbertson had called him into his office at Crockford's and in the presence of two other witnesses, Michael Gottlieb and Walter Beinecke, had told him he had good reason to believe that Karn had been cheating at bridge. For a near professional card player like Karn, with an established reputation, there could be no more serious allegation. Culbertson told Karn that they had been suspicious of him for some time. Culbertson, like many top-class players, had a sort of sixth sense or inner ear that could detect when the rhythm of the game was wrong. Karn had aroused his suspicions once or twice already. Furthermore, his winnings at Crockford's seemed disproportionately large. Rather than confront him outright, Culbertson had arranged for a well-known card detective, Mickey MacDougall, to come to the club and observe him. MacDougall had disguised himself as a waiter and watched him play. With a good 'mechanic' it was almost impossible to tell if he was cheating but MacDougall knew almost immediately from the way Karn held the cards that he was doing so and, as he watched him more closely, he could see that the technique he was using was to interleave the high and low cards whenever he took in a trick on a hand before he was due to shuffle. Then he would use a high speed, pull-through shuffle that none but the most experienced observer could detect was wrong. Technically a pull-through shuffle is meant to divide the pack into two, but Karn did it in such a way that the cards did not change position. Then he would crimp them before they were passed across to be cut. Thus, in one hand out of every four deals, namely when it was his turn to shuffle and the player on his right was the next dealer, he could be certain where some of the cards were placed. It was even suggested he might at times ring in a cold deck (a previously 'prepared' fresh deck of cards) on his own deal.

Culbertson presented these allegations to Karn backed up by MacDougall's testimony. As a result, Karn agreed to withdraw from high-stake and tournament bridge immediately. He later claimed he wanted to issue a statement to the newspapers but was dissuaded from doing so by Culbertson because of the harm it would do to Crockford's and to Contract bridge in general. But he personally stood to lose even more from any such publicity.

Why then did Karn choose to cheat, as was alleged? His background seemed impeccable. Born in Montgomery, Alabama and educated at the Horace Mann School in New York, he went to Cornell University before becoming a First World War pilot. By 1933, Karn was Sales Director of the Eastern half of the USA for National Distilleries. Socially, he was very highly placed, having married the Russian aristocrat, Princess Lilli Davidoff. Why then put all this at risk? One explanation was that he was living beyond his means. The main game at Crockford's had dropped its stake as a result of the Depression, and Karn's winnings had gone down accordingly. He needed to keep up his former level of winning and saw cheating as a means of doing this. A likelier explanation is a psychological one. Karn was one of those men who simply had to win. Winning, for him, was the basis of his self-esteem. He needed constantly to prove to himself that he was one of life's winners, that he had the Midas touch, that fortune smiled on him. Gambling for such individuals is a perpetual questioning of fate with an equally desperate need to get the right confirmation afterwards. After a time such a compulsion becomes an obsession, and a gambler will resort to any methods to achieve his goal. Karn's downfall was that he had chosen a game of a skill to satisfy these egocentric demands, and sooner or later he was bound to be unmasked.

Bridge being a partnership game relies heavily on the observance of high ethical standards to maintain its sense of fair play. Any partnership game potentially lends itself to cheating and the history of competitive bridge is littered with allegations of misconduct – none of them easy to prove. A narrow borderline between gamesmanship and deliberate deception exists, characterized in lighthearted fashion by George Kaufman's memorable line, 'Let's have a review of the bidding – with all the original inflections!' Culbertson, for all his faults in other directions, was always considered a highly ethical player and the evidence seems to confirm this. He was a tough and ruthless competitor, with a 'killer instinct', willing to take on anyone at any time for any stake, but he always stuck to the rules. His 'intolerance' of Karn's behaviour is therefore more explicable. As a student in Paris he too had known what it was like to be a gambler pure and simple.

Karn was not heard of again until five years later in March 1938 when he decided to bring a lawsuit before the New York State Supreme Court alleging conspiracy and claiming $1,000,000 damages. He named as defendants in the action seven bridge experts – Culbertson, Josephine Culbertson, Oswald Jacoby, Waldemar von Zedtwitz, Walter Malowan, William Huske and Lee Langdon – and he alleged that they had 'unlawfully conspired to eliminate him from the bridge world' and had damaged his reputation. Why seven defendants? Karn, or his lawyer, had read their law books carefully and had realized that in a case of conspiracy, the claim, if successful, could be pursued against any one of the defendants. Hence the inclusion of von Zedtwitz, as an acknowledged millionaire! Others were less happy about being included. Bill Huske, the former *Bridge World* editor, on receiving the writ of summons, walked out of his office, took his battered old hat off the hat-rack and threw it in the waste-paper basket. Someone asked him why he had done that. 'Nobody,' he replied, 'who has been sued for a million dollars can afford to wear a hat like that!'

Bridge World was quick to point out some of the other changes in the intervening five years. An article headed 'O Time – What Changes' made it clear that, of the seven defendants, the Culbertsons, formerly the 'living proof of the theorem that married couples can play bridge together and still be happy' were now divorced. Jacoby, previously working for Culbertson, was now not on speaking terms with him while Malowan, another former employee, spoke to Culbertson only 'in muffled growls' now that he was associated with the Regency Club that had taken away so many Crockford's members. Huske was no longer editor of *Bridge World*, nor was von Zedtwitz connected with it, and Lee Langdon lived in California! *Bridge World* and the defendants wanted to know why Karn had waited five years to bring his case. From a legal point of view he could hardly have waited much longer or he would have come up against the Statute of Limitations. Perhaps he hoped there were fewer witnesses around and people's memories may have blurred over the years.

None of the defendants was particularly keen to go to court as conspiracy cases were notoriously hard to disprove. Oswald Jacoby's lawyer advised him to settle and so Jacoby wrote Karn a letter saying that he had never been aware of his cheating whenever he had played as his partner! Culbertson predictably was not prepared to back down. He made it a matter of principle to defy any threat, whether of physical violence, blackmail or even financial disaster! He restricted his comments to calling Karn's lawsuit a 'psychic bid for which at one time Mr Karn was well known'. Karn had also alleged that, at the time in question, Culbertson had sought to damage his reputation by urging him to end his association with Hal Sims and that Mrs Culbertson had warned Karn that 'Ely was a dangerous enemy'. The point of reviving this was to try to substantiate Karn's claim that Culbertson had acted this way originally out of jealousy at his success and had therefore circulated false rumours to discredit him.

As might be expected, when the case did come to court, it simply was not strong enough to stand up. Indeed, Justice Aaron Levy in dismissing it on 13 June stated that the complaint 'violates every known pleading'. Karn tried to reinstate the case a year later but without success. There was an out-of-court settlement whereby Karn was allowed to participate in future ACBL tournaments with one or two respectable players, and he did so for the record but that was all. Through the years, he kept his job with various liquor companies, ending up as National Director of Sales for Schenley Distillers, but his marriage ended in divorce and he never attained any of his former bridge pre-eminence. He died in April 1945 of a heart-attack in his suite at the Hotel Beverly on East 50th Street in New York, at the age of forty-seven.

In April 1938, *Bridge World* announced the formation of Autobridge Inc., headed by Amster Spiro, city editor of the New York *Journal-American*. Autobridge, that surprisingly durable phenomenon, was a self-teaching device whereby a deal-sheet was inserted in a special board so that only the player's own cards were shown. As the deal progressed, the player found that his own bids and plays were automatically corrected, and that the bids and plays of the other players automatically revealed. The board and deal-sheets were accompanied by an explanatory booklet, in which the full hands were set out and the bidding and play explained by experts.

Culbertson thought Autobridge an outstanding invention and proposed to back it up with an extensive lecture tour which he undertook for the second half of 1938. He saw it as a major income-earner, which he would then be able to devote to his peace plan scheme, and in September of that year he bought a controlling interest in it.

By January 1939, Culbertson was putting the finishing touches to his autobiography. The title, *The Strange Lives of One Man*, indicates the structure he chose to give it. For Culbertson, writing an autobiography was more an exercise in self-justification than an Augustinian purging of the soul. Typically he conducted this at several levels or layers. Seven characters were introduced – Ely the Epicurean, Ely the Idealist, Ely the Child, Ely the Family Man, Ely the Business Manager, Ely the Celebrity, and Ely the Philosopher, the radial points of an ever-expanding ego. He handled these characters, usually at war with one another and occasionally summoned to a board meeting, with an assurance that was diminished by the overwrought, verbose nature of his prose style. A man who in his commercial persona managed to effect a light, throwaway style here fell into the trap of thinking he was writing a magnum opus. Prior to writing it he had glanced through Gibbon's *Decline and Fall* in search of stylistic inspiration, but with him the results were often heavy and ponderous.

The book covers the events of his life up to early 1938. Typically, Culbertson wrote it at breakneck speed. In January 1939 he had gone on a two-month cruise to South America with his new secretary and later long-term assistant, Lucinda Hazen. He started work on his autobiography on board in leisurely fashion, but no sooner had he walked down the gang-plank in New York than he secluded himself at his estate in Ridgefield. Six days a week were spent there with two extra secretaries. On the seventh, rather than rest as had been decreed, he went down to New York to attend to his business interests. It was one of his phases of hectic activity. At Ridgefield his routine was as follows: rose at eleven, dictated until two, lunched, dictated from three to eight, dined and listened to the radio, dictated from nine-thirty until twelve-thirty, and then read a few magazines before going to sleep. Sometimes he even dictated during meals. His theory was that rhythm was the most important part of writing and this was achieved best by dictating.

Once the book was completed he hired three editors (Al Moyse one of them) to check it out for grammar and punctuation, then he sent out ten sets of proofs to selected individuals for their criticism and comments. Among these was Jo. Jo was not at all happy with some of the details of their private life and divorce and told him so, but they stayed in all the same. His argument, characteristically, was that the author of a three-dollar book owed his public the truth!

The *New Yorker* sent their reporters round to his apartment on East 62nd Street to interview 'all seven Culbertsons' soon after the book was published. Ushered in by the 'shapely, dark-haired Miss Hazen', they were taken into a big room containing a sofa with a king, queen and a couple of aces woven into its upholstery. There they encountered a 'determined-looking, baldish man wearing an open shirt and a black-figured silk housecoat'. 'Which Ely are you?' they enquired, but Culbertson was giving nothing away. He told them though that he had always planned to write his autobiography, but outside circumstances had intervened. 'I had to delay it. I get in revolutions, I get "rooned", then came bridge.' He told them too that he was now writing a play – entitled *The Queen Twice Guarded*, a mystery thriller that was never produced. Before leaving, he showed them his hideaway by pushing a button to make part of the wall swing open to reveal an enormous room with a bar, dining-table, desk, bed, cardtables and so on, all decorated in modern Spanish. 'It's a six-room apartment in one. I hate walking from one room to another,' he informed them as yet another secret door was opened to show them out.

CHAPTER 14

POLITICAL AMBITIONS

Culbertson's trip to Europe in the summer of 1937 had, as we have seen, reawakened his political interests. On his return he began to use *Bridge World* as a forum for his political views. The October 1937 editorial ran: 'I have left a Europe fatalistically resigned and grimly setting the stage for the coming major war.' Germany and Russia, he predicted, would be the protagonists, while England stood aside 'with a half-worried and half-pleased expression'. The following month he took up the theme again. Now his stance was unequivocally nationalist, that of Fortress America. America should remain aloof and resist all foreign attempts to 'drag us under their ideological mantles of Communism, Fascism, and Democracy. I believe we will gain much more by staying out of the next world war. If we stay out we have a strong chance to dominate the world, bled and weakened by their strife, to our own and our civilization's advantage.'

If there had to be a choice between Russia and Germany, then 'I am for Germany. I do not like Fascism and I greatly deplore the German shortsighted treatment of the Jews who are a wonderful race, although some of them are guilty of internationalism in this ferocious era of nationalism. The Germans may easily save us hundreds of American lives and billions of dollars. So let's encourage them and help them instead of kicking them in the slats ... To have a contented Germany and a non-communistic Russia is the only way to assure peace in Europe for a generation or two.' Communism with its threat to the moneyed and propertied classes was the real enemy – a view shared by many of his contemporaries. However unpleasant the Fascist dictatorships, there was always the hope of doing a deal with them, and they might come round to accepting another viewpoint.

Culbertson had been preoccupied with these ideas for some time. As early as 1935 at a dinner in Boston given by a group of prominent bridge players at the Boston Chess Club where he had been the guest of honour, he had given an after-dinner speech that astounded his audience by announcing that war between the great powers of Europe was inevitable within four to five years. Russia and eventually the USA would be drawn in. At its conclusion, two great powers only would be left in the world, USA and Russia, and they would be at each other's throats. With hindsight, we can but admire the accuracy of his predictions. At the time, most of his listeners thought he was doing his usual posturing and advancing the same grandiloquent, pretentious claims as he was likely to do at bridge.

Indeed this question of credibility was to be Culbertson's major problem over the next few years. People were reluctant to take his political views seriously – they had grown used to him as the flamboyant showman of bridge. He felt his own qualifications were impeccable. As he put it, he had studied at six great universities, attended the little red school house of three forlorn revolutions, had read deep and widely in philosophy, history and economics and also stood in breadlines, picked fruit, planted corn, panhandled, ridden the blind baggage, and gambled scientifically for a living. In addition, he had travelled extensively in Europe and knew Russia and America at first hand. With all this behind him he thought of himself as especially well-equipped to be an authority on the international situation.

By the time war did break out, his peace plan had reached an advanced stage of formulation. He proposed an international umbrella organization, the World Federation, as he called it. The powers of this Federation would be restricted to one aim: to prohibit and prevent war. To this end each nation would be required to give up the 'sovereign' right, of waging war. In exchange each nation would be guaranteed to be defended against aggression. The world would be broken up into the following eleven Regional Federations, decided on a geo-political basis:

American: The United States and the twenty Latin American Republics.

British: The United Kingdom and the British Dominions.

Latin-European: France, Italy, Spain, Portugal, Belgium.

North-European: Germany, Austria, The Netherlands, Scandinavia, Finland.

Middle-European: Poland, Lithuania, Czechoslovakia, Hungary and the Balkans.

Middle Eastern: Turkey, Persia, Afghanistan, Syria, Arabia, a sovereign Jewish state of Palestine, and Egypt.

Russian: The USSR, a continent in itself.

Chinese: Reunited China, including all former foreign concessions, plus sovereign Korea.

Japanese: Japan.

Indian: India, with full Dominion status, temporarily under the trusteeship of Great Britain. Eventually to attain full sovereignty.

Malaysian: The Philippines, the Dutch East Indies (under The Netherlands' sovereignty), Indo-China (under French sovereignty), Thailand and the Western Pacific Islands.

The Governing Council of the World Federation would be under the aegis of a President (rotating on a six-year term), assisted by a World Trustee from each of the eleven Regional Federations. Their task would be to ensure that the constitution of the Federation was adhered to. This would be effected by the World Peace Force. This Force, armed, composed and distributed according to a Quota Force Principle – in other words drawn proportionately from the eleven Regional Federations, each supplying a National Contingent – would be held in reserve in each country of origin. In each country no other troops would be allowed. The National Contingents would swear allegiance both to their country and the World Federation. In addition a Mobile Corps, shock troops and trouble-shooters, would be available as the first to move against any aggressor. The Mobile Corps would be the World Federation's own army, under its control and orders at all times. It would be recruited from only the smaller nations, in other words from those nations who stood most to gain from the security of the World Federation.

Culbertson's plan had undeniable merits. It did attempt to tackle, on a worldwide scale, the issue of the preservation of peace. Its emphasis on active shared responsibility between all participating nations was an attempt to avoid the kind of creeping nationalisitic aggression that, Culbertson argued, had led to the outbreak of the Second World War. At a time when clearly the League of Nations had fallen into disrepute and before the institution of the United Nations, such plans as Culbertson's (Stassen and Baruch put forward others) had some validity. Its emphasis on Regional Federations – the idea had come to him from the Swiss model – seemed its strongest point. It promised a more cohesive structure than the later more amorphous United Nations with its attempt to unify divergent interests. The faults of his plan were typical of the man. It tended to be rigid and autocratic, so well thought-out that if you tampered with the parts, the whole would cease to function. Furthermore, it made little allowance for future political developments within those Regions, particularly those still under the colonial yoke.

Culbertson advocated his plan with a sense of urgency made the more real by his belief that America was now strong, other nations would listen to her. He argued that America had won the First World War on the field of battle but had lost it at the peace table. He did not want the same mistake to be made again. He observed, correctly perhaps, that at the end of war nations would be weary, paralysed by the longing to go spiritually 'home' and to resume their private lives. Culbertson's views had now progressed from their isolationist, Fortress America viewpoint of the 1930s to a more internationalist context.

To get his scheme off the ground he looked around for associates. The one he came closest to inveigling on his side was Bertrand Russell, whom he first came across in 1940. Early in that year Russell had been offered the post of Professor of Philosophy at the College of the City of New York. At the time he was Professor of Philosophy at the University of California in Los Angeles where he had been on a three year contract since the summer of 1939. Russell spent a fair amount of time in the USA in the 1930s; it offered academic opportunities that weren't always available to him in England. No sooner had Russell accepted this appointment than he learnt that the salary for it had been blocked by the combined forces of Mayor La Guardia of New York and the local Catholic hierarchy who viewed Russell as an atheist and unfit to teach the upright citizens of New York. The Jesuit weekly *America* referred to him as a 'dessicated, divorced and decadent advocate of sexual promiscuity', while Mayor La Guardia, himself a staunch Catholic, took an uncompromising stand as he needed the support of the Catholic vote.

After much publicity and the intervention of several prominent academics and intellectuals on Russell's behalf, a lawsuit was brought by a Brooklyn taxpayer, Mrs Jean Kay, a self-elected guardian of public morals, to get the appointment rescinded and was heard before a sympathetic Catholic judge who acceded to her request, deeming Russell's appointment 'an insult to the people of New York' and calling it 'establishing a Chair of Indecency', fearing that Russell would 'make strumpets of our girls'.

Russell thought of appealing against the verdict but while the matter was still *sub judice*, Mayor La Guardia announced that he (or rather the city budget over which he had personal control) would not pay the salary of the post, whether Russell retained the appointment or not. This was where Culbertson came in. He sent Russell the following letter:

14 East 62nd Street, New York
April 25, 1940

Dear Mr Russell,

I am sending to you under separate cover with my compliments an autographed copy of my autobiography, *The Strange Lives of One Man*. I am doing this with particular pleasure, in view of my great admiration for your scientific and educational work, and my indignation at the power that some shrewd politicians still wield in this country through a bigoted populace. I myself have two children, Bruce and Joyce, eleven and twelve years old respectively. Mrs Culbertson and I hope that Bruce will become a scientist. I am sure that if you desired to come to New York it would be an easy matter to underwrite by myself and others a sufficient amount to meet any thing that New York University might pay.

With kindest regards,
Ely Culbertson

It was the beginning of a long friendship. Russell suddenly found himself without a job and with few prospects. A witch hunt was instituted against him. Lecture engagements were cancelled. Newspapers and magazines refused to print his articles. Russell, with a wife and three children to support, was getting desperate. There was no means of getting money out of England now at war, while many Americans assumed that, being the son of an Earl, he was rich. His saviour came from an unlikely source – Dr Barnes, the inventor of the detergent Argyrol, and creator of the Barnes Foundation near Philadelphia. He invited Russell to lecture on philosophy at his Foundation on a five-year contract. Russell came across East to take this up and it was then he had the first of many meetings with Culbertson. Culbertson immediately launched into his peace proposals which he hoped Russell, as an avowed supporter of international government, might support. There was something about Culbertson that Russell immediately took to. This is how Russell described their first meeting in his autobiography.

> I found Culbertson in a flat in New York overflowing with secretaries and clacking typewriters. He worked all day and half the night and was obviously endangering his health by overwork. For visitors he provided exquisite food and drink, but he himself could not touch alcohol and his diet was Spartan. He had a divorced wife who lived in the flat immediately above his, and popped in and out of his flat in the friendliest manner. He regarded bridge solely as a means of procuring money to be spent on the crusade. He is one of that very small company of men who, having decided in youth to make a fortune and then do good work, not only succeed in making the fortune, but when they have made it still retain the public spirit of their youth. Such men are as admirable as they are rare.

As Russell got to know him better he became aware of the duality of his nature, the shrewd American businessman living alongside the passionate Russian mystic. His crusade for world peace had brought the two sides together, as if the lasting peace he was seeking in the political sphere reflected an inner wish to reconcile the warring halves of his nature. In addition, Russell and Culbertson had certain traits in common. Both had a dogmatic side and stuck to their ideas irres-

pective of public opinion, both were womanizers and Culbertson ex-
hibited for Russell something that he too must have shared – the child
in the man. 'It is the child in Culbertson which has caused me to feel
for him a warm affection,' Russell later wrote in 1950. 'The survival
of the child in the adult is one of the characteristics of really remarkable men, and is perhaps the chief cause of the affectionate devotion
they inspire. Something of the child exists in every man who has
strong impersonal passions which dominate his life, for such passions
outweigh the instinct of self-preservation, and lead to heroic actions
from which a sensible adult would shrink.' Indeed in the same article
written for the *Saturday Book* tenth anniversary issue, Russell described Culbertson as 'the most remarkable or at any rate the most
psychologically interesting man it has been my good fortune to know'
when asked to select the most unusual man of his acquaintance. They
both shared the view that America should act now while it was strong.
Indeed Russell, the eventual peace campaigner, was to advocate, in
1948, that America should bomb Russia outright.

Culbertson always liked to think of himself as a little ahead of his
time, a seer into the future. He was ready to go against the mainstream, as this contemporary memoir by Cedric Foster, a radio news
analyst, of a meeting in June 1940 indicates.

Culbertson and I were with, among others, Jack Wheeler, Westford
Pegler, Deac Aylesworth and Bruce Barton. France had just fallen. This
group of people were at Wheeler's home (he was president of the National
Association of News Analysts). We were discussing the dire predicament
in which Britain was. Her army had just come back from Dunkirk; there
was hardly a tank to be found anywhere from Lands End to John
O'Groats. There were many people who had consigned the British people
and the British Isles to the limbo of forgotten things – they had conceded
their defeat. The British army was destroyed as a force in the field. The
French army was encircled, the way was open to cross the English channel
and invade.

Culbertson took no part in the conversation for the first fifteen or twenty
minutes, merely sitting smoking endless cigarettes and listening to the
gloomy principles of the experts. There was a lull in the conversation and
finally it stopped. Culbertson suddenly looked up and addressed Wheeler,
'You're all through?'

Wheeler was startled. 'What do you mean, are we all through?'

'You are all through with this discussion you have been having about
zee Breetish Isles?'

Wheeler said, 'Yes, we are all through. What is on your mind?'

With a wave of his hand, Culbertson said, 'You are stupid all of you,
you are plain stupid fools. You sit here and say Adolf Hitler is going to
invade the British Isles. *With what?* I ask you again, *with what?*' His voice

rose almost to a piercing shriek and his right hand went up in the air, fingers clutching at the sky.

'Don't you realize that it takes just as much material and manpower to cross twenty miles of water as it does almost to cross a whole ocean? In order for Hitler to invade he will have to have set in motion a never-ending stream of men, ships, supplies; the logistical problem in itself is gargantuan. Guns, planes, ammunition, bullets, rifles, everything that goes to make up the panoply of armour of war must be there at the right time. Hitler has none of these things available and he has no ships. I ask you again, with what will he invade? And even if he did have them, I ask you what the hell the British home fleet would be doing all this time? You think it would be sitting on its rear end at Scapa Flow? 1,500 ships? It's ridiculous! You are fools! Come, Cedric, I think it is time we go home.'

Another Englishman whom Culbertson looked to for support in achieving international recognition for his World Federation plan was W.J. Brown, M P, then General Secretary of the Civil Service Clerical Association. Brown was in New York in late 1941 on an official visit to promote the English war effort. He wrote a book about his stay entitled *I Meet America* (Routledge, 1942). Culbertson had heard of his visit and invited him to lunch early in November. He started off by telling him that Americans were divided into two main classes, the materialist type, who wanted to know what the USA was 'going to get out of the war' and the idealist who wanted primarily to put the world right. His plan offered something to both types. Brown was impressed and, like Russell, developed a strong personal liking for Culbertson. Culbertson gave him use of his office facilities at East 62nd Street, and took him on his social round. The contrast with wartime Britain was marked. 'Culbertson took me to "El Morocco" night club for supper and we watched the dancing. It was very like pre-War West End London – crowded tables and a tiny dance floor which became even smaller as fresh tables invaded it. There was no real dancing – only a sort of bottom-waggling walk on the crowded floor. But the women were incredibly lovely. Culbertson said that for every lovely woman you saw in Berlin, you saw ten in Paris and a hundred in New York.' They happened to be together on the night of Pearl Harbor and went down to Times Square packed with tense, expectant crowds watching the electric sign News Bulletin. There was an air of incredulity as if no one could believe that America had been caught napping. Two nights later, Brown went with Culbertson to a newsreel to gauge the public reaction to the war situation. Britain, he noted, did not seem to be any more popular in New York because of the war. The Japs were hissed, Roosevelt applauded, de Gaulle clapped, but Churchill was left in silence.

Brown, Bertrand Russell and Culbertson had regular meetings at East 62nd Street to discuss Culbertson's scheme. Brown recorded one of these in his book.

November 29th 1941

I go for lunch at Culbertson's, where Bertrand Russell joins us. His spare figure is shrunken, and he has aged a good deal since I last saw him. But the fine precise mind and the measured articulation are as pronounced as ever ... Russell's old pacifism is completely gone. He would like to see America in the war, preferably via Japan, and is quite reconciled to the view that any world order must be imposed by force and rest on force as its final sanction. We settle down for an afternoon's discussion of his criticisms and suggestions on Culbertson's peace plan. It is a first rate discussion, with the minds of all three of us at full stretch, and with secretaries making notes of the upshot of the discussion on each point. It is a strange three cornered debate; with Culbertson, a queer genius at cards and a mind saturated in international politics; Russell, the last of the great liberal philosophers, keen, gentle, white-haired, with a mind like a hawk's; and me, intellectual vagabond by birth and Trade Union Secretary by accident. Discussion – keen, vivid, swift, lasts till dinner time, when we go to Gallagher's and have a gargantuan meal, the flood of talk still proceeding. And so at length, after a really good day, home to my hotel – very content at the best argument I've had for a long time.

Culbertson tried hard to co-opt Russell into sponsoring his World Federation plan. In the end, Russell declined and stated his reasons in a long letter to Culbertson dated 12 January 1942. While acknowledging that international government was far and away the most important question at present before the world, Russell declared that he was going to confine himself to 'advocating the *principle* of international government, not this or that special scheme'. Culbertson's scheme had 'great merits' but there were points of detail in the structure of his eleven Regional Federations that he could not agree with, nor did he want to compromise his intellectual independence by associating with one scheme only. In recognizing how 'extraordinarily persuasive' Culbertson was, he mentioned how tempted he was to 'throw in my lot publicly with you'. He wanted Culbertson to know that he had found their talks together 'a great intellectual stimulus' and ended by saying he 'would like to feel that there is a real friendship between us'.

It was a blow to Culbertson who had been hoping for Russell's full support as this would have added considerable weight to his campaign. But their friendship continued. They saw each other frequently enough during the time Russell was lecturing for the Barnes Foundation near Philadelphia. Then in December 1942, Russell and Barnes fell out with each other, Barnes claiming that Russell's lectures were superficial and perfunctory – a view hardly substantiated by the fact that these very same lectures subsequently formed the first two-thirds of Russell's *History of Western Philosophy*, his best-selling and best-known book. Russell stayed on in America until May 1944. Indeed for a time in 1943, he was so hard up that, while giving a course of lectures at Bryn Mawr in New York, he was forced to take a single train ticket from Philadelphia and use the lecture fee to pay his return fare.

Culbertson continued with his peace proposals and World Federation Plan, which he now put into book form, *Total Peace*, published in 1943. In this he compared cards and politics.

> I have always been fascinated by the bizarre world of cards. It was a world of pure power politics where rewards and punishments were meted out immediately. A deck of cards was built like the purest of hierarchies with every card master to those below it and a lackey to those above it. And there were 'masses' – long suits – which always asserted themselves in the end, triumphing over the kings and aces. In bridge every play was in itself a problem of force and timing. And the inexorable rhythm of the law of probabilities dominated the fall of the cards like the beating of a tom-tom. I was at home in this unique world of cards, and I seldom lost.

Clearly he felt confident his success at bridge qualified him for power politics. Nowadays his bridge organization was running smoothly enough for him not to have to concern himself with it. It gave him enough income to pursue his political goals. He compared himself to his adolescent hero Spinoza who ground lenses for a living during the day so as to philosophize at night.

He kept up a busy correspondence with senators and congressmen pressing his viewpoint and wrote several letters to the *New York Times* along those lines. His plan was widely known and talked about. In *Total Peace* he had raised his voice against what he felt was the predominant tendency in many politicians – the belief that war was ineradicable and was inherent in human nature. Power politics, he insisted, by the very rules of the game, led to war. Hence his preoccupation with post-war settlement, and the reconstruction of peace. He saw all this as his war effort.

Culbertson had undeniably played his part in establishing the intellectual climate for the forthcoming international initiatives. In October 1943, the Moscow Conference led to the Dumbarton Oaks proposals of August 1944, which preceded the setting up of the United Nations Charter, signed at San Francisco on 26 June 1945. Culbertson, as a recognized campaigner for international government, was

invited to appear before the Senate Foreign Relations Committee on
11 July 1945, and contribute his views on the UN charter. What he
said to them summarized his position and remained his political stand-
point for the next two or three years.

> The UN Charter, as it now stands, cannot possibly fulfil its stated pur-
> pose. The Security Council is paralysed from the start by the right of any
> big power to veto any action against any aggressor ... the Charter
> abounds in good intentions; but the road to war is paved with good
> intentions ... an iron-clad system of security can only be established by
> adopting three indispensable amendments to the charter – the permanent,
> world-wide limitation of heavy armament, an adequate armed force separ-
> ate from the armed forces of member states, and an international authority
> that can act quickly and efficiently. By incorporating these three amend-
> ments, the US Senate has a god-given opportunity to transform the Charter
> from a timid, appeasing instrument of power politics into a ringing chal-
> lenge to the warlords of the future.

It was after this that he formed the Citizens Committee for United
Nations Reform. He was its Chairman and Lucinda Hazen its Executive Secretary. Its Council contained a wide cross-section of individuals from Sidney Hook to Dorothy Thompson, Max Eastman and
Norman Thomas. Based at 16A East 62nd Street the first issue of its
Bulletin came out in May 1947. Its editorial was pungently written
by Dorothy Thompson, the noted journalist. She had recently
founded the peace-orientated WOMAN (World Organization of Mothers of All Nations), and her line was that it was not enough 'merely
to oppose the power politics manoeuvers of the communist bloc with
power politics manoeuvers by the Anglo-American bloc'. Such stop-
gap solutions would not prevent future aggressors from rearming with
impunity and would, she stated, lead to eventual mutual destruction
by the inexorable laws of power politics. For her the solution lay in
the establishment of a 'real world authority under a higher law, with
a world judge and a world policeman, to prevent the violence of the
few from disturbing the peace of the many'. These arguments, which
were the central tenet of the CCUNR approach, were reiterated elsewhere, notably in a series of articles Culbertson wrote for the high-
circulation *Reader's Digest*, the main ones being 'The Truman Doctrine
is Not Enough' in July 1947, and 'The ABC Plan for World Peace'
published in July 1948.

Outside support for the CCUNR proposals came from many quarters,
with both academic and professional interests strongly represented.
But once again it was the grass roots support that Culbertson was
really after. Just as in his bridge days he looked to them to give his
movement impetus, so now he embarked on a nationwide lecture

tour. At the beginning of 1948 he went in search of Congressional support and installed himself with his helpers in Washington for four months at the Carlton Hotel. He operated as an unpaid lobbyist. Indeed the financing of the whole project from start to finish was out of his own pocket, just as it had been with his promotion of the World Federation Plan. He told a news reporter that since 1940, when he first started on his world peace campaign, it had cost him more than $400,000.

By April his efforts seemed to have paid off. Sixteen senators and fourteen congressmen (the young Richard Nixon, Estes Kefauver, Mike Mansfield among them) agreed to put his ABC plan before Congress. It came at a time of widespread concern over the role and function of the United Nations. Many feared, along with Culbertson, that America was drifting helplessly towards a third World War. The Culbertson-sponsored Resolution proposed three major objectives for the United Nations – the lifting of the veto, the limitation of the arms race and the need for an international police force. Culbertson hoped by this means to achieve his personal objective of including Russia in these changes. Once again the drive to unite his two familial countries was manifesting itself. In May two weeks of public hearings devoted to the question of UN revision were conducted by the House Foreign Affairs Committee. John Foster Dulles, widely expected to be the next Secretary of State after the imminent November elections, expressed his support for Resolution 163 containing the ABC plan. But time was short with the elections looming ahead and no fundamental change of foreign policy could be expected until they were over. His Resolution and others like it were shelved for the time being. The elections came but Dulles was not made Secretary of State and the new administration had other concerns. Culbertson's CCUNR had come close to influencing the course of events and was to remain in existence as a pressure group until the early 1950s. It was the closest Culbertson had got to the corridors of power. He was clearly disappointed he had not got further, and his remaining years were to be saddened by the realization that he had failed to make as much impact in the political field as he had at bridge. He was beginning to justify the contemporary comment by Scott Fitzgerald that there are 'no Second Acts in American lives'.

FINAL YEARS

It was in March 1946 that Culbertson first met his future wife Dorothy Baehne. He had gone to speak at a meeting on 'Tomorrow's World Today' in Chicago, Illinois. Dorothy, in her last year at Vassar, was in the audience. She attended this meeting principally to listen to one of the other speakers, Norman Thomas, the veteran Socialist campaigner, but it was Culbertson who caught her eye. Impressed by his worldly manner and his seeming depth of knowledge, she went up to talk to him afterwards. He told her to look him up if she ever came to New York. Graduating from Vassar that summer, she went to live at her mother's apartment in New York and remembered Culbertson's offer. Meeting her again Culbertson was captivated by her vitality, exuberance and stunning good looks and immediately offered her the post of being in charge of the Students Division of CCUNR.

She began there full time in September. Until then, Culbertson had looked to his daughter Nadya as a replacement for Jo. Nadya was expected to act as hostess at social gatherings. She was young for the job, still only eighteen but Culbertson liked having her around, a young and attractive daughter on display. Then Dorothy appeared, fresh from Vassar, ebullient, radiating confidence. Nadya watched her and saw her father turn his attention more and more to her. Nadya felt rejected, supplanted in her father's affections by this new, glamorous personality. She felt excluded. When she came across a naval captain almost twice her age at one of the 'social teas' she was required to attend at the Waldorf-Astoria, she quickly took up with him – no doubt partly to spite and avenge herself on her father.

Culbertson meanwhile was enchanted by Dorothy's arrival. They were well-matched. Culbertson had obvious charisma and Dorothy was keen to get on in the world and make her mark. Through Culbertson she had access to leaders in political and other influential circles. Culbertson, flattered as any fifty-five-year-old would be by the attentions of a young and extremely attractive girl of twenty, basked in the reflected glory. He saw her as another potential Galatea. Culbertson's perennial quest in life was to dominate the women who surrounded him, mould them according to his own requirements. The

Galatea myth related how the sculptor Pygmalion had carved a statue of a young woman and had so fallen in love with his own creation that he successfully begged the goddess Aphrodite to bring her to life. Culbertson often referred to it in his writings. 'Give me a woman that has within her the elements of greatness. These elements are buried under the crust of everyday existence, prejudices, ignorance and un-awareness of potential greatness. Then place her in a scientifically controlled environment, arouse in her new goals and convictions, sub-ject her to streams of conscious and unconscious influences, teach her new techniques – do all that and much more – and within a few years the results will be astonishing.' It was the old familiar Culbertson Pursuit System again, writ large. Despite the one-sided nature of this arrangement, Dorothy was content for the time being to be on the receiving end of his attentions.

It was a busy time so far as the CCUNR was concerned. The Bulletin was being edited at East 62nd Street and Culbertson was writing articles for *Reader's Digest* and trying to enlist nationwide support for his new proposals. In November his health showed signs of worsening and he decided to leave New York for the kinder climate of Arizona. He wanted to put the finishing touches to his book *The Quota Plan for World Peace*. He asked Dorothy to come and join him there. Away from the distractions of New York, their relationship grew stronger and they decided to get married, although they had only known each other for less than six months. The ceremony took place on 7 January 1947 followed by a small reception in the grounds of the San Marcos Hotel, Chandler where they were staying. No other members of the family were present, nor even the press. Two days later they left for Los Angeles where Culbertson was due to start a lecture tour on behalf of CCUNR, and early in March they were back in New York.

Shortly afterwards Culbertson learnt that Nadya was now pregnant by her Naval Captain, John Stephen Blank III; in June the couple got married and in November their son Stephen was born. In mid August Culbertson was in for another paternal shock. His son Bruce, having left Browning High aged seventeen, was involved in a teenage prank that put paid to his chances of going to Harvard. It was a bizarre episode. Bruce and two New York friends had been tipped off by a merchant seaman that a mass of easily removable radar and radio equipment was lying aboard many of the hundreds of moth-balled naval ships moored off the west shore of the Hudson. Bruce was an amateur radio enthusiast and liked constructing 'ham' sets. On the night in question, under cover of darkness, the threesome set off in a rowing-boat and made their way to a landing dock and proceeded to ransack a radio room on a tanker. Having selected what they wanted they returned to the rowing-boat made fast in the dock but were spotted by a Navy Watch. He alerted the Navy Patrol which sent one of their boats with a searchlight to intercept the fleeing rowing-boat. They contrived to throw the two bags over the side of their boat but one formed a freak air pocket and remained buoyant long enough to be picked up by the patrol. Inside was $500 worth of radar and radio equipment. The boys were held overnight in Rockland County jail and charged with grand larceny. Found guilty, they qualified for the recently-instituted 'youthful offender treatment' programme, and avoided going to prison. But Bruce lost his place at Harvard, which his father had set his heart on. Undeterred, Culbertson fixed up an apartment for him in Boston and made sure he got a place at Massachusetts Institute of Technology. Bruce left after a term – though later, under less parental pressure, he studied for a physics degree at Columbia University.

In the summer of 1947 the newly-wed Culbertsons decided to take a summer residence on the estate of Dorothy Thompson, his colleague on CCUNR, at Twin Falls near Barnard, Vermont. She had moved there while still married to Sinclair Lewis. Now with her present husband the painter, Maxim Kopf, she had recently added two summer cottages by Silver Lake. The Culbertsons took one of these and began to use it more and more as their main residence. They liked the peace and quiet of Vermont, the good clean air and the fine scenery. Nearby lived a number of writers and artists, notably the novelist Niccolo Tucci with his family, Agatha Young, Willy Schlamm, one-time editor of the left-wing paper the *Vienna Weltbuhne* and now on the staff of *Fortune* magazine, and the Zuckmeyers at Backwoods Farm. They were congenial company as were the frequent visitors such as Vincent Sheehan and his wife, Alexander Woollcott and Baroness Hilda Rothschild, who had a house close by at East Barnard where she entertained regularly.

These were the best years of marriage for Dorothy and Culbertson. He was still optimistic about the influence the CCUNR might be able to bring about and he was still lecturing, an activity he always valued. In June 1948 their first child Peter was born. Soon afterwards Nadya's son Stephen came to live with them following the early collapse of her marriage to Blank. Culbertson, with his preoccupations with Dorothy and the CCUNR, had hardly bothered with Nadya and had done little to encourage her marriage. He had disapproved of her choice of husband and had cut short her allowance. The marriage, which to some extent she had undertaken as a reaction to her father's indifference, clearly got off to an unsettled start. After less than two years the couple split up. Nadya's life then became an unfortunate chronicle of tragic mishaps. By this time she had started drinking, taking her cue perhaps from her mother. In 1949 she had a bad car accident. Her face was scarred slightly but she felt it disfigured her. Unable to form any lasting attachments, her drinking became pronounced and she was sent off in search of a cure, first to the Menninger Institute in Kansas, then to the Hartford Institute for Living. Culbertson, now upset to find his daughter beyond control, tried to locate the best specialists for her. A spell in Paris followed, but it made little improvement. Soon she was to be in and out of clinics. For a while she was sent to the public ward of Norwalk State Hospital in an attempt to jolt her out of her 'bad ways'. But it was a misguided attempt, the clash of a blond, New York socialite and the usual inhabitants of the ward only exacerbated her condition. Her son Stephen remained for most of his childhood in the care of his grandfather, with Dorothy being more like a mother to him. Stephen recalls his grandfather as a harsh taskmaster. His stern admonition 'Enunciate, always enunciate' rang frequently in his ears. Nor was he allowed to play with toy guns or cowboy pistols.

The Culbertsons were still spending much of their time in New York and Washington pursuing their political interests. By 1949, they were finding the long seven-hour train journey from New York to Barnard via White River Junction, too long and arduous. They decided to move further south in Vermont, to Brattleboro and bought a small estate on the outskirts of the town known as Brookside Terrace. This consisted of an upper house where they lived and a lower house, with swimming pool, for guests and visitors. In 1952 their second son Alexander was born. That same year another tragedy struck. Their elder son Peter was out playing in the garden below the lower house near the stream. A Finnish *au pair* girl was meant to be looking after him but somehow Peter fell into the stream and was drowned. It was a devastating blow to his parents. Suddenly their joint hopes for the future were shattered. They both felt a sense of guilt as if their concern with outside political interests had caused them to ignore their parental responsibilities. Now they were being made to pay the price. Rather than bring them closer, it only divided them.

At Brattleboro, Culbertson spent most of his day writing in the book-lined Green Room of the upper house. Dorothy was keen to pursue the studies she had left off when she married Culbertson and planned to complete her Ph D. Culbertson put it about that he hoped she would become the first woman senator from Vermont. When winter came Culbertson went to Mexico whose climate suited his chest condition. He bought a house at Cuernavaca and played a prominent part in the expatriate colony there. Dorothy rarely accompanied him. She preferred to remain in Vermont; by now they were tending to go their separate ways more and more.

Culbertson's preoccupation with political matters meant that he had largely ignored his bridge interests. *Bridge World* still carried on and his books still sold but his pre-eminence in the field of bridge was gradually slipping towards Goren. Charles Goren had first come into prominence in 1936 with the publication of his book *Winning Bridge Made Easy* and had soon begun to win more tournaments than anyone else. As his fame spread, so did the popularity of his syndicated newspaper columns and the sale of his books. The next decade saw him edge Culbertson out of the national and international picture. Basically the Goren System was much the same as the Culbertson System. The Point Count, which Goren introduced in 1949, paved the way for 'Standard American' and was easier to learn than honour or quick trick hand evaluation. Its introduction gave the game a boost it had not enjoyed since the early Culbertson years. Culbertson made a belated effort to retaliate by bringing out a revised version of his *Contract Bridge Complete* in 1952 that included a Point Count, but the initiative had gone to Goren. Culbertson was relegated to the position of a Jack Dempsey in boxing or a Babe Ruth in baseball – still an idol to the public but one who had passed his prime.

By now he had sold East 62nd Street and had taken a small apartment on West 57th Street near Carnegie Hall to use as his New York base. Across the road were the Russian Tea Rooms, a favourite haunt. Opened in 1932 by a former Moscow halvah factory owner called Maieff, they were modelled on Cubat's in St Petersburg. For the Russian emigré colony they were an institution, like a Viennese coffee house, a meeting place for gossip and rumour. The famous long bar with every sort of vodka and the three large station-type clocks, none of which, predictably enough, showed the same time, were focal points of interest. Rixi Markus remembers meeting Culbertson there frequently at this period. He would lament how he had lost his position in bridge and how he hoped to make a comeback. He even offered her the franchise for his operations in England. The fact that his political career had not met with the success he had hoped tempted him to try his hand at bridge again.

The strains inherent in his relationship with Dorothy were also beginning to tell. After the birth of their second child Alexander in 1952, her mother came to live with them to free her from domestic ties. Culbertson had recently lost Lucinda Hazen, his chief assistant for the past ten years, who had left in 1950 to get married to Henry Whitney. He advertised in the *New York Times* for a new secretary.

One of his replies came from Cynthia Jefferies, a twenty-five-year-old South African, now in New York at the tail end of an unhappy marriage. She had always wanted to be secretary to a famous writer and had earlier worked for Arthur Koestler in France. As it happened she had booked two appointments on the same morning, the first with Andrew Salter, a friend of Koestler's and author of a book on hypnotism. Salter offered her the job on the spot and she went to ring Culbertson's number to cancel her appointment with him. To her embarrassment, Culbertson answered the phone. 'Where are you? You're late. I'm waiting for you,' he rasped. Confused, she could only stammer she was on her way. Arriving at West 57th Street, she found him sitting at his desk eating lunch off a tray. His Scandinavian maid, Christine, was also there washing dishes in the tiny kitchen of the apartment, able to hear everything that was said. Cynthia found herself telling him much more than she had intended. Shortly afterwards, the door of the sitting-room opened and Dorothy came in and shook hands with her, Dorothy's eyes narrowing slightly as she studied Cynthia.

Culbertson was determined to get her to work for him. He used all the force of his personality to get her to change her mind and turn the other appointment down. The world, he told her, was divided into two sorts of people, those with two-dimensional minds – he waved these aside with a sweep of his hand – and a select few with three-dimensional minds. Cynthia probably had two and a half, he said kindly, but if she stayed working for him, she might end up with three. How could she refuse that!

Her job as Culbertson's secretary meant becoming part of the household and almost a member of the family. She kept the office going in New York and spent part of her time in Vermont. Culbertson was currently writing an abstract of his UN Peace Plan. His correspondence was way behind, letters two and three years old remained unanswered. After a while he would cease dictating, heave a sigh and say despairingly, 'Oh Cyntoushka, won't you bring me some more tea?' When she returned with his Russian tea glass with lemon inside, he would abandon his letter-writing and go back to his beloved peace plan. For him it was a period of lassitude, of inaction, that seemed to punctuate his life more and more these days. On his visits to New York Culbertson would often take her out to dinner. She noticed how the rudeness of New York taxi drivers delighted him. The ruder the better, he stated, since it proved beyond doubt that in America all men were free and equal!

Working for Culbertson brought Cynthia particularly close to Dorothy. Dorothy now confided in her, quite uninhibitedly, about her feelings and experiences. She treated Cynthia as the older sister she had missed as an only child. She told Cynthia of some of the difficulties in her marriage, how Culbertson refused to treat her as an equal and still persisted in viewing her as his youthful Galatea. It was as if he did not want the picture of her as a blond, youthful girl (he referred to her once as Hitler's dream girl) to change. She certainly looked the part with her fair hair, pale blue eyes and golden skin colour. Her parents had originally come from Prussia, moving to America after their marriage. Had Culbertson not gone away so often to Europe and Mexico, she was sure their marriage would have broken down long ago.

Cynthia spent two years working for Culbertson before she left at Koestler's request to rejoin him in London, where they later got married. She was to have told me, as author of this book, much more about life in Brattleboro and New York. I spoke to her on the telephone shortly after learning of her involvement with Culbertson during a research trip to America in 1983. We arranged to meet. The following week on Wednesday, 2 March, I went to the Koestlers' house at three-thirty p.m., as arranged, rang the bell several times, noticed drawn curtains on the first floor and went away, surprised and disappointed. Next day I heard news of their joint suicide pact which had taken place undetected the night before my visit.

Cynthia knew much of what lay behind the manuscript of an unfinished sequel to Culbertson's earlier autobiography which she typed out and which he was still working on by the time he died. The typescript with its many revisions is now in the Albert Morehead Memorial Library at the ACBL Headquarters in Memphis, Tennessee. In it Culbertson revives many of the same themes of the earlier book, a further board meeting of the seven Elys takes place, now motivated by a 'psyche-kick', while a major section focusses on his recent political activities, for whose lack of success he roundly castigates short-sighted politicians. But more puzzling in the manuscript is a lengthy account of various amours and adventures he embarked upon shortly after his divorce from Jo. The episode with Margot Deville and with his White Russian friend in Paris have already been remarked upon. He also chose to dwell at great length on a less flattering episode where he was ruthlessly outmanoeuvred by a young woman half his age who succeeded, he states, in extracting a large sum of money out of him under threat of blackmail. Perhaps as someone who had spent most of his life treating women as objects, he was trying to figure out how one woman had at last contrived to outwit him, or was he trying, by giving such prominence to the sensual side of these attachments, to rekindle dying embers? Certainly Cynthia Koestler must have been able to provide some of the answers.

By the middle of 1954 the Culbertsons had indeed got divorced, as Dorothy feared and half expected. The case was heard on 30 June at Newfane, Vermont, Dorothy bringing the action on grounds of 'intolerable severity', an indication of how little Culbertson's demanding attitude to women had changed over the years. She was given custody of their twenty-month-old son Alexander, and moved with her mother, child and Stephen to another house in Brattleboro on Chestnut Hill. But now she found herself with little money (alimony was hardly likely to be forthcoming, since Culbertson's fortune had been spent on his peace plan). She had to look for a job and found one with NBC in New York in their public affairs department working on religious and educational radio programmes.

Culbertson remained at Brookside Terrace and continued writing. His health was gradually worsening. His doctor advised him to give up smoking. Culbertson, who had smoked incessantly all his life, usually his own blend of the choicest Bulgarian tobacco, was now forced to agree. Ironically this last desperate attempt to improve his lung condition proved only a temporary respite as for most of 1955 he remained in poor health. Dorothy came to see him as often as she could when her work permitted. His main companion was his Afghan dog, Cougar, who, no doubt sensing his master's thoughts, bit anyone in blue jeans. In December his health rapidly deteriorated. Emphysema had set in. He seemed to realize he was going to die. Two days before Christmas, the district nurse visited him. 'I hope I am going to die with dignity,' he told her. By now, most of his family had reunited for Christmas, with the exception of Jo and Nadya. They all stayed in the big house to be near him. It was a typical Vermont Christmas, bright, cold and snowy. His grandson Stephen recalled the stillness in the house, that mantle of silence that falls when someone is dying. Christmas Day itself passed off quietly, with little celebration, Culbertson insisting on his daily bowl of bortsch soup. Two days later on 27 December he died peacefully, attended by his family and now by some of his oldest friends, such as Albert Morehead and Waldemar von Zedtwitz who had arrived to bid him farewell. He was buried in Brattleboro, alongside his young son Peter.

After Culbertson's death, Jo felt adrift and insecure. Though they had been divorced as long ago as 1938, they still remained close. Culbertson looked after her and felt a sense of responsibility towards her. She seldom went out and, modest and unassuming as ever, preferred to keep her social life confined to family and friends. Despite her ill health, she was, as her close friend Madeleine Kerwin recalled, 'never too ill nor too busy to give a helping hand to others. Her generosity was boundless; her sympathy and kindness unfailing.' Gone were the days of chic and beautiful clothes, though she did occasionally make a 'guest' appearance at major bridge tournaments. In a curious way she remained attached and dependent on her former husband. He had allowed her to continue to live not only at East 62nd Street but, at times, in one of the cottages at Ridgefield and even briefly at Brattleboro. Now in the early part of 1956 faced with his death she viewed the future gloomily. Barely three months after his death, she also died. The death certificate records a stroke, although the indications were that she took her own life.

Dorothy continued with her television work and soon became a successful television producer, responsible in 1958 for the highly acclaimed NBC Continental Classroom, a nationwide educational series, which she had devised as part of America's response to the surprise of discovering how far the Russians had advanced scientifically with their launching of Sputnik in October 1957. This had been her idea and it was recognized as a television breakthrough. She was now living in New York and in 1959 had married Jack Marvin, a Wall Street stockbroker. In 1960 they had a son Christopher. She went on working in television and then three years later, in March 1963, she gave birth to a second child, a daughter Lisa. It was a difficult birth and complications set in. Three days later, as a result of a blood disorder, congenital aneurysm, that had been exacerbated by the strains of labour, she died, tragically, at the young age of thirty-seven.

For Culbertson's surviving children, there was precious little left. He had died broke – the millions accumulated in the heyday of the bridge years had long gone. The remaining houses in Brattleboro and Mexico both had to be sold. Nadya continued to move around the country, settling for some time in Florida. After her father's death, her godfather Waldemar von Zedtwitz became her guardian and took responsibility for her. Her condition failed to improve and then she contracted a serious illness. She died of double pneumonia in 1978, aged fifty.

For all the misfortune that seemed to follow in his wake, Culbertson will be best remembered for his achievements. He represents one of those minor but illuminating figures who reflect the age they live in. With its many adventures his life reads like a classic tale of the twentieth century, almost like a movie script. He was involved in some of the major events of the time, the first oil discoveries in the Caucasus, the Russian Revolution, emigré life in America in the 1920s, the American Dream of sudden wealth, the phenomenon of Contract bridge and the first stirrings of international peace plans that preceded the United Nations.

He was a many-sided man, complex, egocentric, often inconsiderate of others. His need to dominate stemmed from an inner compulsion to reconcile the Russian and American halves of his character. He always felt something of an outsider, an 'Amerikanetz' in Russia and a Russian in America where he never entirely lost his Russian accent nor his European manner. This sense of personal difference, isolation even from an early age, led to a fascination with the role of leader and, by extension, the techniques of how to control and dominate the masses. In his bridge life, he succeeded in achieving this, even finding himself in the enviable position of being paid to do what he most enjoyed in life, playing cards.

He belonged at heart to the 1930s, that era of showmanship and display, when he too was convinced that he had a 'rendezvous with destiny'. During that decade, he became a household name, virtually synonymous with Contract bridge. The standard opening remark 'Do you play Culbertson?' was echoed the world over. But like many another twentieth-century public figure, he became trapped as a prisoner of his own image. When he tried to repeat in the political arena what he had achieved in bridge circles, he found he had done his job as bridge promoter too well and was typecast in the public mind as a flamboyant publicist, a victim of his own propaganda. Yet his bridge achievements were outstanding. His flair and his imagination, his readiness to risk all, enabled him to turn the game of bridge from being an elitist and often unadventurous pastime into the richly entertaining and internationally renowned game of today.

THE CULBERTSON SYSTEM

The Culbertson System was first published in the *Blue Book* in 1930. It was to undergo various modifications over the years, sometimes as a result of the Culbertsons' own suggested improvements (for example, strong no trump in 1933, asking bids in 1936) and sometimes in response to changes being introduced elsewhere (for example, Point Count Bidding after Goren had popularized this in 1949), but fundamentally the system remained much the same throughout the 1930s and 1940s. The standard text and reference book was the *Gold Book* of 1936. Rather than list all these modifications, here is an outline of the system as it was first introduced in the *Blue Book*.

The Approach-Forcing system was based on two principles:

Approach Principle: 'When there is a choice between a suit bid and a no trump bid, the suit should be preferred with few exceptions, regardless of distribution or whether the suit be a four-carder, a major, or a minor.'

Forcing Principle: 'A forcing bid shows great honour strength and indicates that a game, or slam, is probable, provided the most satisfactory bid is selected. Partner of forcing bidder must keep the bidding open until a game contract is reached.'

For *Hand valuation* Culbertson introduced his Table of Honour Tricks

Holding		Count
A K		2 honour tricks
A Q		$1\frac{1}{2}$
A		1
K Q	in the same suit	1
K J 10		1
K x		$\frac{1}{2}$
Q J x		$\frac{1}{2}$
Q x and J x		$\frac{1}{2}$

Plus values: King by itself or Q x or J 10 x when unable to combine with another honour in hand. Two such plus values equal about a half honour trick. To give honour trick value to unsupported lower honours was an innovation.

Opening Bids

Culbertson emphasized the importance of valuing the hand in more ways than one. Opening bids were based on honour strength; attacking bids on distributional values; defensive bids on these same values reconsidered in the light of a different trump situation. It was a 'natural' system where bids announced information about the general strength and shape of the hand with the initial call.

A Requirements for opening suit bid of one.
   $2\frac{1}{2}$ honour tricks, and a biddable four- or five-card suit.
B Requirements for opening bid of one no trump.
   $2\frac{1}{2}$ honour tricks distributed in at least three suits, and no biddable suit.
(Both the above require an extra value when vulnerable.)
C Requirements for opening bids of two in a suit (forcing).
   From four and a half to six honour tricks, depending on strength and length of trump suit and distribution of the hand. To justify an opening bid of two a hand should be (1) so strong in playing-tricks that a game is assured with only slight distributional support from partner; and (2) so strong in high cards that a bid of only one would run substantial risk of a pass by all other three players.
D Requirements for opening two no trump bid (not forcing).
   Usually about five (or a shade less) honour tricks distributed in all four suits.
E Opening bids of three are strength showing bids indicating powerful trump suits.
F Opening bids of four are pre-emptive bids and are purely defensive overbids.

Bids by the Responding Hand

Responses by partner may be divided into three categories:

Minimum responses, which suggest that unless opening bidder holds values in excess of a minimum bid, there is no game in the hand, and the bidding should be allowed to die (introduction of two no trump response to a forcing two bid – this was devised by Waldemar von Zedtwitz).

Strong responses – multiple raises and no trump takeouts of more than one, indicating that game should be made if opener has slight added values.

Forcing bids – jump takeouts in a new suit, which announce an almost certain game even though partner has a minimum opening bid.

The last section of the *Blue Book* was devoted to bridge psychology and emphasized the importance of distributional values and the 'language of inference' as the basis for partnership understanding.

Culbertson's innovations were introduced when Auction bridge still dominated the thinking of most bridge players. Albert Morehead wrote in 1954: 'Only a handful of the millions of bridge players have any idea of the extent to which they are following "Culbertson law" each time they play bridge – even when they think they are playing some other system.' When it came out the *Blue Book* had immense influence and went through sixty-five consecutive printings between 1930 and 1933.

STATISTICS OF THE LENZ MATCH

	Culbertson	Lenz
Points won	122,925	113,945
Margin of victory	8,980	....
Rubbers	77	73
Number of two-game rubbers	37	32
Size of average rubber won by each side	934	866
Largest rubber won by each side	2,580	2,285
Smallest rubber won by each side	60	50
Games	195	186
Small Slams made	9	8
Grand Slams defeated	....	1
Opening suit bids of one	366	289
Opening one-no trump bids	43	45
Number of defeated game contracts (voluntarily bid)	48	49
Opening forcing bids	5	5
Successful contracts	273	273
Defeated contracts	142	162
Number of penalties – 600 points or more	7	14
Points lost – penalties of 600 or more	5,900	11,500
Aces	1,745	1,771
Kings	1,775	1,741
Honours–Culbertson honour-trick table	3,649½	3,648

Total number of hands dealt	879
Hands passed out	25

BIBLIOGRAPHY

History of Contract Bridge

David Daniels, *The Golden Age of Contract Bridge* (Stein and Day, 1980).

J. Patrick Dunne and Albert Ostrow, *Championship Bridge* (McGraw Hill, 1949).

Sue Emery, *No Passing Fancy* (American Contract Bridge League, 1977).

Oswald Jacoby and Albert Morehead, *Fireside Book of Cards* (Simon and Schuster, 1957).

Jose le Dentu, *Bridge à La Une* (Fayard, Paris 1965).

Jose le Dentu, *L'Aristocratie du Bridge*, (Balland, Paris 1973).

Rex Mackey, *The Walk of the Oysters* (Allen, 1964).

Victor Mollo, *The Bridge Immortals* (Faber, 1967).

The Official Encyclopedia of Bridge (ACBL, 1964, 1971, 1976, 1984).

Jack Olsen, *The Mad World of Bridge* (Holt, Rinehart and Winston, 1960).

Albert Ostrow, *The Bridge Player's Bedside Companion* (Prentice Hall, 1956).

Guy Ramsey, *Aces All* (Museum Press, 1955).

Terence Reese, *Bridge at the Top* (Faber and Faber, 1977).

Howard Schenken, *The Education of a Bridge Player* (Simon and Schuster, 1973).

Ely Culbertson's books

BRIDGE PUBLICATIONS

1930 *Contract Bridge Blue Book* (Bridge World).

1932 *Contract Bridge for Auction Players* (Garden City).

Famous Hands of the Culbertson–Lenz Match (Bridge World).

The 1932 World Olympic Hands (Bridge World).

Culbertson–Webster Contract System, Laugh While You Learn (Frederick Stokes).

Culbertson's own Summary: *Contract Bridge at a Glance* (Bridge World).

1933 *Contract Bridge Championship of 1933* (News Chronicle).

1934 *Contract Bridge Red Book on Play* (Winston).

How to Lead and Play: Culbertson's own Self-instructor (Bridge World).

1935 *Contract Bridge Self-teacher* (Winston).

Encyclopedia of Bridge (Bridge World).

1936 *Contract Bridge Complete: The Gold Book of Bidding and Play* (Winston).

1937   *Jo-Jotte* (Winston).
1938   *Five Suit Bridge* (Winston).
1940   *The Strange Lives of One Man* (Winston).
1942   *The Official Book of Contract Bridge* (Winston).
1946   *Bidding and Play in Duplicate Contract Bridge* (Winston).
1948   *Contract Bridge for Everyone* (Winston).
1949   *Culbertson on Canasta* (Winston).
1952   *Point Count Bidding* (Winston).

POLITICAL WRITINGS

[Editorials in *Bridge World* 1937–41]
Total Peace (Doubleday, Doran, 1943).
Summary of World Federation Plan (Garden City Publishing Co., 1943).
How to Control the Atomic Threat (Total Peace, 1945).
Must We Fight Russia? (Winston, 1946).
Articles in *Reader's Digest*:
    February 1943: 'A System to win this war – and the peace to come'.
    July 1947: 'The Truman Doctrine is not enough'.
    July 1948: 'The ABC Plan for world peace'.
    December 1950: 'We can really have an effective UN Police Force'.
CCUNR *Bulletin*, Vol. 1 no. 1 (May 1947) – Vol. 2 no. 1 (May 1948) (Citizens
Committee for United Nations Reform, 1947–48).

Jo Culbertson's books

Contract Bridge in Ten Minutes (Winston, 1937).
Contract Bridge for Beginners (Winston, 1938–41).
Contract Bridge Made Easy: The New Point Count Way (Winston, 1955).

Books relating to major Culbertson tournament matches

(All these matches were reported in detail by *Bridge World* and usually by
the *New York Times*, as well as other newspapers)

1. *Buller*
Walter Buller, *Reflections of a Bridge Player* (Methuen, 1929).
International Bridge Test, with introduction by Lt-Col Buller (News Chronicle
Publications, 1930).
2. *Lenz*
Bridge Headquarters Inc., *The Official System of Contract Bridge* (Winston,
1931).
Culbertson, Gruenther, Jacoby, *Famous Hands of the Culbertson–Lenz Match*
(Bridge World, 1932).

William Ashby, *Slam! A Ga-Ga History of the Culbertson–Lenz Bridge War* (Bridge World, 1932).
3. *Beasley*
Culbertson, *Britain v. America: Contract Bridge Championship of 1933* (News Chronicle, 1933).
Colonel Beasley, *Beasley v. Culbertson* (Hutchinson, 1933).
'Criticus', *Contract Simplicitas* (Herbert Jenkins, 1933).
4. *Schwab Trophy 1934*
Ewart Kempson and Dorothy Sims, *Just Bridge* (Allen and Unwin, 1935).
Terence Reese, *Bridge at the Top* (Faber, 1977).
5. *Sims*
See *New York Times*.
The ACBL library has the complete hands of the match.
6. *World Championship 1937 (Budapest)*
Paul Stern, *Beating the Culbertsons: How the Austrians Won the World Contract Bridge Championships* (Laurie, 1938).

Humour and Fiction

William Ashby, *Slam! A Ga-Ga History of the Culbertson–Lenz Bridge War* (Bridge World, 1932).
Culbertson and H. T. Webster, *The Culbertson–Webster Contract System, Laugh While You Learn* (Stokes, 1932).
B. Russell Hertz, *Grand Slam* (Pratt, 1932).
Ewart Kempson and Dorothy Sims, *Just Bridge* (Allen and Unwin, 1935).
Benjamin Levett, *Culbertson in Rime* (Bridge World, 1934).
Warren Lynch, *Culbertson for Morons: A Bridge Primer* (Bridge World, 1932).
C. C. Nicolet, *Death of a Bridge Expert* (Gollancz, 1933).
S. J. Simon, *Why You Lose at Bridge* (Nicholson and Watson, 1945).
Dorothy Sims, *Curiouser and Curiouser* (Simon and Schuster, 1940).
Dorothy Sims, *How to Live on a Hunch* (Vanguard Press, 1944).
H. T. Webster and P. Calhoun, *Who Dealt this Mess?* (Doubleday, 1948).

Periodicals relating to Culbertson

Bridge World, Vol. 1 no. 1 (October 1929) – Vol. 27 no. 7 (April 1956).
Auction Bridge Magazine, February 1924 – September 1929.
British Bridge World, Vol. 1 (November 1932) – Vol. 14 no. 4 (August 1939).
Bridge Magazine, Vol. 1 (May 1926) – Vol. 14 no. 161 (August 1939).
American Bridge League Bulletin (August 1935 – October 1937).
ACBL Contract Bridge Bulletin (November 1937 – May 1956).

INDEX